The Translator and Editors

CONSTANCE CONGDON taught playwriting at the Yale School of Drama, but is based at Amherst College, where she has been Playwright-in-Residence since 1995. She has also adapted Molière's *The Miser* and created a new verse version of *The Misanthrope,* the latter commissioned by the American Conservatory Theater in San Francisco. Her original work has been produced all over the world, particularly *Tales of the Lost Formicans,* most recently translated into Finnish.

VIRGINIA SCOTT is Professor Emeritus of Theater at the University of Massachusetts, Amherst. She is the author of *Molière: A Theatrical Life* and *The Commedia Dell'Art in Paris, 1644–1697.*

A NORTON CRITICAL EDITION

Molière

TARTUFFE

A VERSE TRANSLATION
BACKGROUNDS AND SOURCES
CRITICISM

Verse Translation by

CONSTANCE CONGDON
AMHERST COLLEGE

Edited by

CONSTANCE CONGDON

and

VIRGINIA SCOTT
UNIVERSITY OF MASSACHUSETTS

W • W • NORTON & COMPANY • *New York* • *London*

W. W. Norton & Company has been independent since its founding in 1923, when William Warder Norton and Mary D. Herter Norton first published lectures delivered at the People's Institute, the adult education division of New York City's Cooper Union. The Nortons soon expanded their program beyond the Institute, publishing books by celebrated academics from America and abroad. By midcentury, the two major pillars of Norton's publishing program—trade books and college texts—were firmly established. In the 1950s, the Norton family transferred control of the company to its employees, and today—with a staff of four hundred and a comparable number of trade, college, and professional titles published each year—W. W. Norton & Company stands as the largest and oldest publishing house owned wholly by its employees.

The text of this book is composed in Fairfield Medium
with the display set in Bernhard Modern.
Book design by Antonina Krass.
Composition by Binghamton Valley Composition.
Manufacturing by the Courier Companies—Westford division.
Production manager: Eric Pier-Hocking

Library of Congress Cataloging-in-Publication Data

Molière, 1622–1673.
[Tartuffe. English]
Tartuffe : a verse translation, backgrounds and sources, criticism / Molière ;
verse translation by Constance Congdon ; edited by Constance Congdon and
Virginia Scott. p. cm. — (A Norton critical edition)
Includes bibliographical references.

ISBN 978-0-393-93139-6

1. Molière, 1622–1673 Tartuffe.   I. Congdon, Constance.   II. Scott, Virginia, 1934–   III. Title.
PQ1842.A427   1984
842'.4—dc22   2008037319

W. W. Norton & Company, Inc., 500 Fifth Avenue,
New York, N.Y. 10110
www.wwnorton.com

W. W. Norton & Company Ltd., Castle House,
75/76 Wells Street, London W1T 3QT

Contents

Preface

I have been a playwright for thirty years, and although many of my plays have been published, those playscripts exist to be produced in a theater. I never imagined that I would be doing a book to be used in a classroom, and although I love the idea that my plays are read and studied, I didn't write them to be read—I wrote them to be performed in front of an audience. Even my adaptations of classic plays are written for production and don't appear in print with contextual material. However, this particular play, *Tartuffe*, has such a fascinating history and still packs such a wallop that an acting edition of my new verse version, with no contextual material, didn't seem sufficient. I feel very fortunate to have had such a sterling publishing house as W. W. Norton ask for the volume you are about to read.

Luckily for me, translator and Molière scholar Virginia Scott agreed to do this volume with me. Virginia has spent a lifetime of scholarship on Molière: as a translator, she has completed translations of six of his plays; as a biographer, she published the most recent popular biography in English of Molière's life (*Molière: A Theatrical Life*, Cambridge University Press, 2000). She has spent her life in the theater, first as an actress in New York City, then as a scholar, teacher, and production dramaturg at the University of Massachusetts. We had done a very successful *Misanthrope*, commissioned by and produced at the American Conservatory Theater in San Francisco, and it was with that production that we established our way of working.

Virginia produces a document that contains a "literal translation," in prose, of the play as well as the cultural and historical context of the text, frequently proposing variations of ambiguous or complex passages in the play. I read this document, usually with great enjoyment, and then sit down and begin writing the verse that will make up my playscript. Molière's plays, when in verse, were written in Alexandrine couplets, characterized by a built-in pause called a *caesura* after the sixth syllable of the twelve-syllable line. However, I chose iambic pentameter because that is the meter most English-speaking audiences are familiar with, and it's a meter that works well for English—in medieval and Renaissance poetry and mastered by Shakespeare and Marlowe and their contemporaries.

You have probably noticed that I put the phrase *literal translation* in quotation marks. This is my way of indicating that a literal translation, a word-by-word, line-by-line exact exchange from one language to another is rarely possible. Anyone able to speak another language knows the truth of this. Consider the catchphrase *Got milk?* In French, that is translated as "Lait obtenu?," which translates back into English as "Milk obtained?" And, although that is a very close match, the difference in tone is marked. In fact, the purpose of the advertising catchphrase is undermined by the French version. In an example from *Tartuffe,* Dorine describes the title character as having *"un beau museau."* Literally, *museau* means "muzzle" or "snout," especially of an animal with a protruding nose and mouth. However, *a fine muzzle* in English can mean a restraining device that keeps a dog's mouth shut to prevent the animal from biting. It also refers to the barrel of a rifle or pistol. *Museau* can also be a slang word for face, like *mug* or *kisser* is in English; but these, although clearer, both lack the really amusing reference to an animal. The solution: "He's a dog," a simple English phrase denoting someone who is very unattractive. It's a compromise but, I think, captures the spirit of the French phrase, the comic idea of the moment, and the tone of Dorine in the conversation.

So the playscript I create is actually a re-creation, in that it is made up of many small choices, like the choice I just mentioned, but all in the service of bringing Molière's original French playscript to English-speaking actors and audiences. This is why I call this *Tartuffe,* a new verse version. No matter how hard I try to get to the original play, I'm still writing a "version" of the play.

And the translation process doesn't stop there. Another version of the script emerges in the production. To live on stage, the play must be translated into the language of the theater. I'm referring to the space (that is, the auditorium and the stage), the set, the props, the costumes, the sound, the lighting, even the makeup and hair the actors wear, and—the most important—the movement, the actors' physicality and personae. This is why a playscript is sometimes referred to as a "blueprint," a description that is irritating to many playwrights (because it sounds as though the script were just a schematic representation). As the daughter of someone who spent his life in the building trades, I know that a blueprint contains most of the information one needs to build the building, down to the size of the screws. My point is this: playscripts are different from paintings or sculptures, novels or poems in that a playscript is not in its true form until produced, until the building is built.

Converting Virginia's prose document into verse is challenging but great fun. At times, it's like a puzzle—how can I get everything into a couple of lines? And lines with end rhymes. French, as well as other

Romance languages, rhymes easily and fluidly, whereas rhymes in English call much more attention to themselves. The writers of rap lyrics know this and relish it, not only with couplets at the end of the lines but also in internal rhymes within the lines. Rap has brought rhyme back for the populace. (At the same time, modern poets have eschewed rhyme, with notable exceptions, like Richard Wilbur.) In spite of the power of many rap lyrics, there is a tendency among many actors for the English-speaking stage to bury those end rhymes, as if the rhyming couplets were an embarrassment and somehow detrimental to the emotional import of a speech or a moment on stage. (It's a little like Bill Murray's "lounge singer" doing an aria from a Mozart opera, but unintentionally ridiculous.)

However, plays cannot become themselves without actors and, in the case of rhymed Molière plays, actors who can do verse and meter. Having actors read aloud the first draft of any play is invaluable and essential, but even more so with playscripts in meter and verse. Thus I arranged a reading with actors so Virginia and I could hear what actors found (or didn't find) in the script. After the reading, I went back to work on the draft and rewrote, using notes from Virginia, notes to myself, and notes from the actors. These notes ranged from questions of meaning in word choice, to difficulties with the rhythm and meter of certain passages, to departures so far from the original in French as to be a misinterpretation and/or misrepresentation of Molière's play.

It is here that Molière had a great advantage over many playwrights—he wrote his plays for specific actors to play, including himself. As members of his company, the specific actors' voices and personae were the air he breathed. He also knew the dynamics that worked—for instance, that he was really good and really funny when his character was being irrational and irascible, and that Madeleine Béjart, who played Dorine in *Tartuffe*, as well as all the mouthy female servants, could always get a laugh by being smarter and more reasonable than her master, the role that Molière usually played.

Jean-Baptist Poquelin, sieur de Molière, was an actor first; and even after his theater became known for its playwright's works and had become a theater of the king, Molière remained the leading actor in the company. He created his last play, *The Imaginary Invalid,* as an acting vehicle for himself, by then a real invalid. His tuberculosis was so advanced that he coughed frequently and was often too weak to do the hard physical work of performing. But he missed performing, so he wrote a character who coughed frequently. This character is Argan (not Orgon in *Tartuffe,* but many of Molière's leading men are named versions of Argan or Organ) and is, in fact, described by his wife, Béline, thus: "*sans cesse . . . mouchant, toussant, crachant*"— "always blowing his nose, coughing, spitting." Molière, the man, was often too weak to stand, so he confined his character to a chair. (This chair can still be seen at the Comédie-Française, the theater that is the heir to Molière's theater.) There is the legend that he died sitting in the chair, on stage, during the last scene of the play. In fact, toward the end of the ceremony that ends the play, Molière experienced what has been called a "convulsion" but was probably the beginning of a tubercular hemorrhage. He was rushed to his home, where he died a few hours later. He had been a director, a function seen as separate only since the end of the nineteenth century; frequently a designer because companies did their own stage and costume design; and a producer because companies were their own producers. However, Molière was always an actor first. That was his identity. The rest of the functions he filled for the company were in service to that—he wrote roles for himself to play and he wrote roles for specific actors in his company to play.

After Molière's death, the Comédie-Française, the French national theater established in 1680 and still producing today as The House of Molière, believed that his plays could be handed down in their original translations into the language of the theater and that these exact replicas would preserve the original performances. The original actors would teach their successors, even down to the specific hand movements, tone of voice, and so on. However, each subsequent production, although in French, was still a pale replica of the original production, and fell short. Many would agree that they also fell short in other ways—instead of bringing the original to life, they created museum pieces that were static and dead. (In recent years, the Comédie-Française has changed it policy, and productions of Molière's plays are no longer hobbled to the conventions of the past.)

As a working playwright, I have had the opportunity, the terror, the joy of seeing multiple productions of many of my plays. I recently had the pleasure of seeing my verse version of *Tartuffe* produced—that is, translated for the stage, at Two River Theater in Red Bank, New Jersey. The director chose to set the play in Texas, in a McMansion, in a time contemporary with the production—2006. The text was in no way updated or reconceived, and I believe that Molière would have been pleased and horrified: pleased that the script, through the process of three translations (from the original French verse into English prose, from English prose into English verse, from written language to the language of the theater) still plays so well; horrified that its message is still so apt.

Constance Congdon
Amherst, Massachusetts
September 3, 2007

The Text of
TARTUFFE

Cast List

[5w;7m]

MADAME PERNELLE[1]	*mother of Orgon*
ORGON[2]	*husband of Elmire*
ELMIRE[3]	*wife of Orgon*
DAMIS	*son of Orgon*
MARIANE	*daughter of Orgon, in love with Valère*
VALÈRE	*in love with Mariane*
CLÉANTE	*Orgon's brother-in-law*
TARTUFFE[4]	*falsely devout*
DORINE	*Mariane's suivante[5]*
MONSIEUR LOYAL	*bailiff, or sheriff's officer*
THE EXEMPT[6]	
FLIPOTE[7]	*servant of Madame Pernelle*

The scene is Paris, in ORGON's *house.*

Act One*

Scene 1

MADAME PERNELLE, FLIPOTE, ELMIRE, MARIANE, DORINE,
DAMIS, CLÉANTE

MADAME PERNELLE   Flipote, come on! My visit here is through!
ELMIRE   You walk so fast I can't keep up with you!
MADAME PERNELLE   Then stop! That's your last step! Don't take
    another.
    After all, I'm just your husband's mother.
5 ELMIRE   And, as his wife, I have to see you out,
    Agreed? Now, what is this about?
MADAME PERNELLE   I cannot bear the way this house is run,
    As if I don't know how things should be done!

1. From *peronelle,* "a woman who talks too much in a peremptory manner."
2. From the Greek *orgé,* "anger."
3. From the Spanish *el mira,* "admirable one, beautiful and elegant."
4. The character name is now a common noun in French meaning "someone who is falsely pious, a hypocrite."
5. A lady's maid, in this case one who took over some of the functions of the mother when Orgon's first wife died.
6. An officer of the police, with the power to arrest.
7. From *flipot,* in cabinetry, "a little piece that covers up a flaw."
* Line numbers have been included for the convenience of teachers and students, but do not correspond to the line numbers usually found in texts of *Tartuffe* published in French.

3

No one even thinks about my pleasure,
10   And, if I ask, I'm served at someone's leisure.
It's obvious—the values here aren't good
Or everyone would treat me as they should.
The Lord of Misrule[8] here has his dominion—
DORINE   But—
MADAME PERNELLE   See? A servant with an opinion.
15   You're the former nanny, nothing more.
Were I in charge here, you'd be out the door.
DAMIS   If—
MADAME PERNELLE   —You—be quiet. Now let Grandma spell
Her special word for you: "F-O-O-L."
Oh yes! Your dear grandmother tells you that,
20   Just as I told my son, "Your son's a brat.
He won't become a drunkard or a thief,
And yet, he'll be a lifetime full of grief."
MARIANE   I think—
MADAME PERNELLE   —Oh, don't do that, my dear grandchild.
You'll hurt your brain. You think that we're beguiled
25   By your quietude, you fragile flower,
But as they say, still waters do run sour.
ELMIRE   But Mother—
MADAME PERNELLE   —Daughter-in-law, please take this well—
Behavior such as yours leads straight to Hell.
You spend money like it grows on trees
30   Then wear it on your back in clothes like these.
Are you a princess? No? You're dressed like one!
One wonders whom you dress for, not my son.
Look to these children whom you have corrupted
When their mama's life was interrupted.
35   She spun in her grave when you were wed,
She's still a better mother, even dead.
CLÉANTE   Madame, I do insist—
MADAME PERNELLE   —You do? On what?
That we live life as you do, caring not
For morals? I hear each time you give that speech
40   Your sister memorizing what you teach.
I'd slam the door on you. Forgive my frankness.
That is how I am! And it is thankless.
DAMIS   Tartuffe would, from the bottom of his heart,
If he had one, thank you.
MADAME PERNELLE   Oh, now you start.
45   Grandson, it's "Monsieur Tartuffe," to you.

---

8. Reigns over a court in chaos.

And he's a man who should be listened to.
If you provoke him with ungodly chat,
I will not tolerate it, and that's that.

DAMIS   Yet I should tolerate this trickster who
50   Has become the voice we answer to.
And I'm to be as quiet as a mouse
About this tyrant's power in our house?
All the fun things lately we have planned,
We couldn't do. And why? Because they're banned—

55 DORINE   By him! Anything we take pleasure in
Suddenly becomes a mortal sin.

MADAME PERNELLE   Then he's here just in time is what I say!
Don't you see? He's showing you the way
To Heaven! Yes! So follow where he leads!
60   My son knows he is just what this house needs.

DAMIS   Now Grandmother, listen. Not Father, not you,
No one can make me follow this man who
Rules this house, yet came here as a peasant.
I'll put him in his place. It won't be pleasant.

65 DORINE   When he came here, he wasn't wearing shoes.
But he's no village saint; it's all a ruse.
There was no vow of poverty—he's poor!
And he was just some beggar at the door
Whom we should have tossed. He's a disaster!
70   To think this street bum now plays the master.

MADAME PERNELLE   May God have mercy on me. You're all blind.
A nobler, kinder man you'll never find.

DORINE   So you think he's a saint. That's what he wants.
But he's a hypocrite and merely flaunts
75   This so-called godliness.

MADAME PERNELLE   Will you be quiet!?

DORINE   And that man of his—I just don't buy it—
He's supposed to be his servant? No.
They're in cahoots, I bet.

MADAME PERNELLE   How would you know?
When, clearly, you don't understand, in fact,
80   How a servant is supposed to act?
This holy man you think of as uncouth,
Tries to help by telling you the truth
About yourself. But you can't hear it.
He knows what Heaven wants and that you fear it.

85 DORINE   So, "Heaven" hates these visits by our friends?
I see! And that's why Tartuffe's gone to any ends
To ruin our fun? But it is he who's zealous
About "privacy" and why? He's jealous.

You can't miss it, whenever men come near—
90 He's lusting for our own Madame Elmire.
MADAME PERNELLE Since you, Dorine, have never understood
     Your place, or the concepts of "should"
     And "should not," one can't expect you to see,
     Tartuffe's awareness of propriety.
95   When these men visit, they bring noise and more—
     Valets and servants planted at the door,
     Carriages and horses, constant chatter.
     What must the neighbors think? These things matter.
     Is something going on? Well, I hope not.
100 You know you're being talked about a lot.
CLÉANTE Really, Madame, you think you can prevent
     Gossip? When most human beings are bent
     On rumor mongering and defamation,
     And gathering or faking information
105 To make us all look bad—what can we do?
     The fools that gossip don't care what is true.
     You would force the whole world to be quiet?
     Impossible! And each new lie, deny it?
     Who in the world would want to live that way?
110 Let's live our lives. Let gossips have their say.
DORINE It's our neighbor, Daphne. I just know it.
     They don't like us. It's obvious—they show it
     In the way they watch us—she and her mate.
     I've seen them squinting at us, through their gate.
115 It's true—those whose private conduct is the worst,
     Will mow each other down to be the first
     To weave some tale of lust, and hearts broken
     Out of a simple kiss that's just a token
     Between friends—just friends and nothing more.
120 See—those whose trysts are kept behind a door
     Yet everyone finds out? Well, then, they need
     New stories for the gossip mill to feed
     To all who'll listen. So they must repaint
     The deeds of others, hoping that a taint
125 Will color others' lives in darker tone
     And, by this process, lighten up their own.
MADAME PERNELLE Daphne and her mate are not the point.
     But when Orante says things are out of joint,
     There's a problem. She's a person who
130 Prays every day and should be listened to.
     She condemns the mob who visits here.
DORINE This good woman shouldn't live so near

Those, like us, who run a bawdy house.
I hear she lives as quiet as a mouse,
135   Devout, though. Everyone applauds her zeal.
She needed that when age stole her appeal.
Her passion is policing—it's her duty
And compensation for her loss of beauty.
She's a reluctant prude. And now, her art,
140   Once used so well to win a lover's heart,
Is gone. Her eyes that used to flash with lust,
Are steely from her piety. She must
Have seen that it's too late to be a wife,
And so she lives a plain and pious life.
145   This is a strategy of old coquettes.
It's how they manage once the world forgets
Them. First, they wallow in a dark depression,
Then see no recourse but in the profession
Of a prude. They criticize the lives of everyone.
150   They censure everything, and pardon none.
It's envy. Pleasures that they are denied
By time and age, now, they just can't abide.

MADAME PERNELLE   You do go on and on.
   [*To* ELMIRE]   My dear Elmire,
This is all your doing. It's so clear
155   Because you let a servant give advice.
Just be aware—I'm tired of being nice.
It's obvious to anyone with eyes
That what my son has done is more than wise
In welcoming this man who's so devout,
160   His very presence cast the devils out.
Or most of them—that's why I hope you hear him.
And I advise all of you to stay near him.
You need his protection and advice.
Your casual attention won't suffice.
165   It's Heaven sent him here to fill a need,
To save you from yourselves—oh yes, indeed.
These visits from your friends you seem to want—
Listen to yourselves! So nonchalant!
As if no evil lurked in these events.
170   And you were blind to what Satan invents.
And dances! What are those but food for slander!
It's to the worst desires these parties pander.
I ask you now what purpose do they serve?
Where gossip's passed around like an hors d'oeuvre.
175   A thousand cackling hens, busy with what?

It takes a lot of noise to cover smut.
It truly is the tower of Babylon,[9]
Where people babble on and on and on.
Ah! Case in point—there stands Monsieur Cléante,
180   Sniggering and eyeing me askant,
As if this has nothing to do with him
And nothing that he does would God condemn.
And so, Elmire, my dear, I say farewell.
'Til when? When it is a fine day in Hell.
185   Farewell, all of you. When I pass through that door,
You won't have me to laugh at any more.
Flipote! Wake up! Have you heard nothing I have said?
I'll march you home and beat you till you're dead.
March, slut, march.

Scene 2

DORINE, CLÉANTE

CLÉANTE   I'm staying here. She's scary,
That old lady—
DORINE   I know why you're wary.
Shall I call her back to hear you say,
"That *old* lady"? That would make her day.
5   CLÉANTE   She's lost her mind, she's—now we have the proof—
Head over heels in love with whom? Tartuffe.
DORINE   So here's what's worse and weird—so is her son.
What's more—it's obvious to everyone.
Before Tartuffe and he became entwined,
10   Orgon once ruled this house in his right mind.
In the troubled times, he backed the prince,[1]
And that took courage. We haven't seen it since.
He is intoxicated with Tartuffe—
A potion that exceeds a hundred proof.
15   It's put him in a trance, this Devil's brew.
And so he worships this imposter who
He calls "brother" and loves more than one—
This charlatan—more than daughter, wife, son.
This charlatan hears all our master's dreams,
20   And all his secrets. Every thought, it seems,

---

9. She intends to say the Tower of Babel (Genesis 11). God considered the Tower of Babel to be an example of human arrogance and punished its builders by dividing them into different races that spoke different languages. Cléante laughs at her mistake.
1. Refers to the Fronde, an uprising against the young Louis XIV and his prime minister Cardinal Mazarin in 1648–53. Orgon took the king's side in the conflict.

Is poured out to Tartuffe, like he's his priest![2]
You'd think they'd see the heresy, at least.
Orgon caresses him, embraces him, and shows
More love for him than any mistress knows.
25   Come for a meal and who has the best seat?
Whose preferences determine what we eat?
Tartuffe consumes enough for six, is praised.
And to his health is every goblet raised.
While on his plate are piled the choicest bites
30   Then when he belches, our master delights
In that and shouts, "God bless you!" to the beast,
As if Tartuffe's the reason for the feast.
Did I mention the quoting of each word,
As if it's the most brilliant thing we've heard?
35   And, oh, the miracles Tartuffe creates!
The prophecies! We write while he dictates.
All that's ridiculous. But what's evil
Is seeing the deception and upheaval
Of the master and everything he owns.
40   He hands him money. They're not even loans—
He's giving it away. It's gone too far.
To watch Tartuffe play him like a guitar!

And this Laurent, his man, found some lace.
Shredded it and threw in my face.
45   He'd found it pressed inside *The Lives of Saints*,[3]
I thought we'd have to put him in restraints.
"To put the Devil's finery beside
The words and lives of saintly souls who died—
Is action of satanical transgression!"
50   And so, of course, I hurried to confession.

Scene 3

ELMIRE, MARIANE, DAMIS, CLÉANTE, DORINE

ELMIRE [*To* CLÉANTE]   Lucky you, you stayed. Yes, there was more,
And more preaching from Grandma, at the door.
My husband's coming! I didn't catch his eye.
I'll wait for him upstairs. Cléante, good-bye.
5   CLÉANTE   I'll see you soon. I'll wait here below,
Take just a second for a brief hello.

2. Tartuffe is not a priest; he is a lay director of conscience, a fairly common occupation in the period. He advises people on how to avoid sin and achieve salvation.
3. Being handmade and delicate, lace was frequently put between the pages of books to press it flat. A copy of *Lives of the Saints* would be found in many households.

DAMIS   While you have him, say something for me?
    My sister needs for Father to agree
    To her marriage with Valère, as planned.
10   Tartuffe opposes it and will demand
    That Father break his word, and that's not fair;
    Then I can't wed the sister of Valère.
    Listening only to Tartuffe's voice,
    He'd break four hearts at once—
DORINE   He's here.

Scene 4

ORGON, CLÉANTE, DORINE

ORGON   Rejoice!
    I'm back.
CLÉANTE   I'm glad to see you, but I'm on my way.
    Just stayed to say hello.
ORGON   No more to say?
    Dorine! Come back! And Cléante, why the hurry?
5   Indulge me for a moment. You know I worry.
    I've been gone two days! There's news to tell.
    Now don't hold back. Has everyone been well?
DORINE   Not quite. There was that headache Madame had
    The day you left. Well, it got really bad.
10   She had a fever—
ORGON   And Tartuffe?
DORINE   He's fine—
    Rosy nosed and red cheeked, drinking your wine.
ORGON   Poor man!
DORINE   And then, Madame became unable
    To eat a single morsel at the table.
ORGON   Ah, and Tartuffe?
DORINE   He sat within her sight,
15   Not holding back, he ate with great delight,
    A brace of partridge, and a leg of mutton.
    In fact, he ate so much, he popped a button.
ORGON   Poor man!
DORINE   That night until the next sunrise,
    Your poor wife couldn't even close her eyes.
20   What a fever! Oh, how she did suffer!
    I don't see how that night could have been rougher.
    We watched her all night long, worried and weepy
ORGON   Ah, and Tartuffe?
DORINE   At dinner he grew sleepy.
    After such a meal, it's not surprising.

25   He slept through the night, not once arising.
ORGON   Poor man!
DORINE   At last won over by our pleading,
         Madame agreed to undergo a bleeding.
         And this, we think, has saved her from the grave.
ORGON   Ah, and Tartuffe?
DORINE   Oh, he was very brave.
30   To make up for the blood Madame had lost
         Tartuffe slurped down red wine, all at your cost.
ORGON   Poor man!
DORINE   Since then, they've both been fine, although,
         Madame needs me. I'll go and let her know
         How anxious you have been about her health,
35   And that you prize it more than all your wealth.

Scene 5

ORGON, CLÉANTE

CLÉANTE   You know that girl was laughing in your face.
         I fear I'll make you angry, but in case
         There is a chance you'll listen, I will try
         To say that you are laughable and why.
5   I've never known of something so capricious
         As letting this man do just as he wishes
         In your home and to your family.
         You brought him here, relieved his poverty,
         And, in return—
ORGON   Now you listen to me!
10   You're just my brother-in-law, Cléante. Quiet!
         You don't know this man. And don't deny it!
CLÉANTE   I don't know him, yes, that may be so,
         But men like him are not so rare, you know.
ORGON   If you only could know him as I do,
15   You would be his true disciple, too.
         Your ecstasy, the universe would span.
         This is a man . . . who . . . ha! . . . well, such a man.
         Behold him. Let him teach you profound peace.
         When first we met, I felt my troubles cease.
20   Yes, I was changed after I talked with him.
         I saw my wants and needs as just a whim!
         Everything that's written, all that's sung,
         The world, and you and me, well, it's all dung!
         Yes, it's crap! And isn't that a wonder!
25   The real world—it's just some spell we're under!
         He's taught me to love nothing and no one!

Mother, father, wife, daughter, son—
They could die right now, I'd feel no pain.
CLÉANTE   What feelings you've developed, how humane.
30 ORGON   You just don't see him in the way I do,
But if you did, you'd feel what I feel, too.
Every day he came to church and knelt,
And from his groans, I knew just what he felt.
Those sounds he made from deep inside his soul,
35 Were fed by piety he could not control.
Of the congregation, who could ignore
The way he humbly bowed and kissed the floor?
And when they tried to turn away their eyes,
His fervent prayers to Heaven and deep sighs
40 Made them witness his deep spiritual pain.
Then something happened I can't quite explain.
I rose to leave—he quickly went before
To give me holy water at the door.
He knew what I needed, so he blessed me.
45 I found his acolyte, he'd so impressed me,
To ask who he was and there I learned
About his poverty and how he spurned
The riches of this world. And when I tried
To give him gifts, in modesty, he cried,
50 "That is too much," he'd say, "A half would do."
Then gave a portion back, with much ado.
"I am not worthy. I do not deserve
Your gifts or pity. I am here to serve
The will of Heaven, that and nothing more."
55 Then takes the gift and shares it with the poor.
So Heaven spoke to me inside my head.
"Just bring him home with you," is what it said.
And so I did. And ever since he came,
My home's a happy one. I also claim
60 A moral home, a house that's free of sin,
Tartuffe's on watch—he won't let any in.
His interest in my wife is reassuring,
She's innocent of course, but so alluring,
He tells me whom she sees and what she does.
65 He's more jealous than I ever was.
It's for my honor that he's so concerned.
His righteous anger's all for me, I've learned,
To the point that just the other day,
A flea annoyed him as he tried to pray,
70 Then he rebuked himself, as if he'd willed it—
His excessive anger when he killed it.

CLÉANTE   Orgon, listen. You're out of your mind.
   Or you're mocking me. Or both combined.
   How can you speak such nonsense without blinking?
75 ORGON   I smell an atheist! It's that freethinking![4]
   Such nonsense is the bane of your existence.
   And that explains your damnable resistance.
   Ten times over, I've tried to save your soul
   From your corrupted mind. That's still my goal.
80 CLÉANTE   You have been corrupted by your friends,
   You know of whom I speak. Your thought depends
   On people who are blind and want to spread it
   Like some horrid flu, and, yes, I dread it.
   I'm no atheist. I see things clearly.
85   And what I see is loud lip service, merely,
   To make exhibitionists seem devout.
   Forgive me, but a prayer is not a shout.
   Yet those who don't adore these charlatans
   Are seen as faithless heathens by your friends.
90   It's as if you think you'd never find
   Reason and the sacred intertwined.
   You think I'm afraid of retribution?
   Heaven sees my heart and their pollution.
   So we should be the slaves of sanctimony?
95   Monkey see, monkey do, monkey phony.
   The true believers we should emulate
   Are not the ones who groan and lay prostate.
   And yet you see no problem in the notion
   Of hypocrisy as deep devotion.
100   You see as one: the genuine and the spurious.
   You'd extend this to your money? I'm just curious.
   In your business dealings, I'd submit:
   You'd not confuse the gold with counterfeit.
   Men are strangely made, I'd have to say.
105   They're burdened with their reason, 'til one day,
   They free themselves with such force, that they spoil
   The noblest of things for which they toil.
   Because they must go to extremes. It's a flaw.
   Just a word in passing, Brother-in-Law.
110 ORGON   Oh, you are the wisest man alive, so
   You know everything there is to know.
   You are the one enlightened man, the sage.

---

4. In French, *libertinage*. The libertine was often accused of being both free living and free-
thinking, meaning he or she had doubts about religious orthodoxy and was interested in
the new scientific ideas of people like Galileo and Descartes.

You are Cato, the Elder,[5] of our age.
Next to you, all men are dumb as cows.

115 CLÉANTE   I'm not the wisest man, as you espouse,
     Nor do I know—what—all there is to know?
     But I do know, Orgon, that quid pro quo[6]
     Does not apply at all to "false" and "true,"
     And I would never trust a person who
120 Cannot tell them apart. See, I revere
     Everyone whose worship is sincere.
     Nothing is more noble or more beautiful
     Than fervor that is holy, not just dutiful.
     So nothing is more odious to me
125 Than the display of specious piety
     Which I see in every charlatan
     Who tries to pass for a true holy man.
     Religious passion worn as a facade
     Abuses what's sacred and mocks God.
130 These men who take what's sacred and most holy
     And use it as their trade, for money, solely.
     With downcast looks and great affected cries
     Who suck in true believers with their lies
     Who ceaselessly will preach and then demand
135 "Give up the world!" and then by sleight of hand,
     End up sitting pretty at the court,
     The best in lodging and new clothes to sport,
     If you're their enemy, then Heaven hates you.
     That's their claim when one of them berates you.
140 They'll say you've sinned. You'll find yourself removed
     And wondering if you'll be approved
     For anything, at all, ever again.
     Because so heinous was this fictional "sin."
     When these men are angry, they're the worst,
145 There's no place to hide, you're really cursed.
     They use what we call righteous as their sword,
     To coldly murder in the name of the Lord.
     But next to these imposters faking belief,
     The devotion of the true is a relief.
150 Our century has put before our eyes
     Glorious examples we can prize.
     Look at Ariston, and look at Periandre,
     Oronte, Alcidamas, Polydore, Clitandre:[7]

---

5. A statesman who from 204 to 195 B.C.E served the ancient Roman republic and was known especially for his public speaking and his wisdom.
6. Indicates a more or less equal exchange or substitution.
7. Like Orante, earlier, these are invented names, not actual people.

Not one points out his own morality,
155   Instead they speak of their mortality.
They don't form cabals, they don't have factions,
They don't censure other people's actions.
They see the flagrant pride in such correction
And know that humans can't achieve perfection.
160   They know this of themselves and yet their lives
Good faith, good works, all good, epitomize.
They don't exhibit zeal that's more intense
Than Heaven shows us in its own defense.
They'd never claim a knowledge that's divine
165   And yet they live in virtue's own design.
They concentrate their hatred on the sin,
And when the sinner grieves, invite him in.
They leave to others the arrogance of speech.
Instead they practice what others only preach.
170   These are the men who show us how to live.
Their lives, the best example I can give.
These are my men, the ones that I would follow.
Your man and his life, honestly, are hollow.
I believe you praise him quite sincerely,
175   I also think you'll pay for this quite dearly.
He's a fraud, this man whom you adore.

ORGON   Oh, you've stopped talking. Is there any more?

CLÉANTE   No.

ORGON   I am your servant, sir.[8]

CLÉANTE   No! wait!
There's one more thing—no more debate—
180   I want to change the subject, if I might.
I heard that you said the other night,
To Valère, he'd be your son-in-law.

ORGON   I did.

CLÉANTE   And set the date?

ORGON   Yes.

CLÉANTE   Did you withdraw?

ORGON   I did.

CLÉANTE   You're putting off the wedding? Why?

ORGON   Don't know.

CLÉANTE   There's more?

ORGON   Perhaps.

185 CLÉANTE   Again I'll try:
You would break your word?

ORGON   I couldn't say.

---

8. A conventional way to end a conversation.

CLÉANTE   Then, Orgon, why did you change the day?
ORGON   Who knows?
CLÉANTE   But we need to know, don't we now?
    Is there a reason you would break your vow?
ORGON   That depends.
190 CLÉANTE   On what? Orgon, what is it?
    Valère was the reason for my visit.
ORGON   Who knows? Who knows?
CLÉANTE   So there's some mystery there?
ORGON   Heaven knows.
CLÉANTE   It does? And now, Valère—
    May he know, too?
ORGON   Can't say.
CLÉANTE   But, dear Orgon,
195   We have no information to go on.
    We need to know—
ORGON   What Heaven wants, I'll do.
CLÉANTE   Is that your final answer? Then I'm through.
    But your pledge to Valère? You'll stand by it?
ORGON   Good-bye.

                                        [ORGON *exits.*]

CLÉANTE   More patience, yes, I should try it.
200   I let him get to me. Now I confess
    I fear the worst for Valère's happiness.

                    End of Act One

Act Two

Scene 1

ORGON, MARIANE

ORGON   Mariane
MARIANE   Father.
ORGON   Come. Now. Talk with me.
MARIANE   Why are you looking everywhere?
ORGON   To see
    If everyone is minding her own business.
    So. Child, I've always loved your gentleness.
5 MARIANE   And for your love, I'm grateful, Father dear.
ORGON   Well said. And so to prove that you're sincere,
    And worthy of my love, you have the task
    Of doing for me anything I ask.

MARIANE   Then my obedience will be my proof.
10 ORGON   Good. What do you think of our guest, Tartuffe?
MARIANE   Who, me?
ORGON   Yes, you. Watch what you say right now.
MARIANE   Then, Father, I will say what you allow.
ORGON   Wise words, Daughter. So this is what you say:
   "He is a perfect man in every way,
15   In body and soul, I find him divine."
   And then you say, "Please Father, make him mine."
   Huh?
MARIANE   Huh?
ORGON   Yes?
MARIANE   I heard . . .
ORGON   Yes.
MARIANE   What did you say?
   Who is this perfect man in every way,
   Whom in body and soul, I find divine,
20   And ask of you, "Please, Father, make him mine?"
ORGON   Tartuffe.
MARIANE   All that I've said, I now amend
   Because you wouldn't want me to pretend.
ORGON   Absolutely not—that's so misguided.
   Have it be the truth, then. It's decided.
MARIANE   What?! Father, you want—
25 ORGON   Yes, my dear, I do—
   To join in marriage my Tartuffe and you.
   And since I have—

Scene 2

DORINE, ORGON, MARIANE

ORGON   Dorine, I know you're there!
   Any secrets in this house you don't share?
DORINE   "Marriage"—I think, yes, I heard a rumor,
   Someone's failed attempt at grotesque humor,
5   So when I heard the story, I said, "No!
   Preposterous! Absurd! It can't be so."[1]
ORGON   Oh, you find it preposterous? And why?
DORINE   It's so outrageous, it must be a lie.

---

1. In seventeenth-century France, until you were twenty-five, the law said you had to have your parents' consent to get married. However, parents were also meant to consult their children, who supposedly could not be forced into an unwanted marriage. The latter part of the law was not always honored, however, and Molière was especially concerned with the issue of girls forced into marriage by their fathers.

ORGON   Yet it's the truth and you will believe it.

10   DORINE   Yet as a joke is how I must receive it.

ORGON   But it's a story that will soon come true.

DORINE   A fantasy!

ORGON   I'm getting tired of you.

    Mariane, it's not a joke—

DORINE   Says he,

    Laughing up his sleeve for all to see.

ORGON   I'm telling you—

15   DORINE   —more make-believe for fun.

    It's very good—you're fooling everyone.

ORGON   You have made me really angry now.

DORINE   I see the awful truth across your brow.

    How can a man who looks as wise as you

    Be such a fool to want—

20   ORGON   What can I do

    About a servant with a mouth like that?

    The liberties you take! Decorum you laugh at!

    I'm not happy with you—

DORINE   Oh sir, don't frown.

    A smile is just a frown turned upside down.

25   Be happy, Sir, because you've shared your scheme,

    Even though it's just a crazy dream.

    Because, dear Sir, your daughter is not meant

    For this zealot—she's too innocent.

    She'd be alarmed by his robust desire

30   And question Heaven's sanction of this fire

    And then the gossip! Your friends will talk a lot,

    Because you're a man of wealth and he is not.

    Could it be your reasoning has a flaw—

    Choosing a beggar for a son-in-law?

35   ORGON   You, shut up! If he has nothing now

    Admire that, as if it were his vow,

    This poverty. His property was lost

    Because he would not pay the deadly cost

    Of daily duties nibbling life away,

40   Leaving him with hardly time to pray.

    The grandeur in his life comes from devotion

    To the eternal, thus his great emotion.

    And at those moments, I can plainly see

    What my special task has come to be:

45   To end the embarrassment he feels

    And the sorrow he so nobly conceals

    Of the loss of his ancestral domain.

    With my money, I can end his pain.

I'll raise him up to be, because I can,
50   With my help, again, a gentleman.
     DORINE   So he's a gentleman. Does that seem vain?
     Then what about this piety and pain?
     Those with "domains" are those of noble birth.
     A holy man's domain is not on earth.
55   It seems to me a holy man of merit
     Wouldn't brag of what he might inherit,
     Even gifts in Heaven, he won't mention.
     To live a humble life is his intention.
     Yet he wants something back? That's just ambition
60   To feed his pride. Is that a holy mission?
     You seem upset. Is it something I said?
     I'll shut up. We'll talk of her instead.
     Look at this girl, your daughter, your own blood.
     How will her honor fare covered with mud?
65   Think of his age. So from the night they're wed,
     Bliss, if there is any, leaves the marriage bed,
     And she'll be tied unto this elderly person.
     Her dedication to fidelity will worsen
     And soon he will "sprout horns,"[2] your holy man,
70   And no one will be happy. If I can
     Have another word, I'd like to say
     Old men and young girls are married every day,
     And the young girls stray, but who's to blame
     For the loss of honor and good name?
75   The father, who proceeds to pick a mate,
     Blindly, though it's someone she may hate,
     Bears the sins the daughter may commit,
     Imperiling his soul because of it.
     If you do this, I vow you'll hear the bell,
80   As you die, summoning you to hell.
     ORGON   You think that you can teach me how to live.
     DORINE   If you'd just heed the lessons that I give.
     ORGON   Can Heaven tell me why I still endure
     This woman's ramblings? Yet, of this I'm sure,
85   I know what's best for you—I'm your father.
     I gave you to Valère, without a bother.
     But I hear he gambles and what's more,
     He thinks things that a Christian would abhor.
     It's from freethinking that all evils stem.
90   No wonder, then, at church, I don't see him.

---

2. He will be a cuckold—that is, his wife will be unfaithful to him.

DORINE   Should he race there, if he only knew
   Which Mass you might attend, and be on view?
   He could wait at the door with holy water.

ORGON   Go away. I'm talking to my daughter.

95   Think, my child, he is Heaven's favorite!
   And age in marriage? It can flavor it,
   A sweet confit suffused with deep, deep pleasure.
   You will be loving, faithful, and will treasure
   Every single moment—two turtle doves—

100   Next to Heaven, the only thing he loves.
   And he will be the only one for you
   No arguments or quarrels. You'll be true.
   Like two innocent children, you will thrive,
   In Heaven's light, thrilled to be alive.

105   And as a woman, surely you must know
   Wives mold husbands, like making pies from dough.

DORINE   Four and twenty cuckolds baked in a pie.

ORGON   Ugh! What a thing to say!

DORINE   Oh, really, why?
   He's destined to be cheated on, it's true.

110   You know he'd always question her virtue.

ORGON   Quiet! Just be quiet. I command it!

DORINE   I'll do just that, because you do demand it!
   But your best interests—I will protect them.

ORGON   Too kind of you. Be quiet and neglect them.

DORINE   If I weren't fond of you—

115 ORGON   —Don't want you to.

DORINE   I will be fond of you in spite of you.

ORGON   Don't!

DORINE   But your honor is so dear to me,
   How can you expose yourself to mockery?

ORGON   Will you never be quiet!

DORINE   Oh, dear Sir,

120   I can't let you do this thing to her.
   It's against my conscience—

ORGON   You vicious asp!

DORINE   Sometimes the things you call me make me gasp.
   And anger, Sir, is not a pious trait.

ORGON   It's your fault, girl! You make me irate!

125   I am livid! Why won't you be quiet!

DORINE   I will. For you, I'm going to try it.
   But I'll be thinking.

ORGON   Fine. Now, Mariane,
   You have to trust—your father's a wise man.
   I have thought a lot about this mating.

I've weighed the options—
130   DORINE   It's infuriating
    Not to be able to speak.
  ORGON   And so
    I'll say this. Of up and coming men I know,
    He's not one of them, no money in the bank,
    Not handsome.
  DORINE   That's the truth. Arf! Arf! Be frank.
    He's a dog!
135   ORGON   He has manly traits.
    And other gifts.
  DORINE   And who will blame the fates
    For failure of this marriage made in hell?
    And whose fault will it be? Not hard to tell.
    Since everyone you know will see the truth:
140   You gave away your daughter to Tartuffe.
    If I were in her place, I'd guarantee
    No man would live the night who dared force me
    Into a marriage that I didn't want.
    There would be war with no hope of détente.
145   ORGON   I asked for silence. This is what I get?
  DORINE   You said not to talk to *you*. Did you forget?
  ORGON   What do you call what you are doing now?
  DORINE   Talking to myself.
  ORGON   You insolent cow!
    I'll wait for you to say just one more word.
    I'm waiting . . .
        [*He prepares to give her a smack, but each time he looks over*
        at her, DORINE *stands silent and still.*]
150   Just ignore her. Look at me.
    I've chosen you a husband who would be,
    If rated, placed among the highest ranks
        [*To* DORINE] Why don't you talk?
  DORINE   Don't feel like it, thanks.
  ORGON   I'm watching you.
  DORINE   Do you think I'm a fool?
155   ORGON   I realize that you may think me cruel.
    But here's the thing, child, I will be obeyed,
    And this marriage, child, will not be delayed.
  DORINE [*Running from him, she throws a line to* MARIANE.]
    You'll be a joke with Tartuffe as a spouse.
        [ORGON *tries to slap her but misses.*]
  ORGON   What we have is a plague in our own house!
160   It's her fault that I'm in the state I'm in,
    So furious, I might commit a sin.

She'll drive me to murder. Or to curse.
I need fresh air before my mood gets worse.

[ORGON *exits.*]

Scene 3

DORINE, MARIANE

DORINE   Tell me, have you lost the power of speech?
   I'm forced to play your role and it's a reach.
   How can you sit there with nothing to say
   Watching him tossing your whole life away?
5 MARIANE   Against my father, what am I to do?
DORINE   You want out of this marriage scheme, don't you?
MARIANE   Yes.
DORINE   Tell him no one can command a heart.
   That when you marry, you will have no part
   Of anyone unless he pleases you.
10 And tell your father, with no more ado,
   That you will marry for yourself, not him,
   And that you won't obey his iron whim.
   Since he finds Tartuffe to be such a catch,
   He can marry him himself. There's a match.
15 MARIANE   You know that fathers have such sway
   Over our lives that I've nothing to say.
   I've never had the strength.
DORINE   Let's think. All right?
   Didn't Valère propose the other night?
   Do you or don't you love Valère?
20 MARIANE   You know the answer, Dorine—that's unfair.
   Just talking about it tears me apart.
   I've said a hundred times, he has my heart.
   I'm wild about him. I know. And I've told you.
DORINE   But how am I to know, for sure, that's true?
25 MARIANE   Because I told you. And yet you doubt it?
   See me blushing when I speak about it?
DORINE   So, you do love him?
MARIANE   Yes, with all my might.
DORINE   He loves you just as much?
MARIANE   I think that's right.
DORINE   And it's to the altar you're both heading?
MARIANE   Yes.
30 DORINE   So what about this other wedding?
MARIANE   I'll kill myself. That's what I've decided.
DORINE   What a great solution you've provided!
   To get out of trouble, you plan to die!

Immediately? Or sometime, by and by?
35 MARIANE   Oh, really, Dorine, you're not my friend,
Unsympathetic—
DORINE   I'm at my wit's end,
Talking to you whose answer is dying,
Who in a crisis, just gives up trying.
MARIANE   What do you want of me, then?
DORINE   Come alive!
40 Love needs a resolute heart to survive.
MARIANE   In my love for Valère, I'm resolute.
But the next step is his.
DORINE   And so, you're mute?
MARIANE   What can I say? It's the job of Valère,
His duty, before I go anywhere,
To deal with my father—
45 DORINE   —Then, you'll stay.
"Orgon was born bizarre," is what some say.
If there were doubts before, we have this proof—
He is head over heels for his Tartuffe,
And breaks off a marriage that he arranged.
50 Valère's at fault if your father's deranged?
MARIANE   But my refusal will be seen as pride
And, worse, contempt. And I have to hide
My feelings for Valère, I must not show
That I'm in love at all. If people know,
55 Then all the modesty my sex is heir to
Will be gone. There's more: how can I bear to
Not be a proper daughter to my father?
DORINE   No, no, of course not. God forbid we bother
The way the world sees you. What people see,
60 What other people think of us, should be
Our first concern. Besides, I see the truth:
You really want to be Madame Tartuffe.
What was I thinking, urging opposition
To Monsieur Tartuffe! This proposition,
65 To merge with him—he's such a catch!
In fact, for you, he's just the perfect match.
He's much respected, everywhere he goes.
And his ruddy complexion nearly glows.
And as his wife, imagine the delight
70 Of being near him, every day and night.
And vital? Oh, my dear, you won't want more.
MARIANE   Oh, Heaven help me!
DORINE   How your soul will soar,
Savoring this marriage down to the last drop,

With such a handsome—

MARIANE   All right! You can stop!

75   Just help me. Please. And tell me there's a way
To save me. I'll do whatever you say.

DORINE   Each daughter must choose always to say yes
To what her father wants, no more and no less.
If he wants to give her an ape to marry,
80   Then she must do it, without a query.
But it's a happy fate! What is this frown?
You'll go by wagon to his little town,
Eager cousins, uncles, aunts will greet you
And will call you "Sister" when they meet you
85   Because you're family now. Don't look so grim.
You will so adore chatting with them.
Welcomed by the local high society,
You'll be expected to maintain propriety
And sit straight, or try to, in the folding chair[3]
90   They offer you, and never, ever stare
At the wardrobe of the bailiff's wife
Because you'll see her every day for life.
Let's not forget the village carnival!
Where you'll be dancing at a lavish ball
95   To a bagpipe orchestra of locals,
An organ grinder's monkey doing vocals—
And your husband—

MARIANE   —Dorine, I beg you, please,
Help me. Should I get down here on my knees?

DORINE   Can't help you.

MARIANE   Please, Dorine, I'm begging you!

DORINE   And you deserve this man.

100   MARIANE   That just not true!

DORINE   Oh yes? What changed?

MARIANE   My darling Dorine . . .

DORINE   No.

MARIANE   You can't be this mean.
I love Valère. I told you and it's true.

DORINE   Who's that? Oh. No, Tartuffe's the one for you.

105   MARIANE   You've always been completely on my side.

DORINE   No more. I sentence you to be Tartuffified!

MARIANE   It seems my fate has not the power to move you,
So I'll seek my solace and remove to
A private place for me in my despair.

3. There was a hierarchy of chairs in the seventeenth century. The most important people sat
in armchairs, the next most important in regular chairs, the next in folding chairs, and the
next on stools. Those of no importance did not sit down.

110   To end the misery that brought me here.
         [*She starts to exit.*]
   DORINE   Wait! Wait! Come back! Please don't go out that door.
      I'll help you. I'm not angry anymore.
   MARIANE   If I am forced into this martyrdom,
      You see, I'll have to die, Dorine.
   DORINE   Oh come,
115   Give up this torment. Look at me—I swear.
      We'll find a way. Look, here's your love, Valère.

Scene 4

VALÈRE, MARIANE, DORINE

   VALÈRE   So I've just heard some news that's news to me,
      And very fine news it is, do you agree?
   MARIANE   What?
   VALÈRE   You have plans for marriage I didn't know.
      You're going to marry Tartuffe. Is this so?
5   MARIANE   My father has that notion, it is true.
   VALÈRE   Madame, your father promised—
   MARIANE   —me to you?
      He changed his mind, announced this change to me,
      Just minutes ago . . .
   VALÈRE   Quite seriously?
   MARIANE   It's his wish that I should marry this man.
10   VALÈRE   And what do you think of your father's plan?
   MARIANE   I don't know.
   VALÈRE   Honest words—better than lies.
      You don't know?
   MARIANE   No.
   VALÈRE   No?
   MARIANE   What do you advise?
   VALÈRE   I advise you to . . . marry Tartuffe. Tonight.
   MARIANE   You advise me to . . .
   VALÈRE   Yes.
   MARIANE   Really?
   VALÈRE   That's right.
15   Consider it. It's an obvious choice.
   MARIANE   I'll follow your suggestion and rejoice.
   VALÈRE   I'm sure that you can follow it with ease.
   MARIANE   Just as you gave it. It will be a breeze.
   VALÈRE   Just to please you was my sole intent.
20   MARIANE   To please you, I'll do it and be content.
   DORINE   I can't wait to see what happens next.
   VALÈRE   And this is love to you? I am perplexed.

Was it a sham when you—

MARIANE   That's in the past
Because you said so honestly and fast

25 That I should take the one bestowed on me.
I'm nothing but obedient, you see,
So, yes, I'll take him. That's my declaration,
Since that's your advice and expectation.

VALÈRE   I see, you're using me as an excuse,

30 Any pretext, so you can cut me loose.
You didn't think I'd notice—I'd be blind
To the fact that you'd made up your mind?

MARIANE   How true. Well said.

VALÈRE   And so it's plain to see,
Your heart never felt a true love for me.

35 MARIANE   If you want to, you may think that is true.
It's clear this thought has great appeal for you.

VALÈRE   If I want? I will, but I'm offended
To my very soul. But your turn's ended,
And I can win this game we're playing at:
I've someone else in mind.

40 MARIANE   I don't doubt that.
Your good points—

VALÈRE   Oh, let's leave them out of this.
I've very few—in fact, I am remiss.
I must be. Right? You've made that clear to me.
But I know someone, hearing that I'm free,

45 To make up for my loss, will eagerly consent.

MARIANE   The loss is not that bad. You'll be content
With your new choice, replacement, if you will.

VALÈRE   I will. And I'll remain contented still,
In knowing you're as happy as I am.

50 A woman tells a man her love's a sham.
The man's been fooled and his honor blighted.
He can't deny his love is unrequited,
Then he forgets this woman totally,
And if he can't, pretends, because, you see,

55 It is ignoble conduct and weak, too,
Loving someone one who does not love you.

MARIANE   What a fine, noble sentiment to heed.

VALÈRE   And every man upholds it as his creed.
What? You expect me to keep on forever

60 Loving you after you blithely sever
The bond between us, watching as you go
Into another's arms and not bestow
This heart you've cast away upon someone

Who might welcome—
MARIANE   I wish it were done.
65   That's exactly what I want, you see.
VALÈRE   That's what you want?
MARIANE   Yes.
VALÈRE   Then let it be.
I'll grant your wish.
MARIANE   Please do.
VALÈRE   Just don't forget,
Whose fault it was when you, filled with regret,
Realize that you forced me out the door.
MARIANE   True.
70   VALÈRE   You've set the example and what's more,
I'll match you with my own hardness of heart.
You won't see me again, if I depart.
MARIANE   That's good!
        [VALÈRE *goes to exit, but when he gets to the door, he returns.*]
VALÈRE   What?
MARIANE   What?
VALÈRE   You said . . . ?
MARIANE   Nothing at all.
VALÈRE   Well, I'll be on my way, then.
        [*Goes, stops*]
                              Did you call?
MARIANE   Me? You must be dreaming.
75   VALÈRE   I'll go away.
Good-bye, then.
MARIANE   Good-bye.
DORINE   I am here to say,
You both are idiots! What's this about?
I left you two alone to fight it out,
To see how far you'd go. You're quite a pair
80   In matching tit for tat—Hold on, Valère!
Where are you going?
VALÈRE   What, Dorine? You spoke?
DORINE   Come here.
VALÈRE   I'm upset and will not provoke
This lady. Do not try to change my mind.
I'm doing what she wants.
DORINE   You are so blind.
Just stop.
VALÈRE   No. It's settled.
85   DORINE   Oh, is that so?
MARIANE   He can't stand to look at me, I know.
He wants to go away, so please let him.

No, I shall leave so I can forget him.
DORINE   Where are you going?
MARIANE   Leave me alone.
DORINE   Come back here at once.
90 MARIANE   No. Even that tone
Won't bring me. I'm not a child, you see.
VALÈRE   She's tortured by the very sight of me.
It's better that I free her from her pain.
DORINE   What more proof do you need? You are insane!
95 Now stop this nonsense! Come here both of you.
VALÈRE   To what purpose?
MARIANE   What are you trying to do?
DORINE   Bring you two together! And end this fight.
It's so stupid! Yes?
VALÈRE   No. It wasn't right
The way she spoke to me. Didn't you hear?
100 DORINE   Your voices are still ringing in my ear.
MARIANE   The way he treated me—didn't you see?
DORINE   Saw and heard it all. Now listen to me.
The only thing she wants, Valère, is you.
I can attest to that right now. It's true.
105 And Mariane, he wants you for his wife,
And only you. On that I'll stake my life.
MARIANE   He told me to be someone else's bride!
VALÈRE   She asked for my advice and I replied!
DORINE   You're both impossible. What can I do?
Give your hand—
VALÈRE   What for?
110 DORINE   Come on, you.
Now yours, Mariane, Don't make me shout.
Come on!
MARIANE   All right. But what is this about?
DORINE   Here. Take each other's hand and make a link.
You love each other better than you think.
115 VALÈRE   Mademoiselle, this is your hand I took,
You think you could give me a friendly look?
        [MARIANE *peeks at* VALÈRE *and smiles.*]
DORINE   It's true. Lovers are not completely sane.
VALÈRE   Mariane, haven't I good reason to complain?
Be honest. Wasn't it a wicked ploy?
To say—
120 MARIANE   You think I told you that with joy?
And you confronted me.
DORINE   Another time.
This marriage to Tartuffe would be a crime,

We have to stop it.
MARIANE   So, what can we do?
    Tell us.
DORINE   All sorts of things involving you.
125   It's all nonsense and your father's joking.
    But if you play along, say, without choking,
    And give your consent, for the time being,
    He'll take the pressure off, thereby freeing
    All of us to find a workable plan
130   To keep you from a marriage with this man.
    Then you can find a reason every day
    To postpone the wedding, in this way:
    One day you're sick and that can take a week.
    Another day you're better but can't speak,
135   And we all know you have to say "I do,"
    Or the marriage isn't legal. And that's true.
    Now bad omens—would he have his daughter
    Married when she's dreamt of stagnant water,
    Or broken a mirror or seen the dead?
140   He may not care and say it's in your head,
    But you will be distraught in your delusion,
    And require bed rest and seclusion.
    I do know this—if we want to succeed,
    You can't be seen together.
    [*To* VALÈRE]   With all speed,
145   Go, and gather all your friends right now,
    Have them insist that Orgon keep his vow.
    Social pressure helps. Then to her brother.
    All of us will work on her stepmother.
    Let's go.
VALÈRE   Whatever happens, can you see?
150   My greatest hope is in your love for me.
MARIANE   Though I don't know just what Father will do,
    I do know I belong only to you.
VALÈRE   You put my heart at ease! I swear I will . . .
DORINE   It seems that lovers' tongues are never still.
    Out, I tell you.
VALÈRE [*Taking a step and returning*]   One last—
155 DORINE   No more chat!
    You go out this way, yes, and you go that.

End of Act Two

Act Three

Scene 1

DAMIS, DORINE

DAMIS   May lightning strike me dead, right here and now,
Call me a villain, if I break this vow:
Forces of Heaven or earth won't make me sway
From this my—

DORINE   Let's not get carried away.
5   Your father only said what he intends
To happen. The real event depends
On many things and something's bound to slip,
Between this horrid cup and his tight lip.

DAMIS   That this conceited fool Father brought here
10   Has plans? Well, they'll be ended—do not fear.

DORINE   Now stop that! Forget him. Leave him alone.
Leave him to your stepmother. He is prone,
This Tartuffe, to indulge her every whim.
So let her use her power over him.
15   It does seem pretty clear he's soft on her,
Pray God that's true. And if he will concur
That this wedding your father wants is bad,
That's good. But he might want it, too, the cad.
She's sent for him so she can sound him out
20   On this marriage you're furious about,
Discover what he feels and tell him clearly
If he persists that it will cost him dearly.
It seems he can't be seen while he's at prayers,
So I have my own vigil by the stairs
25   Where his valet says he will soon appear.
Do leave right now, and I'll wait for him here.

DAMIS   I'll stay to vouch for what was seen and heard.

DORINE   They must be alone.

DAMIS   I won't say a word.

DORINE   Oh, right. I know what you are like. Just go.
30   You'll spoil everything, believe me, I know.
Out!

DAMIS   I promise I won't get upset.
        [*She pinches him as she used to do when he was a child.*]
                  Ow!

DORINE   Do as I say. Get out of here right *now!*

Scene 2

TARTUFFE, LAURENT, DORINE

TARTUFFE [*Noticing* DORINE]   Laurent, lock up my scourge and hair
    shirt, too.[1]
    And pray that our Lord's grace will shine on you.
    If anyone wants me, I've gone to share
    My alms at prison with the inmates there.

5   DORINE   What a fake! What an imposter! What a sleaze!

TARTUFFE   What do you want?

DORINE   To say—

TARTUFFE [*Taking a handkerchief from his pocket*]
                             Good Heavens, please,
    Do take this handkerchief before you speak.

DORINE   What for?

TARTUFFE   Cover your bust. The flesh is weak.
    Souls are forever damaged by such sights,

10   When sinful thoughts begin their evil flights.

DORINE   It seems temptation makes a meal of you—
    To turn you on, a glimpse of flesh will do.
    Inside your heart, a furnace must be housed.
    For me, I'm not so easily aroused.

15   I could see you naked, head to toe—
    Never be tempted once, and this I know.

TARTUFFE   Please! Stop! And if you're planning to resume
    This kind of talk, I'll leave the room

DORINE   If someone is to go, let it be me.

20   Yes, I can't wait to leave your company.
    Madame is coming down from her salon,
    And wants to talk to you, if you'll hang on.

TARTUFFE   Of course. Most willingly.

DORINE   [*Aside*] Look at him melt.
    I'm right. I always knew that's how he felt.

TARTUFFE   Is she coming soon?

25   DORINE   You want me to leave?
    Yes, here she is in person, I believe.

Scene 3

ELMIRE, TARTUFFE

TARTUFFE   Ah, may Heaven in all its goodness give
    Eternal health to you each day you live,

---

1. To whip oneself, to wear a shirt made out of animal hair, and other kinds of self-inflicted
   punishment were practices of penitence meant to make up for sin. Tartuffe's performance
   of penitence is part of his fraudulent piety.

Bless your soul and body, and may it grant
The prayerful wishes of this supplicant.

5   ELMIRE   Yes. Thank you for that godly wish, and please,
Let's sit down so we can talk with ease.

TARTUFFE   Are you recovered from your illness now?

ELMIRE   My fever disappeared, I don't know how.

TARTUFFE   My small prayers, I'm sure, had not the power,

10   Though I was on my knees many an hour.
Each fervent prayer wrenched from my simple soul
Was made with your recovery as its goal.

ELMIRE   I find your zeal a little disconcerting.

TARTUFFE   I can't enjoy my health if you are hurting.

15   Your health's true worth, I can't begin to tell.
I'd give mine up, in fact, to make you well.

ELMIRE   Though you stretch Christian charity too far,
Your thoughts are kind, however strange they are.

TARTUFFE   You merit more, that's in my humble view.

20   ELMIRE   I need a private space to talk to you.
I think that this will do—what do you say?

TARTUFFE   Excellent choice. And this is a sweet day,
To find myself here tête-à-tête[2] with you,
That I've begged Heaven for this, yes, is true,

25   And now it's granted to my great relief.

ELMIRE   Although our conversation will be brief,
Please open up your heart and tell me all.
You must hide nothing now, however small.

TARTUFFE   I long to show you my entire soul,

30   My need for truth I can barely control.
I'll take this time, also, to clear the air—
The criticisms I have brought to bear
Around the visits that your charms attract,
Were never aimed at you or how you act,

35   But rather were my own transports of zeal,
Which carried me away with how I feel,
Consumed by impulses, though always pure,
Nevertheless, intense in how—

ELMIRE   I'm sure
That my salvation is your only care.

TARTUFFE [Pressing the ends of her fingers]

40   Yes, you're right, and so my fervor there—

ELMIRE   Ouch! You're squeezing too hard.

TARTUFFE   —comes from this zeal . . .
I didn't mean to squeeze. How does this feel?

_____
2. Alone and face to face.

[*He puts his hand on her knee.*]

ELMIRE   Your hand—what is it doing . . . ?

TARTUFFE   So tender,
    The fabric of your dress, a sweet surrender
    Under my hand—

45 ELMIRE   I'm quite ticklish. Please, don't.
        [*She moves her chair back, and* TARTUFFE *moves his forward.*]

TARTUFFE   I want to touch this lace—don't fret, I won't.
    It's marvelous! I so admire the trade
    Of making lace. Don't tell me you're afraid.

ELMIRE   What? No. But getting back to business now,
50 It seems my husband plans to break a vow
    And offer you his daughter. Is this true?

TARTUFFE   He mentioned it, but I must say to you,
    The wondrous gifts that catch my zealous eye,
    I see quite near in bounteous supply.

55 ELMIRE   Not earthly things for which you would atone.

TARTUFFE   My chest does not contain a heart of stone.

ELMIRE   Well, I believe your eyes follow your soul,
    And your desires have Heaven as their goal.

TARTUFFE   The love that to eternal beauty binds us
60 Doesn't stint when temporal beauty finds us.
    Our senses can as easily be charmed
    When by an earthly work we are disarmed.
    You are a rare beauty, without a flaw,
    And in your presence, I'm aroused with awe
65 But for the Author of All Nature, so,
    My heart has ardent feelings, even though
    I feared them at first, questioning their source.
    Had I been ambushed by some evil force?
    I felt that I must hide from this temptation:
70 You. My feelings threatened my salvation.
    Yes, I found this sinful and distressing,
    Until I saw your beauty as a blessing!
    So now my passion never can be wrong,
    And, thus, my virtue stays intact and strong.
75 That is how I'm here in supplication,
    Offering my heart in celebration
    Of the audacious truth that I love you,
    That only you can make this wish come true,
    That through your grace, my offering's received,
80 And accepted, and that I have achieved
    Salvation of a sort, and by your grace,
    I could be content in this low place.
    It all depends on you, at your behest:

Am I to be tormented or be blest?
85   You are my welfare, solace, and my hope
But, whatever your decision, I will cope.
Will I be happy? I'll rely on you.
If you want me to be wretched, that's fine, too.
ELMIRE   Well, what a declaration! How gallant!
90   But I'm surprised you want the things you want.
It seems your heart could use a talking to—
It's living in the chest of someone who
Proclaims to be pious—
TARTUFFE   —And so I am.
My piety's a true thing—not a sham,
95   But I'm no less a man so when I find
Myself with you, I quickly lose my mind.
My heart is captured and, with it, my thought.
Yet since I know the cause, I'm not distraught.
Words like these from me must be alarming,
100   But it is your beauty that's so charming,
I cannot help myself, I am undone.
And I'm no angel, nor could I be one.
If my confession earns your condemnation,
Then blame your glance for the annihilation
105   Of my command of this: my inmost being.
A surrender of my soul is what you're seeing.
Your eyes blaze with more than human splendor,
And that first look had the effect to render
Powerless the bastions of my heart.
110   No fasting, tears or prayers, no pious art
Could shield my soul from your celestial gaze
Which I will worship 'til the End of Days.
A thousand times my eyes, my sighs have told
The truth that's in my heart. Now I am bold,
115   Encouraged by your presence, so I say,
With my true voice, will this be the day
You condescend to my poor supplication,
Offered up with devout admiration,
And save my soul by granting this request:
120   Accept this love that I've lovingly confessed?
Your honor has, of course, all my protection,
And you can trust my absolute discretion.
For those men that all the women die for,
Love's a game whose object is a high score.
125   Although they promise not to talk, they will.
They need to boast of their superior skill,
Receive no favors not as soon revealed,

Exposing what they vowed would be concealed.
And in the end, this love is over priced,
130   When a woman's honor's sacrificed.
But men like me burn with a silent flame,
Our secrets safe, our loves we never name,
Because our reputations are our wealth.
When we transgress, it's with the utmost stealth.
135   Your honor's safe as my hand in a glove,
So I can offer, free from scandal, love,
And pleasure without fear of intervention.
    ELMIRE   Your sophistry does not hide your intention.
In fact, you know, it makes it all too clear.
140   What if, through me, my husband were to hear
About this love for me you now confess
Which shatters the ideals you profess?
How would your friendship fare, then, I wonder?
    TARTUFFE   It's your beauty cast this spell I suffer under.
145   I'm made of flesh, like you, like all mankind.
And since your soul is pure, you will be kind,
And not judge me harshly for my brashness
In speaking of my love in all its rashness.
I beg you to forgive me my offense,
150   I plead your perfect face as my defense.
    ELMIRE   Some might take offense at your confession,
But I will show a definite discretion,
And keep my husband in the dark about
These sinful feelings for me that you spout.
155   But I want something from you in return:
There's a promised marriage, you will learn,
That supercedes my husband's recent plan—
The marriage of Valère and Mariane.
This marriage you will openly support,
160   Without a single quibble, and, in short,
Renounce the unjust power of a man
Who'd give his own daughter, Mariane,
To another when she's promised to Valère.
In return, my silence—

Scene 4

ELMIRE, DAMIS, TARTUFFE

DAMIS [*Jumping out from where he had been hiding*]
                —Hold it right there!
No, no! You're done. All this will be revealed.
I heard each word. And as I was concealed,

Something besides your infamy came clear:
5   Heaven in its great wisdom brought me here,
To witness and then give my father proof
Of the hypocrisy of his Tartuffe,
This so-called saint anointed from above.
Speaking to my father's wife of love!
10 ELMIRE   Damis, there is a lesson to be learned,
And there is my forgiveness to be earned.
I promised him. Don't make me take it back.
It's not my nature to see as an attack
Such foolishness as this, or see the need
15   To tell my husband of the trivial deed.
DAMIS   So, you have your reasons, but I have mine.
To grant this fool forgiveness? I decline.
To want to spare him is a mockery,
Because he's more than foolish, can't you see?
20   This fanatic in his insolent pride,
Brought chaos to my house, and would divide
Me and my father—unforgivable!
What's more, he's made my life unlivable,
As he undermines two love affairs,
25   Mine and Valère's sister, my sister and Valère's!
Father must hear the truth about this man.
Heaven helped me—I must do what I can
To use this chance. I'd deserve to lose it,
If I dropped it now and didn't use it.
ELMIRE   Damis—
30 DAMIS   No, please, I have to follow through.
I've never felt as happy as I do
Right now. And don't try to dissuade me
I'll have my revenge. If you forbade me,
I'd still do it, so you don't have to bother.
35   I'll finish this for good. Here comes my father.

Scene 5

ORGON, DAMIS, TARTUFFE, ELMIRE

DAMIS   Father! You have arrived. Let's celebrate!
I have a tale that I'd like to relate.
It happened here and right before my eyes,
I offer it to you—as a surprise!
5   For all your love, you have been repaid
With duplicity. You have been betrayed
By your dear friend here, whom I just surprised
Making verbal love, I quickly surmised,

To your wife. Yes, this is how he shows you
10   How he honors you—he thinks he knows you.
But as your son, I know you much better—
You demand respect down to the letter.
Madame, unflappable and so discreet,
Would keep this secret, never to repeat.
15   But, as your son, my feelings are too strong,
And to be silent is to do you wrong.
ELMIRE   One learns to spurn without being unkind,
And how to spare a husband's peace of mind.
Although I understood just what he meant,
20   My honor wasn't touched by this event.
That's how I feel. And you would have, Damis,
Said nothing, if you had listened to me.

Scene 6

ORGON, DAMIS, TARTUFFE

ORGON   Good Heavens! What he said? Can it be true?
TARTUFFE   Yes, my brother, I'm wicked through and through.
The most miserable of sinners, I.
Filled with iniquity, I should just die.
5   Each moment of my life's so dirty, soiled,
Whatever I come near is quickly spoiled.
I'm nothing but a heap of filth and crime.
I'd name my sins, but we don't have the time.
And I see that Heaven, to punish me,
10   Has mortified my soul quite publicly.
What punishment I get, however great,
I well deserve so I'll accept my fate.
Defend myself? I'd face my own contempt,
If I thought that's something I'd attempt.
15   What you've heard here, surely, you abhor,
So chase me like a criminal from your door.
Don't hold back your rage, please, let it flame,
For I deserve to burn, in my great shame.
ORGON [*To his son*]   Traitor! And how dare you even try
20   To tarnish this man's virtue with a lie?
DAMIS   What? This hypocrite pretends to be contrite
And you believe him over me?
ORGON   That's spite!
And shut your mouth!
TARTUFFE   No, let him have his say.
And don't accuse him. Don't send him away.
25   Believe his story—why be on my side?

You don't know what motives I may hide.
Why give me so much loyalty and love?
Do you know what I am capable of?
My brother, you have total trust in me,
30   And think I'm good because of what you see?
No, no, by my appearance you're deceived,
And what I say you think must be believed.
Well, believe this—I have no worth at all.
The world sees me as worthy, yet I fall
35   Far below. Sin is so insidious.
[*To* DAMIS]
Dear Son, do treat me as perfidious,
Infamous, lost, a murderer, a thief,
Speak on, because my sins, beyond belief,
Can bring this shameful sinner to his knees,
40   In humble, paltry effort to appease.
ORGON [*To* TARTUFFE]   Brother, there is no need . . .
    [*To* DAMIS]   Will you relent?
DAMIS   He has seduced you!
ORGON   Can't you take a hint?
    Be quiet!
    [*To* TARTUFFE]
            Brother, please get up.
    [*To* DAMIS]   Ingrate!
DAMIS   But Father, this man—
ORGON   —whom you denigrate.
DAMIS   But you should—
ORGON   Quiet!
45   DAMIS   But I saw and heard—
ORGON   I'll slap you if you say another word.
TARTUFFE   In the name of God, don't be that way.
    Brother, I'd rather suffer, come what may,
    Than have this boy receive what's meant for me.
ORGON [*To his son*]   Heathen!
50   TARTUFFE   Please! I beg of you on bended knee.
ORGON [*To* DAMIS]   Wretch! See his goodness?!
DAMIS   But—
ORGON   No!
DAMIS   But—
ORGON   Be still!
    And not another word from you until
    You admit the truth. It's plain to see
    Although you thought that I would never be
55   Aware and know your motives, yet I do.
    You all hate him. And I saw today, you,

Wife, servants—everyone beneath my roof,
Are trying everything to force Tartuffe,
Out of my house, this holy man, my friend.
60   The more you try to banish him and end
Our sacred brotherhood, the more secure
His place is. I have never been more sure
Of anyone. I give him as his bride
My daughter. If that hurts the family pride,
65   Then good. It needs humbling. You understand?
DAMIS   You're going to force her to accept his hand?
ORGON   Yes, traitor, and this evening. You know why?
To infuriate you. Yes, I defy
You all. I am master and you'll obey.
70   And you, you ingrate, now I'll make you pay
For your abuse of him, kneel on the floor,
And beg his pardon, or go out the door.
DAMIS   Me? Kneel and ask the pardon of this fraud?
ORGON   What? You refuse? Someone get me a rod!
A stick! Something!
[*To* TARTUFFE]   Don't hold me.
75   [*To* DAMIS]   Here's your whack!
Out of my house and don't ever come back!
DAMIS   Yes, I'll leave, but—
ORGON   Get out of my sight!
I disinherit you, you traitor, you're a blight
On this house. And you'll get nothing now
80   From me, except my curse!

Scene 7

ORGON, TARTUFFE

ORGON   You have my vow,
He'll never more question your honesty.
TARTUFFE [*To Heaven*]   Forgive him for the pain he's given me.
[*To* ORGON]   How I suffer. If you could only see
5   What I go through when they disparage me.
ORGON   Oh no!
TARTUFFE   The ingratitude, even in thought,
Tortures my soul so much, it leaves me fraught
With inner pain. My heart's stopped. I'm near death,
I can barely speak now. Where is my breath?
ORGON
[*Running in tears to the door through which he chased his son*]
10   You demon! I held back, you little snot

I should have struck you dead right on the spot!
[*To* TARTUFFE] Get up, Brother. Don't worry any more.
TARTUFFE   Let us end these troubles, Brother, I implore.
For the discord I have caused, I deeply grieve,
15 So for the good of all, I'll take my leave.
ORGON   What? Are you joking? No!
TARTUFFE   They hate me here.
It pains me when I see them fill your ear
With suspicions.
ORGON   But that doesn't matter.
I don't listen.
TARTUFFE   That persistent chatter
20 You now ignore, one day, you'll listen to.
Repetition of a lie can make it true.
ORGON   No, my brother. Never.
TARTUFFE   A man's wife
Can so mislead his soul and ruin his life.
ORGON   No, no.
TARTUFFE   Brother, let me, by leaving here,
25 Remove any cause for doubt or fear.
ORGON   No, no. You will stay. My soul is at stake.
TARTUFFE   Well, then, a hefty penance I must make.
I'll mortify myself, unless . . .
ORGON   No need!
TARTUFFE   Then we will never speak of it, agreed?
30 But the question of your honor still remains,
And with that I'll take particular pains
To prevent rumors. My absence my defense—
I'll never see your wife again, and hence—
ORGON   No. You spend every hour with her you want,
35 And be seen with her. I want you to flaunt,
In front of them, this friendship with my wife.
And I know how to really turn the knife
I'll make you my heir, my only one,
Yes, you will be my son-in-law and son.
40 A good and faithful friend means more to me
Than any member of my family.
Will you accept this gift that I propose?
TARTUFFE   Whatever Heaven wants I can't oppose.
ORGON   Poor man! A contract's what we need to write.
45 And let all the envious burst with spite.

End of Act Three

Act Four

Scene 1

CLÉANTE, TARTUFFE

CLÉANTE   Yes, everyone is talking and each word
Diminishes your glory, rest assured.
Though your name's tainted with scandal and shame,
I'm glad I ran across you, all the same,
5   Because I need to share with you my view
On this disaster clearly caused by you.
Damis, let's say for now, was so misguided,
He spoke before he thought. But you decided
To just sit back and watch him be exiled
10   From his own father's house. Were he a child,
Then, really, would you dare to treat him so?
Shouldn't you forgive him, not make him go?
However, if there's vengeance in your heart,
And you act on it, tell me what's the part
15   That's Christian in that? And are you so base,
You'd let a son fall from his father's grace?
Give God your anger as an offering,
Bring peace and forgive all for everything.

TARTUFFE   I'd do just that, if it were up to me.
20   I blame him for nothing, don't you see?
I've pardoned him, already. That's my way.
And I'm not bitter, but have this to say:
Heaven's best interests will have been served,
When wrongdoers have got what they deserved.
25   In fact, if he returns here, I would leave,
Because God knows what people might believe.
Faking forgiveness to manipulate
My accuser, silencing the hate
He has for me could be seen as my goal.
30   When I would only wish to save his soul.
What he said to me, though unforgivable,
I give unto God to make life livable.

CLÉANTE   To this conclusion, Sir, I have arrived:
Your excuses could not be more contrived.
35   Just how did you come by the opinion
Heaven's business is in your dominion,
Judging who is guilty and who is not?
Taking revenge, is Heaven's task, I thought.
And if you're under Heaven's sovereignty,
40   What human verdict would you ever be

The least bit moved by. No, you wouldn't care—
Judging other's lives is so unfair.
Heaven seems to say live and let live,
And our task, I believe, is to forgive.

45 TARTUFFE   I said I've pardoned him. I take such pains
To do exactly what Heaven ordains.
But after his attack on me, it's clear,
Heaven does not ordain that he live here.

    CLÉANTE   Does it ordain, Sir, that you nod and smile,
50 When taking what is not yours, all the while?
On this inheritance you have no claim
And yet you think it's yours. Have you no shame?

    TARTUFFE   That this gift was, in any way, received
Out of self-interest, would not be believed
55 By anyone who knows me well. They'd say,
"The world's wealth, to him, holds no sway."
I am not dazzled by gold nor its glitter,
So lack of wealth has never made me bitter.
If I take this present from the father,
60 The source of all this folderol and bother,
I am saving, so everyone understands,
This wealth from falling into the wrong hands.
Waste of wealth and property's a crime,
And that is what would happen at this time.
65 But I would use it as part of my plan:
For glory of Heaven, and the good of man.[1]

    CLÉANTE   Well, Sir, I think these small fears that plague you,
In fact, may cause the rightful heir to sue.
Why trouble yourself, Sir, couldn't you just
70 Let him own his property, if he must?
Let others say his property's misused
By him, rather than have yourself accused
Of taking it from its rightful owner.
Wouldn't a pious man be a donor
75 Of property? Unless there is a verse,
Or proverb about how you fill your purse
With what's not yours, at all, in any part.
And if Heaven has put into your heart,
This obstacle to living with Damis,
80 The honorable thing, you must agree,

---

1. A group of ultra-conservative Catholics called The Company of the Holy Sacrament accused Molière of attacking them, based partly on his use here of the expression *"Pour la gloire du Ciel et le bien du prochain"* (For the glory of Heaven and the good of mankind), which appeared in many of their writings.

As well as, certainly, the most discreet
Is pack your bags and, quickly, just retreat.
To have the son of the house chased away,
Because a guest objects, is a sad day.
85   Leaving now would show your decency,
Sir . . .
TARTUFFE   Yes. Well, it is half after three;
Pious duties consume this time of day,
You will excuse my hurrying away.
CLÉANTE
Ah!

Scene 2

ELMIRE, MARIANE, DORINE, CLÉANTE

DORINE   Please, come to the aid of Mariane.
She's suffering because her father's plan
To force this marriage, impossible to bear,
Has pushed her from distress into despair.
5   Her father's on his way here. Do your best,
Turn him around. Use subtlety, protest,
Whatever way will work to change his mind.

Scene 3

ORGON, ELMIRE, MARIANE, CLÉANTE, DORINE

ORGON   Ah! Here's everyone I wanted to find!
[*To* MARIANE] This document I have here in my hand
Will make you very happy, understand?
MARIANE   Father, in the name of Heaven, I plead
5   To all that's good and kind in you, concede
Paternal power, just in this sense:
Free me from my vows of obedience.
Enforcing that inflexible law today
Will force me to confess each time I pray
10   My deep resentment of my obligation.
I know, Father, that I am your creation,
That you're the one who's given life to me.
Why would you now fill it with misery?
If you destroy my hopes for the one man
15   I've dared to love by trying now to ban
Our union, then I'm kneeling to implore,
Don't give me to a man whom I abhor.
To you, Father, I make this supplication.

Don't drive me to some act of desperation,
20   By ruling me simply because you can.
ORGON [*Feeling himself touched*]   Be strong! Human weakness
      shames a man!
MARIANE   Your affection for him doesn't bother me:
      Let it erupt, give him your property,
      And if that's not enough, then give him mine.[2]
25   Any claim on it, I do now decline.
      But in this gifting, don't give him my life.
      If I must wed, then I will be God's wife,
      In a convent, until my days are done.
ORGON   Ah! So you will be a holy, cloistered nun,
30   Because your father thwarts your love affair.
      Get up! The more disgust you have to bear,
      The more of Heaven's treasure you will earn.
      And then Heaven will bless you in return.
      Through this marriage, you'll mortify[3] your senses.
35   Don't bother me with any more pretenses.
DORINE   But . . . !
ORGON   Quiet, you! I see you standing there.
      Don't speak a single word! Don't even dare!
CLÉANTE   If you permit, I'd like to say a word . . .
ORGON   Brother, the best advice the world has heard
40   Is yours—its reasoning, hard to ignore.
      But I refuse to hear it anymore.
ELMIRE [*To her husband*]   And now I wonder, have you lost your
      mind?
      Your love for this one man has made you blind.
      Can you stand there and say you don't believe
45   A word we've said? That we're here to deceive?
ORGON   Excuse me—I believe in what I see.
      You, indulging my bad son, agree
      To back him up in this terrible prank,
      Accusing my dear friend of something rank.
50   You should be livid if what you claim took place,
      And yet this look of calm is on your face.
ELMIRE   Because a man says he's in love with me,
      I'm to respond with heavy artillery?
      I laugh at these unwanted propositions.
55   Mirth will quell most ardent ambitions.
      Why make a fuss over an indiscretion?

___

2. Mariane has inherited property from her mother.
3. To subdue or deaden (as the body or bodily appetites) especially by abstinence or self-
   inflicted pain or discomfort.

My honor's safe and in my possession.
You say I'm calm? Well, that's my constancy,
It won't need a defense, or clemency.
60 I know I'll never be a vicious prude
Who always seems to hear men being rude,
And then defends her honor tooth and claw,
Still snarling, even as the men withdraw.
From honor like that Heaven preserve me,
65 If that's what you want, you don't deserve me.
Besides, you're the one who has been betrayed.
ORGON   I see through this trick that's being played.
ELMIRE   How can you be so dim? I am amazed
How you can hear these sins and stay unfazed.
70 But what if I could show you what he does?
ORGON   Show?
ELMIRE   Yes.
ORGON   A fiction!
ELMIRE   No, the truth because
I am quite certain I can find a way
To show you in the fullest light of day . . .
ORGON   Fairy tales!
ELMIRE   Come on, at least answer me.
75 I've given up expecting you to be
My advocate. What have you got to lose,
By hiding somewhere, any place you choose,
And see for yourself. And then we can
Hear what you say about your holy man.
80 ORGON   Then I'll say nothing because it cannot be.
ELMIRE   Enough. I'm tired. You'll see what you see.
I'm not a liar, though I've been accused.
The time is now and I won't be refused.
You'll be a witness. And we can stop our rants.
85 ORGON   All right! I call your bluff, Miss Smarty Pants.
ELMIRE [*To* DORINE]   Tell Tartuffe to come.
DORINE   Watch out. He's clever.
Men like him are caught, well, almost never.
ELMIRE   Narcissism is a great deceiver,
And he has lots of that. He's a believer
In his charisma.
90 [*To* CLÉANTE *and* MARIANE] Leave us for a bit.

Scene 4

ELMIRE, ORGON

ELMIRE See this table? Good. Get under it.
ORGON What!
ELMIRE You are hiding. Get under there and stay.
ORGON Under the table?
ELMIRE Just do as I say.
  I have a plan, but for it to succeed,
5 You must be hidden. So are we agreed?
  You want to know? I'm ready to divulge it.
ORGON This fantasy of yours—I'll indulge it.
  But then I want to lay this thing to rest.
ELMIRE Oh, that'll happen. Because he'll fail the test.
10 You see, I'm going to have a conversation
  I'd never have—just as an illustration
  Of how this hypocrite behaved with me.
  So don't be scandalized. I must be free
  To flirt. Clearly, that's what it's going to take
15 To prove to you your holy man's a fake.
  I'm going to lead him on, to lift his mask,
  Seem to agree to anything he'll ask,
  Pretend to respond to his advances.
  It's for you I'm taking all these chances.
20 I'll stop as soon as you have seen enough;
  I hope that comes before he calls my bluff.
  His plans for me must be circumvented,
  His passion's strong enough to be demented,
  So the moment you're convinced, you let me know
25 That I've revealed the fraud I said I'd show.
  Stop him so I won't have a minute more
  Exposure to your friend, this lecherous boor.
  You're in control. I'm sure I'll be all right.
  And . . . here he comes: so hush, stay out of sight.

Scene 5

TARTUFFE, ELMIRE, ORGON [under the table]

TARTUFFE I'm told you want to have a word with me.
ELMIRE Yes. I have a secret but I'm not free
  To speak. Close that door, have a look around,
  We certainly do not want to be found
5 The way we were just as Damis appeared.
  I was terrified for you and as I feared,
  He was irate. You saw how hard I tried

To calm him down and keep him pacified.
I was so upset; I never had the thought,
10 "Deny it all," which might have helped a lot,
But as it turns out, we've nothing to fear.
My husband's not upset, it would appear.
Things are good, to Heaven I defer,
Because they're even better than they were.
15 I have to say I'm quite amazed, in fact,
His good opinion of you is intact.
To clear the air and quiet every tongue,
And to kill any gossip that's begun—
You could've pushed me over with a feather—
20 He wants us to spend all our time together!
That's why, with no fear of a critical stare,
I can be here with you or anywhere.
Most important, I am completely free
To show my ardor for you, finally.

25 TARTUFFE   Ardor? This is a sudden change of tone
From the last time we found ourselves alone.

ELMIRE   If thinking I was turning you away
Has made you angry, all that I can say
Is that you do not know a woman's heart!
30 Protecting our virtue keeps us apart,
And makes us seem aloof, and even cold.
But cooler outside, inside the more bold.
When love overcomes us, we are ashamed,
Because we fear that we might be defamed.
35 We must protect our honor—not allow
Our love to show. I fear that even now,
In this confession, you'll think ill of me.
But now I've spoken, and I hope you see
My ardor that is there. Why would I sit
40 And listen to you? Why would I permit
Your talk of love, unless I had a notion
Just like yours, and with the same emotion?
And when Damis found us, didn't I try
To quiet him? And did you wonder why,
45 In speaking of Mariane's marriage deal,
I not only asked you, I made an appeal
That you turn it down? What was I doing?
Making sure I'd be the one you'd be wooing.

TARTUFFE   It is extremely sweet, without a doubt,
50 To watch your lips as loving words spill out.
Abundant honey there for me to drink,
But I have doubts. I cannot help but think,

"Does she tell the truth, or does she lie,
To get me to break off this marriage tie?
55 Is all this ardor something she could fake,
And just an act for her stepdaughter's sake?"
So many questions, yet I want to trust.
But need to know the truth, in fact, I must.
Pleasing you, Elmire, is my main task,
60 And happiness, and so I have to ask
To sample this deep ardor felt for me
Right here and now, in blissful ecstasy.

ELMIRE [*Coughing to alert her husband*]
You want to spend this passion instantly?
I've been opening my heart consistently,
65 But for you, it's not enough, this sharing.
Yet for a woman, it is very daring.
So why can't you be happy with a taste,
Instead of the whole meal consumed in haste?

TARTUFFE   We dare not hope, all those of us who don't
70 Deserve a thing. And so it is I won't
Be satisfied with words. I'll always doubt
Assume my fortune's taken the wrong route
On its way to me. And that is why
I don't believe in anything 'til I
75 Have touched, partaken until satisfied.

ELMIRE   So suddenly, your love can't be denied.
It wants complete dominion over me,
And what it wants, it wants violently.
I know I'm flustered, I know I'm out of breath—
80 Your power over me could be the death
Of my reason. Does this seem right to you?
To use my weakness against me, just to
Conquer? No one's gallant anymore.
I invite you in. You break down the door.

85 TARTUFFE   If your passion for me isn't a pretence,
Then why deny me its best evidence?

ELMIRE   But, Heaven, Sir, that place that you address
So often, would judge us both if we transgress.

TARTUFFE   That's all that's in the way of my desires?
90 These judgments Heaven makes of what transpires?
All you fear is Heaven's bad opinion.

ELMIRE   But I am made to fear its dominion.

TARTUFFE   And I know how to exorcise these fears.
To sin is not as bad as it appears
95 If, and stay with me on this, one can think
That in some cases, Heaven gives a wink

[*It is a scoundrel speaking.*][4] When it comes to certain needs of
   men
Who can remain upright but only when
There is a pure intention. So you see,
                00   If you just let yourself be led by me,
You'll have no worries, and I can enjoy
You. And you, me. Because we will employ
This way of thinking—a real science
And a secret, thus, with your compliance,
05   Fulfilling my desires without fear,
Is easy now, so let it happen here.
That cough, Madame, is bad.
ELMIRE   I'm in such pain.
TARTUFFE   A piece of licorice might ease the strain.
ELMIRE [*Directed to* ORGON]   This cold I have is very obstinate.
10   It stubbornly holds on. I can't shake it.
TARTUFFE   That's most annoying.
ELMIRE   More than I can say.
TARTUFFE   Let's get back to finding you a way,
Finally, to get around your scruples:
Secrecy—I'm one of its best pupils
15   And practitioners. Responsibility
For any evil—you can put on me.
I will answer up to Heaven if I must,
And give a good accounting you can trust.
There'll be no sins for which we must atone,
20   'Cause evil exists only when it's known.
Adam and Eve were public in their fall.
To sin in private is not to sin at all.
ELMIRE [*After coughing again*]   Obviously, I must give in to you,
Because, it seems, you are a person who
25   Refuses to believe anything I say.
Live testimony only can convey
The truth of passion here, no more, no less.
That it should go that far, I must confess,
Is such a pity. But I'll cross the line,
30   And give myself to you. I won't decline
Your offer, Sir, to vanquish me right here.
But let me make one point extremely clear:
If there's a moral judgment to be made,
If anyone here feels the least betrayed,
35   Then none of that will be my fault. Instead,

---

4. Molière wanted to make certain that everyone understood that Tartuffe's argument here
   is clever sophistry designed to deceive.

The sin weighs twice as heavy on your head.
You forced me to this brash extremity.
TARTUFFE   Yes, yes, I will take all the sin on me.
ELMIRE   Open the door and check because I fear
140   My husband—just look—might be somewhere near.
TARTUFFE   What does it matter if he comes or goes?
The secret is, I lead him by the nose.
He's urged me to spend all my time with you.
So let him see—he won't believe it's true.
145   ELMIRE   Go out and look around. Indulge my whim.
Look everywhere and carefully for him.

Scene 6

ORGON, ELMIRE

ORGON [*Coming out from under the table*]   I swear that is the most
    abominable man!
How will I bear this? I don't think I can.
I'm stupefied!
ELMIRE   What? Out so soon? No, no.
You can't be serious. There's more to go.
5   Get back under there. You can't be too sure.
It's never good relying on conjecture.
ORGON   That kind of wickedness comes straight from Hell.
ELMIRE   You've turned against this man you know so well?
Good lord, be sure the evidence is strong
10   Before you are convinced. You might be wrong.
    [*She steps in front of her husband.*]

Scene 7

TARTUFFE, ELMIRE, ORGON

TARTUFFE   Yes, all is well; there's no one to be found,
And I was thorough when I looked around.
To my delight, my rapture, at last . . .
ORGON [*Stopping him*]   Just stop a minute there! You move too fast!
5   Delight and rapture? Fulfilling desire?
Ah! Ah! You are a traitor and a liar!
Some holy man you are, to wreck my life,
Marry my daughter? Lust after my wife?
I've had my doubts about you, but kept quiet,
10   Waiting for you to slip and then deny it.
Well, now it's happened and I'm so relieved,
To stop pretending that I am deceived.

ELMIRE [*To* TARTUFFE]   I don't approve of what I've done today,
    But I needed to do it, anyway.
TARTUFFE   What? You can't think . . .
15 ORGON   No more words from you.
    Get out of here, you . . . You and I are through.
TARTUFFE   But my intentions . . .
ORGON   You still think I'm a dunce?
    You shut your mouth and leave this house at once!
TARTUFFE   You're the one to leave, you, acting like the master.
20   Now I'll make it known, the full disaster:
    This house belongs to me, yes, all of it,
    And I'll decide what's true, as I see fit.
    You can't entrap me with demeaning tricks,
    Yes, here's a situation you can't fix.
25   Here nothing happens, without my consent,
    You've offended Heaven. You must repent.
    But I know how to really punish you.
    Those who harm me, they know not what they do.

Scene 8

    ELMIRE, ORGON

ELMIRE   What was that about? I mean, the latter.
ORGON   I'm not sure, but it's no laughing matter.
ELMIRE   Why?
ORGON   I've made a mistake I now can see,
    The deed I gave him is what troubles me.
ELMIRE   The deed?
5 ORGON   And something else. I am undone.
    I think my troubles may have just begun.
ELMIRE   What else?
ORGON   You'll know it all. I have to race,
    To see if a strongbox is in its place.

End of Act Four

Act Five

Scene 1

ORGON, CLÉANTE

CLÉANTE   Where are you running to?

ORGON   Who knows.

CLÉANTE   Then wait.
It seems to me we should deliberate,
Meet, plan, and have some family talks.

ORGON   I can't stop thinking about the damned box
5   More than anything, that's the loss I fear.

CLÉANTE   What about this box makes it so dear?

ORGON   I have a friend whom I felt sorry for,
Because he chose the wrong side in the war;
Before he fled, he brought it to me,
10   This locked box. He didn't leave a key.
He told me it has papers, this doomed friend,
On which his life and property depend.

CLÉANTE   Are you saying you gave the box away?

ORGON   Yes, that's true, that's what I'm trying to say.
15   I was afraid that I would have to lie,
If I were confronted. That is why
I went to my betrayer and confessed
And he, in turn, told me it would be best
If I gave him the box, to keep, in case
20   Someone were to ask me to my face
About it all, and I might lie and then,
In doing so, commit a venial sin.

CLÉANTE   As far as I can see, this is a mess,
And with a lot of damage to assess.
25   This secret that you told, this deed you gave,
Make the situation hard to save.
He's holding all the cards, your holy man,
Because you gave them to him. If you can
Restrain yourself a bit and stay away.
30   That would be best. And do watch what you say.

ORGON   What? With his wicked heart and corrupt soul,
And I'm to keep my rage under control?
Yes, me who took him in, right off the street?
Damn all holy men! They're filled with deceit!
35   I now renounce them all, down to the man,
And I'll treat them worse than Satan can.

CLÉANTE   Listen to yourself! You're over the top,
Getting carried away again. Just stop.

"Moderation." Is that word you know?
40 I think you've learned it, but then off you go,
Always ignoring the strength in reason,
Flinging yourself from loyalty to treason.
Why can't you just admit that you were swayed
By the fake piety that man displayed?
45 But no. Rather than change your ways, you turned
Like that.
      [*Snaps fingers*]
            Attacking holy men who've earned
The right to stand among the true believers.
So now all holy men are base deceivers?
Instead of just admitting your delusion,
50 "They're all like that!" you say—brilliant conclusion.
Why trust reason, when you have emotion?
You've implied there is no true devotion.
Freethinkers are the ones who hold that view,
And yet, you don't agree with them, do you?
55 You judge a man as good without real proof.
Appearances can lie—witness: Tartuffe.
If your respect is something to be prized,
Don't toss it away to those disguised
In a cloak of piety and virtue.
60 Don't you see how deeply they can hurt you?
Look for simple goodness—it does exist.
And just watch for imposters in our midst,
With this in mind, try not to be unjust
To true believers, sin on the side of trust.

Scene 2

DAMIS, ORGON, CLÉANTE

DAMIS   Father, what? I can't believe it's true,
That scoundrel has the gall to threaten you?
And use the things you gave him in his case
'Gainst you? To throw you out? I'll break his face.
5 ORGON   My son, I'm in more pain than you can see.
DAMIS   I'll break both his legs. Leave it to me.
We must not bend under his insolence.
I'll finish this business, punish his offense,
I'll murder him and do it with such joy.
10 CLÉANTE   Damis, you're talking like a little boy,
Tantrums head the list of your main flaws.
We live in modern times, with things called "laws."
Murder is illegal. At least for us.

Scene 3

MADAME PERNELLE, MARIANE, ELMIRE, DORINE, DAMIS, ORGON,
CLÉANTE

MADAME PERNELLE   It's unbelievable! Perposterous!
ORGON   Believe it. I've seen it with my own eyes.
    He returned kindness with deceit and lies.
    I took in a man, miserable and poor,
5   Brought him home, gave him the key to my door,
    I loaded him with favors every day,
    To him, my daughter, I just gave away,
    My house, my wealth, a locked box from a friend.
    But to what depths this devil would descend.
10 This betrayer, this abomination,
    Who had the gall to preach about temptation,
    And know in his black heart he'd woo my wife,
    Seduce her! Yes! And then to steal my life,
    Using my property, which I transferred to him,
15 I know, I know—it was a stupid whim.
    He wants to ruin me, chase me from my door,
    He wants me as he was, abject and poor.
DORINE   Poor man!
MADAME PERNELLE   I don't believe a word, my son,
    This isn't something that he could have done.
ORGON   What?
20 MADAME PERNELLE   Holy men always arouse envy.
ORGON   Mother, what are you trying to say to me?
MADAME PERNELLE   That you live rather strangely in this house;
    He's hated here, especially by your spouse.
ORGON   What has this got to do with what I said?
25 MADAME PERNELLE   Heaven knows, I've beat into your head:
    "In this world, virtue is mocked forever;
    Envious men may die, but envy never."
ORGON   How does that apply to what's happened here?
MADAME PERNELLE   Someone made up some lies; it's all too clear.
30 ORGON   But I saw it myself, you understand.
MADAME PERNELLE   "Whoever spreads slander has a soiled hand."
ORGON   You'll make me, Mother, say something not nice.
    I saw it for myself; I've told you twice.
MADAME PERNELLE   "No one should trust what gossips have to say,
35 Yet they'll be with us until Judgment Day."
ORGON   You're talking total nonsense, Mother!
    I said I saw him, this man I called "Brother!"
    I saw him with my wife, with these two eyes.
    The word is "saw," past tense of "see." These "lies"

40   That you misnamed are just the truth.
       I saw my wife almost beneath Tartuffe.
       MADAME PERNELLE   Oh, is that all? Appearances deceive.
       What we think we see, we then believe.
       ORGON   I'm getting angry.
       MADAME PERNELLE   False suspicions, see?
45   We are subject to them, occasionally,
       Good deeds can be seen as something other.
       ORGON   So I'm to see this as a good thing, Mother,
       A man trying to kiss my wife?
       MADAME PERNELLE   You must.
       Because, to be quite certain you are just,
50   You should wait until you're very very sure.
       And not rely on faulty conjecture.
       ORGON   Goddamm it! You would have me wait until . . . ?
       And just be quiet while he has his fill,
       Right before my very eyes, Mother, he'd—
55   MADAME PERNELLE   I can't believe that he would do this "deed"
       Of which he's been accused. There is no way.
       His soul is pure.
       ORGON   I don't know what to say!
       Mother!
       DORINE   Just deserts, for what you put us through.
       You though we lied, now she thinks that of you.
60   CLÉANTE   Why are we wasting time with all of this?
       We're standing on the edge of the abyss.
       This man is dangerous! He has a plan!
       DAMIS   How could he hurt us? I don't think he can.
       ELMIRE   He won't get far, complaining to the law,
65   You'll tell the truth, and he'll have to withdraw.
       CLÉANTE   Don't count on it; trust me, he'll find a way
       To use these weapons you gave him today.
       He has legal documents, and the deed.
       To kick us out, just what else does he need?
70   And if he's doubted, there are many ways
       To trap you in a wicked legal maze.
       You give a snake his venom, nice and quick.
       And after that you poke him with a stick?
       ORGON   I know. But what was I supposed to do?
75   Emotions got the best of me, it's true.
       CLÉANTE   If we could placate him, just for a while,
       And somehow get the deed back with a smile.
       ELMIRE   Had I known we had all this to lose,
       I never would have gone through with my ruse.
       I would've—

[*A knock on the door*]

80   ORGON   What does that man want? You go find out.
      But I don't want to know what it's about.

Scene 4

MONSIEUR LOYAL, MADAME PERNELLE,
ORGON, DAMIS, MARIANE, DORINE, ELMIRE, CLÉANTE

MONSIEUR LOYAL [*To* DORINE]   Dear Sister, hello; please, I beg
      of you,
      Your master is the one I must speak to.
DORINE   He's not receiving visitors today.
MONSIEUR LOYAL   I bring good news so don't send me away.
5   My goal in coming is not to displease;
      I'm here to put your master's mind at ease.
DORINE   And you are . . . whom?
MONSIEUR LOYAL   Just say that I have come
      For his own good and with a message from
      Monsieur Tartuffe.
DORINE [*To* ORGON]   It's a soft-spoken man,
10   Who says he's here to do just what he can
      To ease your mind. Tartuffe sent him.
CLÉANTE   Let's see
      What he might want.
ORGON   Oh, what's my strategy?
      He's come to reconcile us, I just know.
CLÉANTE   Your strategy? Don't let your anger show,
15   For Heaven's sake. And listen for a truce.
MONSIEUR LOYAL   My greetings, sir. I'm here to be of use.
ORGON   Just what I thought. His language is benign.
      For the prospect of peace, a hopeful sign.
MONSIEUR LOYAL   Your family's dear to me, I hope you know.
20   I served your father many years ago.
ORGON   I humbly beg your pardon, to my shame,
      I don't know you, nor do I know your name.
MONSIEUR LOYAL   My name's Loyal. I'm Norman by descent.
      My job of bailiff[1] is what pays my rent.
25   Thanks be to Heaven, it's been forty years
      I've done my duty free of doubts or fear.
      That you invited me in, I can report,
      When I serve you with this writ from the court.
ORGON   What? You're here . . .

---

1. In seventeenth-century France, the one who served legal writs and seized property.

MONSIEUR LOYAL   No upsetting outbursts, please.
30   It's just a warrant saying we can seize,
    Not me, of course, but this Monsieur Tartuffe,
    Your house and land as his. Here is the proof.
    I have the contract here. You must vacate
    These premises. Please, now, don't be irate.
35   Just gather up your things now, and make way
    For this man, without hindrance or delay.
ORGON   Me? Leave my house?
MONSIEUR LOYAL   That's right, sir, out the door.
    This house, at present, as I've said before,
    Belongs to good Monsieur Tartuffe, you see.
40   He's lord and master of this property
    By virtue of this contract I hold right here.
    Is that not your signature? It's quite clear.
DAMIS   He's so rude, I do almost admire him.
MONSIEUR LOYAL   Excuse me. Is it possible to fire him?
45   My business is with you, a man of reason,
    Who knows resisting would be seen as treason.
    You understand that I must be permitted
    To execute the orders as committed.
DAMIS   I'll execute him, Father, to be sure.
50   His long black nightgown won't make him secure.
MONSIEUR LOYAL   He's your son! I thought he was a servant.
    Control the boy. His attitude's too fervent,
    His anger is a bone of contention,
    Throw him out, or I will have to mention
55   His name in this, my official report.
DORINE   "Loyal" is loyal only to the court.
MONSIEUR LOYAL   I have respect for all God-fearing men,
    So instantly I knew I'd come here when
    I heard your name attached to this assignment.
60   I knew you'd want a bailiff with refinement.
    I'm here for you, to just accommodate,
    To make removal something you won't hate.
    Now if I hadn't come, then you would find
    You got a bailiff who would be less kind.
65 ORGON   I'm sorry, I don't see the kindness in
    An eviction order.
MONSIEUR LOYAL   Let me begin:
    I'm giving you time. I won't carry out
    This order you are so upset about.
    I've come only to spend the night with you,
70   With my men, who will be coming through.
    All ten of them, as quiet as a mouse.

Oh, you must give me the keys to the house.
We won't disturb you, you will have your rest,
You need a full night's sleep—that's always best.
75 There'll be no scandal, secrets won't be bared,
Tomorrow morning you must be prepared,
To pack your things, down to the smallest plate,
And cup, and then these premises vacate.
You'll have helpers; the men I chose are strong,
80 And they'll have this house empty before long.
I can't think of who would treat you better
And still enforce the law down to the letter,
Just later with the letter is my gift.
So, no resistance. And there'll be no rift.

85 ORGON   From that which I still have, I'd give this hour,
One hundred coins of gold to have the power
To sock this bailiff with a punch as great
As any man in this world could create.

CLÉANTE   That's enough. Let's not make it worse.
                                              The nerve
DAMIS
90 Of him. Let's see what my right fist can serve.

DORINE   Mister Loyal, you have a fine, broad back,
And if I had a stick, you'd hear it crack.

MONSIEUR LOYAL   Words like that are punishable, my love,
Be careful when a push becomes a shove.

95 CLÉANTE   Oh, come on, there's no reason to postpone,
Just serve your writ and then leave us alone.

MONSIEUR LOYAL   May Heaven keep you, 'til we meet again!

ORGON   And strangle you, and him who sent you in!

Scene 5

ORGON, CLÉANTE, MARIANE, ELMIRE, MADAME PERNELLE,
DORINE, DAMIS

ORGON   Well, Mother, look at this writ. Here is proof
Of treachery supreme by your Tartuffe.
Don't jump to judgment—that's what you admonished.

MADAME PERNELLE   I'm overwhelmed, I'm utterly astonished.

5 DORINE   I hear you blaming him and that's just wrong.
You'll see his good intentions before long.
"Just love thy neighbor" is here on this writ,
Between the lines, you see him saying it.
Because men are corrupted by their wealth.
10 Out of concern for your spiritual health,
He's taking, with a pure motivation,

Everything that keeps you from salvation.
ORGON   Aren't you sick of hearing, "Quiet!" from me?
CLÉANTE   Thoughts of what to do now? And quickly?
15   ELMIRE   Once we show the plans of that ingrate;
His trickery can't get him this estate.
As soon as they see his disloyalty,
He'll be denied, I hope, this property.

Scene 6

VALÈRE, ORGON, CLÉANTE, ELMIRE, MARINE, *etc.*

VALÈRE   I hate to ruin your day—I have bad news.
Danger's coming. There's no time to lose.
A good friend, quite good, as it turns out,
Discovered something you must know about,
5   Something at the court that's happening now.
That swindler, sorry, if you will allow,
That holy faker has gone to the king,
Accusing you of almost everything.
But here's the worst, he says that you have failed
10   Your duty as a subject, which entailed
The keeping of a strongbox so well hidden,
That you could deny knowledge, if bidden,
Of a traitor's whereabouts. What's more,
That holy fraud will come right through that door,
15   Accusing you. You can't do anything.
He had this box and gave it to the king.
So there's an order out for your arrest!
And evidently, it's the king's behest,
That Tartuffe come, so justice can be done.
20   CLÉANTE   Well, there it is, at last, the smoking gun.
He can claim this house, at the very least.
ORGON   The man is nothing but a vicious beast.
VALÈRE   You must leave now, and I will help you hide.
Here's ten thousand in gold.[2] My carriage is outside.
25   When a storm is bearing down on you
Running is the best thing one can do.
I have a place where both of us can stay.
ORGON   My boy, I owe you more than I can say.
I pray to Heaven, that before too long,
30   I can pay you back and right the wrong
I've done to you.

---

2. This illustrates how appropriate a match Valère is for Mariane and heightens the unsuitability of Tartuffe.

[*To* ELMIRE] Good-bye. Take care, my dear.

CLÉANTE   We'll plan. You go while the way is still clear.

Scene 7

THE EXEMPT, TARTUFFE, VALÈRE, ORGON, ELMIRE, MARIANE, DORINE, *etc.*

TARTUFFE   Easy, just a minute, you move too fast.
   Your cowardice, dear Sir, is unsurpassed.
   What I have to say is uncontested.
   Simply put, I'm having you arrested.

5   ORGON   You villain, you traitor, your lechery
   Is second only to your treachery.
   And you arrest me—that's the crowning blow.

TARTUFFE   Suffering for Heaven is all I know,
   So revile me. It's all for Heaven's sake.

10   CLÉANTE   Why does he persist when we know it's fake?

DAMIS   He's mocking Heaven. What a loathsome beast.

TARTUFFE   Get mad—I'm not bothered in the least.
   It is my duty, what I'm doing here.

MARIANE   You really think that if you persevere

15   In this lie, you'll keep your reputation?

TARTUFFE   My honor is safeguarded by my station,
   As I am on a mission from the king.

ORGON   You dog, have you forgotten everything?
   Who picked you up from total poverty?

20   TARTUFFE   I know that there were things you did for me.
   My duty to our monarch is what stifles
   Memory, so your past gifts are trifles.
   My obligations to him are so rife,
   That I would give up family, friends, and life.

ELMIRE   Fraud!

25   DORINE   Now there's a lie that beats everything,
   His pretended reverence for our king!

CLÉANTE   This "duty to our monarch," as you say,
   Why didn't it come up before today?
   You had the box, you lived here for some time,

30   To say the least, and yet this crime
   That you reported—why then did you wait?
   Orgon caught you about to desecrate
   The holy bonds of marriage with his wife.
   Suddenly, your obligations are so "rife"

35   To our dear king, that you're here to turn in
   Your former friend and "brother" and begin

To move into his house, a gift, but look,
Why would you accept gifts from a crook?
TARTUFFE [*To* THE EXEMPT]   Save me from this whining!
   I have had my fill!
40 Do execute your orders, if you will.
EXEMPT   I will. I've waited much too long for that.
   I had to let you have your little chat.
   It confirmed the facts our monarch knew,
   That's why, Tartuffe, I am arresting you.
TARTUFFE   Who, me?
THE EXEMPT   Yes, you.
45 TARTUFFE   You're putting me in jail?
THE EXEMPT   Immediately. And there will be no bail.[3]
   [*To* ORGON] You may compose yourself now, sir, because
   We're fortunate in leadership and laws.
   We have a king who sees into mens' hearts,
50 And cannot be deceived, so he imparts
   Great wisdom, and a talent for discernment.
   So frauds are guaranteed a quick internment.
   Our Prince of Reason sees things as they are,
   So hypocrites do not get very far.
55 But saintly men and the truly devout,
   He cherishes and has no doubts about.
   This man could not begin to fool the king
   Who can defend himself against the sting
   Of much more subtle predators. And, thus,
60 When this craven pretender came to us,
   Demanding justice and accusing you,
   He betrayed himself. Our king could view
   The baseness lurking in his coward's heart.
   Evil like that can set a man apart.
65 And so Divine Justice nodded her head,
   The king did not believe a word he said.
   It was soon confirmed, he has a crime
   For every sin, but why squander the time
   To list them or the aliases he used.
70 For the king, it's enough that he abused
   Your friendship and your faith. And though we knew
   Each accusation of his was untrue,
   Our monarch himself, wanting to know
   Just how far this imposter planned to go,
75 Had me wait to find this out, then pounce,

3. The significance of The Exempt's speech that follows can be best understood by studying the documents in the "The Quarrel of *Tartuffe*" (see pp. 65–81 herein).

Arrest this criminal, quickly denounce
The man and all his lies. And now, the king
Orders delivered to you, everything
This scoundrel took, the deed, all documents,
80   This locked box of yours and all its contents,
And nullifies the contract giving away
Your property, effective today.
And finally, our monarch wants to end
Your worries about aiding your old friend
85   Before he went into exile because,
In that same way, and in spite of the laws,
You openly defended our king's right
To his throne. And you were prepared to fight.
From his heart and because it makes good sense
90   That a good deed deserves a recompense,
He pardons you. And wanted me to add:
He remembers good longer than the bad.

DORINE   May Heaven be praised!

MADAME PERNELLE   I am so relieved.

ELMIRE   A happy ending!

MARIANE   Can it be believed?

ORGON [*To* TARTUFFE]   Now then, you traitor . . .

95   CLÉANTE   Stop that, Brother, please.
You're sinking to his level. Don't appease
His expectations of mankind. His fate
Is misery. But it's never too late
To take another path, and feel remorse.
100   So let's wish, rather, he will change his course,
And turn his back upon his life of vice,
Embrace the good and know it will suffice.
We've all seen the wisdom of this great king,
Whom we should go and thank for everything.

105   ORGON   Yes, and well said. So come along with me,
To thank him for his generosity.
And then once that glorious task is done,
We'll come back here for yet another one,
I mean a wedding for which we'll prepare,
110   To give my daughter to the good Valère.

End of Play

BACKGROUNDS
AND SOURCES

The Quarrel of *Tartuffe*

[All the documents below have been translated by Virginia Scott]

Molière struggled for five years before his play Tartuffe *was given permission to be performed. He first introduced it, in a three-act version, during a court festival given by Louis XIV in May 1664. According to the official festival program:*

[May 12] In the evening, His Majesty had a comedy entitled *Tartuffe* performed, that the sieur de Molière had written against the hypocrites; but even though it was found to be very entertaining, the king recognized that there was so much agreement between those whom true devotion put on the path to heaven and those whose vain affectation of good works did not prevent them from committing bad ones, that given his extreme sensitivity to matters of religion, he could not allow this resemblance of vice and virtue * * * and that although he had no doubt about the good intentions of the author, he must nonetheless forbid it [the play] in public, depriving himself of this pleasure so that others, less capable than he of just discernment, would not be abused. [André Félibien, *Les Plaisirs de l'Île enchantée* (Paris, 1674).]

The Gazette, *a semi-official newspaper, also praised the king for the discernment he showed:*

[May 17] * * * when he recently forbade performances of a theatre play entitled *The Hypocrite*, that His Majesty, fully enlightened in all things, judged to be absolutely injurious to religion and capable of having some very dangerous effects.

The gazetteer Jean Loret, whose weekly Muze historique *is a doggerel record of events in Molière's day, concludes that, although the playwright had made trip after trip to court complaining to the king of the censorship of his play:*

[MAY 24]

All his impassioned pleading
Had no chance of succeeding;
I'll not contribute to the fuss;
I'll follow old Pythagoras,
Be silent, pay no heed to it,
Not knowing what's the seed of it.

A few months later Molière was stunned to read a polemic published against him by Pierre Roullé, the pastor of the parish of Saint-Barthélemy, who praises the king for being deaf to those impious and abominable atheists, those innovators of religion, those disturbers of the public tranquility, the worst of whom was Molière. The king, Roullé notes, is presently vacationing at Fontainebleau after a heroic action:

[August 1] * * * truly worthy of the greatness of his heart and of his piety and the respect he has for God and for the Church, which he offers willingly to the ministers who are responsible for conferring the graces necessary to salvation. A man, or rather a Demon clothed in flesh and dressed like a man and the most notable and impious freethinker who has ever lived, has had the wickedness and abomination to bring from his diabolical mind a play ready to be shown on the public stage to the derision of the Church, scorning what is most sacred, sneering at the most divine function, mocking what is most holy in the Church, ordained by the Savior for the sanctification of souls, with the intention of rendering it ridiculous, contemptible, and odious. He would deserve, as a result of this sacrilegious and impious attack, to be tortured publicly as an example, and to be burned at the stake, in advance of the fires of Hell, to expiate so grievous a crime of divine lèse-majesté, which would ruin the Catholic religion, condemning and making fun of its most religious and holy practice, which is the conduct and the direction of individual souls and families by wise guides and pious leaders. But His Majesty, animated by righteous anger, after severely reproaching him, with his usual lenience, in which he imitates the essential clemency of God, has pardoned his insolence and his demonic audacity, to give him the time to do solemn and public penance for the rest of his life [*Le Roi glorieux du monde*].

Molière was certainly in no mood for "solemn and public penance": quite the opposite. His answer was to appeal again to the king and to begin writing his play Don Juan, *an even more bitter attack on religious hypocrisy and a satire of those men, defended by Roullé, who attached themselves to great nobles as "directors of conscience."*

Molière's First Petition to the King on Tartuffe *appeared in August 1664, shortly after Roullé's rant:*

Sire—
The duty of comedy being to correct men while entertaining them, I believe that, given the trade in which I find myself, I could do nothing better than attack the vices of my century by painting them as ridiculous; and, as hypocrisy is one of the most common and most troublesome, and the most dangerous, I thought I would be doing some small service to all the decent people of your kingdom if I wrote a play that discredited the hypocrites and showed all the calculated dissimulations of these excessively pious people, all the covert mischief of these counterfeiters of devotion, who try to entrap men with feigned zeal and insincere love of their neighbors.

I have written it, Sire, so I believe, with all the care and all the circumspection that the delicacy of the subject calls for; and to better preserve the esteem and the respect owed to the truly devout, I have distinguished them as best I could from the character with whom I am concerned. I have left nothing equivocal, I have deleted whatever could confuse good and evil, and I have painted only essential features and with the necessary colors that make a genuine and out and out hypocrite recognizable.

Nonetheless, all my precautions have been useless. There are those who have profited, Sire, from the delicacy of your judgment in matters of religion, for the only weak point in your defenses is your respect for holy things. The Tartuffes, in secret, have cleverly found their way into Your Majesty's good graces, and the originals have finally suppressed the copy, however innocent it may be, and however great its resemblance to them.

Although the suppression of my work has been a painful blow, my unhappiness has been assuaged by the way in which Your Majesty expressed his views on the subject; and I believed, Sire, that this relieved me of any cause for complaint, you having had the goodness to declare that you found nothing reprehensible in this play that you have forbidden me to produce in public.

But in spite of that glorious declaration by the greatest and most enlightened king in the world, in spite of the approbation of the Legate [Cardinal Chigi, in Paris on a mission from the pope] as well, and of the greatest percentage of our bishops, all of whom, after the private readings that I have given them of my work, found themselves in agreement with the sentiments of Your Majesty; in spite of all of that, I say, a book appears written by the pastor of . . . [Molière leaves out Roullé's name], which impudently contradicts all these eminent witnesses. Your Majesty has spoken in vain, and the Legate and the bishops have given their judgment in vain: my play, although unseen, is diabolical and diabolical is my brain; I am a demon clothed in flesh and dressed like a man, a freethinker, an impious man who deserves torture as an example. It is not enough that my offense be expiated publicly by fire, that would be leaving me off too cheaply: the charitable zeal of this gallant man of piety would not stop there. He does not want me to have God's mercy, he wants me to be damned. The matter is settled.

This book, Sire, has been presented to Your Majesty, and without doubt you will judge for yourself how difficult it is for me to see myself exposed daily to the insults of these gentlemen, what wrongs are done me in the world by such slanders, that I must tolerate, and, finally, that it is in my interest to free myself of his false imputations, and to show the public that my play is nothing other than what I say it is.

I do not speak, Sire, to ask you to restore my reputation and to justify to everyone the innocence of my play: enlightened kings like you do not need to be told what is wanted. They see, like God, what is called for and know better than we do what wishes should be granted. It is enough to place my interests in Your Majesty's hands, and I await, with respect, whatever it pleases you to ordain in this matter.

Molière echoes this last thought—though in a less servile mode—in Don Juan, *when Don Luis, Don Juan's disgusted father, laments:*

Alas, we think we know better than God what we need and we importune him with our blind wishes and thoughtless demands. I wanted a son with all my heart. I incessantly begged God for one with inconceivable fervor, and now this son, sent by a God weary of my prayers, is not the joy and consolation I expected but the sorrow and agony of my life [Act IV, scene 4].

Unlike the God who finally gave in to Don Luis, Molière's God-King stayed silent, and the playwright himself, speaking through Don Juan, publicly scourged Roullé and his ilk:

Hypocrisy is a fashionable vice, and all the fashionable vices pass for virtues. The best character you can play is the devout man, and the profession of hypocrite has some marvelous advantages. The artful imposter is always respected, and even when he's found out, no one dares say anything against him. * * * The hypocrites with their phony piety stick like glue to the devout party, and if you offend one of them, the whole pack rises up in arms. * * * So, I propose to take cover under this handy shelter myself. I have no intention of abandoning my pleasurable activities, but I'll keep them quiet. If I should be found out I won't have to do a thing. I'll just rouse the cabal of hypocrites and they will defend me and take my side. * * * I'll set myself up as the censor of other people's behavior, criticize everyone, approve no one, and have a good opinion only of myself. If anyone offends me, I will never pardon him but secretly preserve a relentless hatred of him. I will be God's avenger and, under this accommodating pretext, I will press my enemies, accuse them of impiety, set the zealots on them, who—without knowing why—will publicly attack them and damn them on their personal authority. That's how to profit from human weakness and how a clever man can adapt to the vices of his century [Act V, scene 2].

Don Juan opened on February 15, 1665, was censored, but ran for fourteen more performances until the Easter recess. It then closed and was never performed again while Molière was alive. Two and a half years later, Molière opened a revised version of Tartuffe, now titled l'Imposteur, with the central character rechristened Panulphe, at his theater in Paris at the Palais-Royal. He must have believed that the king had approved or would approve the production, but the king was away at the siege of Lille. The actor Charles Varlet de La Grange, a member of Molière's troupe, explains what happened in his Registre:

[August 6, 1667] An officer of the Court of the Parlement came on behalf of the first President, Monsieur de Lamoignon, to prohibit the play. On the 8th, La Thorillière and I left Paris by coach to go speak to the King on the subject of this prohibition. His Majesty was at the siege of Lille in Flanders, where we were well received. Monsieur [the king's brother] took us under his protection as usual and His Majesty said that on his return to Paris he would examine the play *Tartuffe* and that we could perform it. After which, we returned. The trip cost the Troupe 1000 livres.

Although Molière did not go himself to see the king in Lille, he did send along his second petition:

It is very rash of me to importune a great monarch in the midst of his glorious conquests; but in the state in which I find myself, Sire, where else can I find protection? And whose help can I solicit against the authority of the power that condemns me but the source of all power and authority, the just dispenser of absolute orders, the sovereign judge and the master of all things?

My play, Sire, has not been able to enjoy Your Majesty's favors. In vain I have produced it under the title of *The Imposter* and disguised the character in the costume of a man of the world. In vain I gave him a grand wig and a little hat, a big collar, a sword, and lace on everything. I toned down several passages, and carefully excised what I thought would furnish the shadow of a pretext to the celebrated originals of the portrait I was painting: all that served for nothing. * * *

My play had no sooner appeared than it was struck by the lightning bolt of a power we are forced to respect; and all that I could do to save myself from the violence of the storm was to say that Your Majesty had had the goodness to permit the performance of [my play], and that I did not think it was necessary to ask the permission of others, since it was you alone who had forbidden it.

I have no doubt, Sire, that the people I depict in the play will make every effort to turn Your Majesty against me and to attract to their party, as they have done before, the truly pious people, who are easily led because they judge others by themselves. They may dress their intentions in fine colors, but it is not the interest of God that moves them. They have demonstrated that with the plays they have allowed to be produced in public over and over without saying a word. Those plays only attack piety and religion, about which they care very little, but this play attacks them and makes fun of them, and that is what they cannot permit. They will not forgive me for revealing their impostures to the eyes of everyone; and, without a doubt, none of them will miss the chance to tell Your Majesty that they are scandalized by my play. But the pure truth, Sire, is that all Paris is scandalized by its being prohibited, that the most scrupulous have found its performance to be profitable, and what is astonishing is that persons of well-known probity have shown such great deference to people who should horrify everyone and who are so opposed to the true piety they appear to profess.

I respectfully await the judgment that Your Majesty will deign to pronounce on this matter; but it is very certain, Sire, that I will no longer think of writing plays if the Tartuffes have the advantage; they would claim the right to persecute me more than ever, and would denounce the most innocent things that might come from my pen.

Deign of your benevolence, Sire, to protect me from their poisonous rages; and may I be permitted, upon your return from a so-glorious campaign, to revive Your Majesty after the fatigues of your conquests, give you some innocent pleasure after your noble work, and make the monarch laugh who makes all Europe tremble.

As Sganarelle says in Don Juan: *"This damned servility!" But along with the expected servility, Molière dared to threaten; the king's favorite entertainer might put down his pen. He also went to beard the lion Lamoignan in his den. The story is told by his friend Boileau, who went with him:*

Molière explained the subject of his visit; the first President answered him as follows: Sir, I hold your merit in great esteem; I know that you are not only an excellent actor, but also a very clever man who does honor to your profession and to France; however, with all the good

will in the world, I cannot permit you to play your comedy. I am per-
suaded that it is very well-written and very instructive, but actors are
not meant to instruct mankind on matter of Christian morality and
religion; it is not the business of the theatre to preach the gospel.
[*Correspondence Boileau/Brossette*, 563–65.]

*Molière tried to defend his play, but he became so angry that he could
only sputter, and Lamoignon excused himself, saying that he was afraid
he would be late for church. Lamoignon was a member of the Company
of the Holy Sacrament, a brotherhood of the very fanatics and hyp-
ocrites Molière had targeted, and in Molière's mind one of the Tartuffes
who were so eager to see him silenced. What appeared to be a final blow
was struck a day or two later when the archbishop of Paris issued an
ordonnance, or decree:*

[August 11, 1667] Hardouin, by the Grace of God and of the Holy
See, archbishop of Paris, Greetings in the name of Our Lord:
* * * We, knowing how dangerous it is to permit true piety to be
injured by such a scandalous performance and that the King himself
had in the past expressly forbidden it, and considering moreover that
in a time when this great monarch exposes his life freely for the good
of his State, and when our principal care is to exhort all to make con-
tinual prayers for the conservation of his sacred person and for the
success of his arms, believe it would be impious to occupy ourselves
with spectacles capable of attracting the wrath of Heaven. We have
forbade and do expressly forbid all persons of our diocese to per-
form, read, or hear read the aforesaid comedy, in public or in private,
under whatever name or pretext, and this under pain of excommu-
nication.

*Not everyone agreed with the official assessment of the play. On August
20 an anonymous pamphlet appeared, probably written and published
with Molière's approval. Among other justifications, it attempts to
defend the play against Lamoignan's point that the religion is not the
business of the theatre. After several pages that summarize the play—
and that enable modern scholars to detect some minor differences
between The Imposter and the final Tartuffe—the anonymous author
reflects on the play and defends it as moral philosophy:*

There it is, sir, that's the play that has been forbidden. It may be that
the poisons among the flowers cannot be seen, and that the eyes of
those who have the power are more refined than those of the com-
mon people. If so, it seems that the religious persecutors of the mis-
erable Panulphe might have the kindness to reveal the poison that the
others swallow unawares. * * *

As you know, I am afraid of making a fuss, so I will be content with two reflections. * * * The first is on the way that the minds of certain people are disposed to assume or believe, in good faith, that although nothing specifically said or done in the play has a dangerous effect (which is the issue), it should be condemned in general for the single reason that religion is mentioned in it, and that the theatre, so they say, is not a place where religion should be taught. Their perfect rage against Molière must have distracted them; there is no more feeble commonplace behind which the passion to criticize and censure could be entrenched, daring to fortify itself with such a miserable and ridiculous defense. What? Even though Truth was represented with the dignity that must accompany it everywhere, even though the slightest troublesome consequences that could happen were anticipated and avoided, even though all precautions were taken against corrupting the minds of the age, including a perfect knowledge of ancient morality, a solid veneration of religion, a profound meditation on the nature of the soul, the experience of several years, and a frightful amount of work, even then, after all that, there are people capable of so horrible an error as to proscribe a work which is the result of such excellent preparation for the sole reason that to present religion in a theatre is new and has never been seen before, no matter how well, how worthily, how discretely, necessarily, and usefully is it done. I do not hesitate to confess to you that this sentiment appears to me to be one of the most serious consequences of the corruption of the century in which we live. It is by this principle of false propriety that reason and truth are relegated * * * to schools and churches, where their powerful virtue is almost useless, because they are sought out only by those who know and love them, as if their strength and their authority are mistrusted and they cannot be exposed in a place where they might meet their enemies. But there is where they should appear. It is in the most profane places, in public squares, courts of law, the palaces of the great, that they find the means of their triumph; and as they are, properly speaking, truth and reason only when they persuade men's minds, and drive away the shadows of error and ignorance by their absolute divine light, it may be said that their essence consists in their action, that these places where their operation is the most necessary are their natural places, and that to reduce their appearance only among those who love them is in some way to destroy them. * * *

It was * * * our fathers who, for the edification of the people and wanting to profit, from their natural inclination for spectacles, first instituted plays to represent the passion of the Savior of the world and similar pious subjects. But if the corruption that has crept into our morals since that happy time and rendered profane what should be sacred, why—if we are fortunate enough that Heaven has given birth in our time to some genius capable of returning it to its state of sanctity—why do we prevent him and forbid ourselves a thing we would eagerly seek, if charity reigned in our souls, and if there were not such a need as there is today among us to discredit hypocrisy and preach true devotion?

The second of my reflections is on a fruit, truly accidental, but also very important, that I think can be harvested from the performance of *The Imposter*. No harsher blow against what is politely called gallantry has ever been struck than by this play; and if anything is capable of sheltering the fidelity of marriage from the artful devices of those who would corrupt it, it is certainly this play, because the most common and most forceful avenues by which women are assaulted are ridiculed in such a lively and powerful way that anyone who tried them after this would appear ridiculous and would not succeed.

Some might find what I advance here strange, but I beg them not to judge it if they have not seen the play performed or asked those who have seen it; for a reading of the play will not make it possible to judge the full effect of its performance. I know, too, that I will be told that the vice of which I speak, being the most natural of all, will never lack attractions capable of surmounting whatever ridicule of it this play can muster. I have two answers: one, that in the opinion of those who know the world, this sin, morally speaking, is the most universal of all, and, two, that the sin arises, especially among women, from the loose manners, the freedom, and the frivolity of our Nation, rather than from any natural penchant, since what is certain is that of women in all civilized countries, none are less given to it than French women. That granted, I am persuaded that the degree to which this play ridicules all the arguments and rationalizations which are the natural prelude to a tête-à-tête (the most dangerous form of gallantry), this degree of ridicule, I say, through representation in performance would be powerful enough and forceful enough to counterbalance the attractions of gallantry for three quarters of the women who see it. * * *

The ridiculous is the exterior and perceptible form that the providence of nature has attached to all that is unreasonable, so that we can *recognize* it and flee from it. To recognize what is ridiculous we must know what is reasonable and recognize how it is deformed. At bottom, reason is characterized by *la convenance* [conformity to truth], and its perceptible mark is *la bienséance* [propriety, what is fitting], the famous *quod decet* of the ancients. *La bienséance* is to *la convenance* what the Platonists say beauty is to goodness—that is, beauty is the flower of goodness, its body and external appearance. So, *la bienséance* is reason made perceptible, and *la convenance* is the essence of reason. From that, we see that what is fitting is always based on conformity to truth, as what is not fitting is based on nonconformity to truth, that is to say, that the ridiculous is based on lack of reason. If nonconformity to truth is the essence of the ridiculous, it is easy to see why the seductive behavior of Panulphe appears to be ridiculous, and hypocrisy in general as well; for the secret actions of the bigots do not conform to the idea that their devout facial expressions and the austerity of their conversation has created of them in the public mind. * * *

And after many pages of philosophical argument on the subject of the ridiculous:

There it is, sir, the proof of my reflection; it is not up to me to judge if it is good, but I know that if it is, its importance is without a doubt extreme; and if remedies must be more greatly esteemed the more the illnesses are incurable, you will admit that this play is an excellent remedy, since all the other efforts made against seduction are absolutely vain. In fact, preachers thunder, confessors exhort, pastors threaten, good souls tremble, parents, husbands, and teachers keep watch ceaselessly, and make constant efforts as useless as they are great, to rein in the force of the torrent of impurity that ravages France: nonetheless, if one does not go along, one is ridiculed in society, and some find no less glory in loving debauchery than others do in correcting it. The disorder proceeds from no other cause than the impious opinion of most of today's worldly people that this sin is morally indifferent, and that it is a point of religion directly contrary to natural reason. But can one combat this perverted opinion more powerfully than by uncovering its natural immorality and showing by the lights of nature itself, as in this play, not only that this passion is criminal, unjust, and unreasonable, but even that it is extremely so, enough to appear ridiculous. * * *

I obviously render a very bad service to Molière with this reflection, although that is not my intention, because I shall make him enemies of all the gallants of Paris, who are perhaps not the least enlightened nor the least powerful people. But the fault is entirely his. This would not happen to him if, following in the footsteps of the ancient comic writers and the moderns who preceded him, he censured his plays * * * without any care for morals, neglecting, as he has done, all the customary laws and usages of the fashionable world, in favor of virtue and truth. * * *

I speak on assumptions I make myself. * * * With that in mind, it little matters to me who is right; for although this business appears to me to have some importance, I see many other things of the same kind today, which are either treated as trifles or settled according to principles that are the opposite of what they should be. But not being strong enough to resist the bad examples of the century, I gradually accustom myself, thank God, to laughing at everything like all the others do, and regarding all the things that happen in the world as diverse scenes of the great comedy played on the earth by mankind [*Lettre sur la comédie de* l'Imposteur].

Finally, on February 5, 1669, nearly five years after it was first performed at Versailles, Tartuffe *was performed with great success at the Palais-Royal and settled in for a long and highly profitable run. Molière took advantage of the event to thank the king and ask another favor in a third petition:*

Sire—

A very fine gentleman and doctor, whose invalid I have the honor to be, promises me—and will oblige himself before a notary—to keep me alive for another thirty years, if I can obtain for him a favor from Your Majesty. I have told him, as to his promise, that I would not ask so much of him, and that I will be satisfied with him so long as he does not kill me. The favor, sir, is an appointment as a canon [for the doctor's son] at your royal chapel at Vincennes, vacant since the death of . . .

Dare I ask another favor of Your Majesty the very day of the great resurrection of *Tartuffe*, revived by your benevolence? I am, by that first favor, reconciled with the devout; and I will be, by the second, with the doctors. This is, without a doubt, too much favor all at once for me; but perhaps not too much for Your Majesty, and I await, with a bit of respectful hope, for the answer to my petition.

Tartuffe, *as we know, succeeded with the Paris audience, and the king saw the revised version on February 21 in a private performance. The gazetteer Charles Robinet celebrated the opening in two of his weekly* Lettres in vers:

[FEBRUARY 9, 1669]

Speaking of the unexpected,
My surprise was not affected
When word arrived from Molière—
His great *Tartuffe!* A première!
I saw it on that very day,
Though getting in was not child's play;
For curiosity, I presume,
Like Nature abhors a vacuum.
No vacuum at the Palace Royal,
A thousand fans, all deeply loyal,
Came crowding in, and in distress,

Were nearly smothered in the press.
"I'm suffocating. I can't stand
This" were the cries on every hand.
"Alas, Alas, Monsieur Tartuffe,
We die to see you. That's the truth."
And while we laughed at every antic,
We saw Tartuffe, so sycophantic,
Disguising his malignity
Under a mask of piety,
Deceive, seduce, and have his fun,
And dupe Orgon, that simpleton.
Molière paints with careful strokes a
Speaking portrait of the hoaxer,
With so much art and so much truth,
So subtly that I think, in sooth,
The true devout will be delighted,
The false will all remain benighted.
The other characters, I swear,
Are so well cast, beyond compare,
So unaffected on the stage,
They are the idols of the age.
There's ne'er been such a comedy,
Or such applause, I guarantee.

[FEBRUARY 23, 1669]

Still running at the Royal Palace,
Tartuffe, who symbolizes malice,
Has for its scribe, Orgon by name,   Molière
Been raking in both cash and fame.
And no less highly I revere
His youthful wife who plays Elmire,   Mlle Molière
There is no actress of our age
Who is more natural on the stage.
Also the one who makes us chuckle,   Mlle Béjart
The servant girl who will not truckle,
You know the actress that I mean,
In this play she is called Dorine.
And there's Cléante, who's nothing worse,   La Thorillière
Who entertains with first-rate verse.
There are the children of Orgon,
Damis and little Mariane,   Hubert and Mlle de Brie
Marvels both, so I declare,
And there's the lover, young Valère,   La Grange
A model gallant, I would say,

A perfect man in every way.
And then, of course, there is Tartuffe,   Du Croisy
Who'll charm the chimney off the roof.
Our lovely queen, the belle Marie,
One night this week, for all to see,
Invited to her private rooms
These actors, who are royal grooms,
And laughed aloud when she observed
The Hypocrite get what he deserved.

Molière decided to have Tartuffe published almost immediately, not his usual way of proceeding, since once a play was in print, any acting troupe could perform it. One editor suggests that Molière hurried into print, worried that the king might change his mind. Whatever the motive, Molière applied for and received, on March 15, 1669, the privilege or royal approval for publication, which followed rapidly on March 23. In the preface to this first edition, Molière had the last word on the play and his struggle to produce it. He was not entirely mollified:

Here is a play, much talked about and long persecuted; and the people it mocks have shown that they are more powerful in France than all the others I have satirized up to now. The marquises, the pretentious society women, the betrayed husbands, and the doctors have suffered in silence when they've been put on the stage, and they have pretended to be amused by their portraits along with everyone else; but the hypocrites have not wanted to hear jokes about themselves. They are shocked, and they have found it strange that I would have the nerve to make fun of their pious faces and would want to disparage a profession adopted by so many gentlemen. This is a crime they cannot forgive, and they have taken up arms against my play with terrible fury. But they have not attacked it because of what actually wounded them: they are too politic for that, and know too well how not to reveal the depths of their souls. Following their praiseworthy custom, they have covered their self-interest with the cause of God; and *Tartuffe*, in their mouths, is a play that offends piety. It is, from beginning to end, filled with abominations, nothing is to be found there that does not deserve the fire. Every syllable is impious; even the gestures are criminal, and the least wink, the least wag of the head, the least step to right or left hides mysteries that they find a way to explicate to my disadvantage.

I have listened to the ideas of my friends and to the critiques of everyone; the corrections I have made, the judgment of the king and the queen, who have seen it, the approbation of the great princes and the ministers, who have honored it publicly with their presence; the testimony of truly devout men, who have found it profitable, all of that has served for nothing. They will not budge an inch, and still every day the indiscrete zealots cry out in public, piously slandering me and charitably damning me.

I would care very little for what they say were it not for their artful way of making me enemies of those I respect, and winning to their party some truly devout people, whose good faith they count on, and who, thanks to the ardor they feel for the cause of heaven, are only too impressionable. That is what obliges me to defend myself. It is to the truly devout that I want to justify the way I have written my play; and I beg them, with all my heart, not to condemn things before seeing them, and to rid themselves of all prejudices and not serve the purposes of those whose dissimulation dishonors them.

Anyone who takes the trouble to examine my play in good faith will see without any doubt that my intentions are entirely innocent, and that it nowhere trifles with things that ought to be revered; that I have treated the subject with all the delicacy it requires; and that I have used all possible art and care to distinguish the character of the hypocrite from that of the truly devout. I have taken two whole acts to prepare for the entrance of my scoundrel. The audience is not left in doubt for a single moment; he is instantly recognizable by the way he has been described and, from beginning to end, he says not a single word nor takes a single action that does not paint for the spectator the character of a wicked man, clearly shown in opposition to that of a truly devout man.

I know perfectly well that, in answer, these gentlemen will try to insinuate that it is not for the theatre to speak of these matters; but I ask them, with their permission, upon what grounds they base this proposition, which is only a supposition and which they cannot prove in any way. And, without a doubt, it would not be difficult to show them that the theatre, during ancient times, had its origin in religion and was part of its mysteries; that the Spanish, our neighbors, celebrate no feast day without a play; that—even among us— the theatre owes its birth to the cares of a religious fraternity that still today owns the Hôtel de Bourgogne, a place where the most important mysteries of our faith were once performed; that some plays are still printed in gothic letters, in the name of a doctor of the Sorbonne; and that there have been performed, in our times, plays on holy subjects by Monsieur Corneille, that have been admired by all France.

If the purpose of comedy is to correct the vices of men, I do not see for what reason some vices are privileged. That would have, within the State, the most dangerous consequence; and we have seen that the theatre has a great power to correct. The most beautiful moral writings are often less powerful than the darts of satire; and nothing corrects most men better than seeing their faults imitated. Vices are best attacked when they are exposed to the laughter of everyone. We easily endure reprimands, but not being laughed at. We want to be wicked, but not ridiculous.

I have been reproached for putting the language in piety in the mouth of my Imposter. So, should I forbid myself to use such words to properly represent the character of a hypocrite? It is enough, or so it seems to me, that I have made clear the criminal motives that lead him to say these things, and that I have cut out the sacred words that might be troubling when used improperly by him. But in the fourth act, he spouts a pernicious doctrine. Yet isn't that doctrine something which everyone has heard over and over? Is it new in my play? Should we be afraid that something so generally detested might make an impression on someone's mind? That by putting it on the stage I make it dangerous? That it gains authority in the mouth of a scoundrel? There are no grounds for that; and the play *Tartuffe* must be approved, or all plays must be condemned.

There's the real reason for this attack, for never has such fury been unleashed against the stage as it has been recently. I cannot deny that there were fathers of the Church who have condemned the theatre; but it also cannot be denied that some have treated it more gently. Thus the authority claimed to support censure is balanced by the other; and the only conclusion that can be drawn from the diversity of opinion in these minds of equal intelligence is that they have seen the theatre differently, and that some have considered it in its pure form while others have looked at its corrupt form and confused it with all those vile spectacles that are rightly called depraved. In effect, since we should speak of things and not of words, and since most contradictions arise from lack of understanding and from confounding opposing meanings in a single word, it remains only to lift the veil of ambiguity, and look at what theatre is, in itself, to see if it should be condemned. We will discover, without a doubt, that being no other thing than an ingenious poem, which reproves men's faults by means of agreeable lessons, theatre cannot be censured without injustice; and if we will listen to the testimony of the ancients, we will learn that the most celebrated philosophers, those who made profession of austere virtue and who cried out ceaselessly against the vices of their century, have praised the theatre; we will learn that Aristotle devoted some evenings to the theatre and took the trouble to reduce to precepts the art of writing plays. We will learn that the greatest men, the first in dignity, have gloried in writing plays themselves, while others have not disdained to publicly recite those they have composed; that Greece showed its esteem for this art by glorious prizes and by the superb theatres with which she honored it; and that, finally, in Rome this same art received some extraordinary honors: I do not speak of debauched Rome given license by the emperors, but of a disciplined Rome, ruled by the consuls, in the time of the vigor of Roman virtue.

I confess there have been times when theatre became corrupt. But what is there that never becomes corrupt in this world? There is nothing so innocent that men cannot make it criminal, no art so healthy that they cannot reverse its intentions, nothing so good that they cannot put it to bad use. Medicine is a beneficial art, and everyone reveres it as one of the most excellent arts we have; and yet, at times it is rendered odious, and often has become an art of poisoning. Philosophy is a gift of heaven; it has been given to us to bring our minds to the knowledge of God through contemplation of the marvels of nature; and yet, we are not ignorant of the fact that it has often been diverted from its purpose, and used publicly to support impiety. Even the most holy things are not protected from the corruption of men and we see scoundrels who, every day, abuse piety and make it maliciously serve the greatest crimes. But we do not fail to make the necessary distinctions. We do not confuse the essential goodness of what has been corrupted with the malice of the corrupters. We separate bad practice from the intention of the art and, as we do not forbid medicine because the Romans banished it, nor philosophy for having been publicly condemned in Athens, so we should not prohibit the theatre because it was censured in certain times. There were reasons for that censure which do not exist here. Censure now restricts itself to what it sees; we should not allow it beyond the limits it has set itself, extend it farther than it needs to go, and force it to embrace the innocent with the guilty. The theatre that needs to be censured is not at all the theatre we want to defend. We must be careful not to confound the one with the other. They are two entities whose morals are completely opposed. They have no connection with each other, although their names are the same; and it would be a frightful injustice to condemn Olympia the virtuous woman because there was once another Olympia who was debauched. Such actions, without a doubt, would make a great disorder in the world. Nothing would exist that could not be condemned; but since we do not observe that rigor regarding so many things that are abused every day, we must grant the same grace to the theatre, and approve plays in which instruction and decency reign.

I know that there are some minds so delicate they cannot endure plays of any kind, who say that the most decent are the most dangerous; that the passions depicted in them are all the more moving because they are virtuous, and that souls are softened by these sorts of performances. I do not see what great crime it is to be moved by the sight of decent emotion; the total lack of sensibility to which these persons seek to raise our souls is virtue at its highest, but I doubt if human nature is strong enough to reach such perfection, and I don't know if it is not better to work to rectify and soften the passions of men than to want to remove them entirely.

I confess there are some places that are better to frequent than the theatre; and if you want to avoid all things that do not relate directly to God and our salvation, plays must be among them, and I do not find it wrong if they are condemned with all the rest. But let us suppose, as is the case, that there are intervals between exercises of piety and that men need diversions—then I maintain that nothing more innocent than the theatre can be found.

But I am running on and on. Let us finish with a word from a great prince [probably the prince of Condé] on the play of *Tartuffe*:

A week after it was prohibited, a play entitled *Scaramouche the Hermit* was performed for the court; and the king, as he was leaving, said to the great prince I mentioned: "I would really like to know why the people who are so scandalized by Molière's play say nothing about Scaramouche's play." To which the prince replied: "The reason for that is that Scaramouche's play mocks heaven and religion, for which these gentlemen care nothing; but Molière's play mocks them; that's what they cannot abide."

CRITICISM

Reviews

HAROLD CLURMAN

Theatre[†]

The 1977–78 season has begun, as far as I am concerned, with French fare. And it has been good. At the Broadway Circle in the Square there is an entirely pleasant production of Molière's *Tartuffe*, in Richard Wilbur's brilliant translation.

* * *

Tartuffe has a most interesting history. It is hard to say in exactly what frame of mind it was first received at its private performance in 1664 and in the public one in 1667. Was it taken to be the wonderful and very nearly perfect comedy it so patently is, or was there a more somber note in its reception? A religious faction, supported perhaps by Mme. de Maintenon, Louis XIV's last wife, had it suppressed because it mocked the hypocrisy of severe piety, after which Molière, to mollify the hounds, played still another trick and had Tartuffe punished by the King so that everyone was assured that religious fanatacism was not to be ascribed to His Majesty's court (which had indeed become bigoted) and that Tartuffe was a rare exception to the temper of the times.

I have seen the play in France acted as if it were a grave document. Or so it seemed, when as Louis Jouvet put it, the Comédie Française produced Molière as though he were dead! Jouvet himself once portrayed Tartuffe as a person almost justified in his machinations against the silly religiosity of the home into which he had been invited. The actor-director, Roger Planchon, in turn suggested that Orgon, the wealthy bourgeois who had picked up the beggarly Tartuffe, allowed himself to be totally hoodwinked by the imposter because he (Orgon) was homosexually attracted to him. When objections were made to such interpretations or, as many averred, distortions, Jouvet countered with, "Do you have Molière's telephone number?"

[†] Reprinted with permission from the October 8, 1977, issue of *The Nation*.

The play is a classic comedy, or perhaps farce, with all the possible changes rung on the situation in a fashion that even in the 17th century was familiar to the audiences. Today we might call it hokum. But the genius of Molière makes its hokum serve our delight. For the very fact that from the beginning we are in on the joke, instead of spoiling the fun, adds to it. It is the author's dramatic guile—the swift and incisive traits in his portraitures, his sovereign pleasure in the game, his common sense, the dance of his dialogue which darts and swirls, his scenic joy—which makes *Tartuffe* so consummate an entertainment and a masterpiece.

The production at the Circle in the Square, directed by Stephen Porter, is more or less traditional in the sense that it depends largely on speech, that is, on the play's verbal vigor, its spring, dash, fluency. (There is, however, one contemporary American bit of action in the scene of the attempted sexual possession by Tartuffe of Elmire, Orgon's wife. Original I believe with Porter, it is hilariously effective.) As a traditional production this *Tartuffe* is very well done by a most engaging company in Zack Brown's properly designed setting and fitting costumes. Each of the players fills the bill with dispatch and in the right key, while several are outstandingly gratifying.

John Wood uses his voice in a special sonority; his lank body with its large, lean face which lend his acting here an exhilaratingly nervous and quasi-demonic verve keeps the total picture in just the right balance. Tammy Grimes's Elmire is champagne dry, unerringly crisp, unsparingly witty.

JOHN PETER

Review of *Tartuffe*[†]

Molière transposed to an Islamic setting? John Peter on a French production of Tartuffe *that speaks to our times.*

I have just seen one of the most thrillingly topical political plays in Ariane Mnouchkine's Theatre du Soleil in Paris. It was written by Molière, in 1664.

Already, in its own time, *Tartuffe,* or *The Impostor,* was all-too topical. Molière was a protege of Louis XIV, who liked the play but that was not enough. It was about religious hypocrisy, which was a sensitive topic. There was an influential right-wing ecclesiastical body called the Company of the Blessed Sacrament, which was hot on Molière's heels.

[†] From *The Sunday Times*, November 12, 1995. Reprinted by permission of NI Syndication Ltd.

Someone must have leaked the contents of the play because a month before its very first, and private, performance before the king, the Company held a secret meeting and decided to press for its suppression. Intense lobbying followed; Louis XIV had to give way, and *Tartuffe*, twice rewritten, was only performed in public in 1669. It was a huge success. This is the play Mnouchkine has redirected for the 1990s.

The first surprise is Guy-Claude Francois's set. We are in a land of shared cultures. The decor has Christian, Islamic and Judaic features. This could be southern Spain in the 16th century, when Moorish, Christian and Jewish civilisations mingled with and fertilised one another; or Egypt or somewhere in the Levant, where the architecture shows Venetian, possibly French, influence. We are in a spacious forecourt of a prosperous but somewhat neglected house: the once elegant tall iron railings are in poor repair and the gate is rusting badly. A merchant trundles by with a loaded cart and a ghetto-blaster playing garishly westernised Arab music; but he is soon chased away and Molière's play begins, with the imperious Madame Pernelle, Orgon's mother (Myriam Azencot), reading the riot act to her son's family about their hostility to his house guest and protege, the saintly Tartuffe.

Mnouchkine's production is like the setting: both precise and generalised. The acting has an extraordinary realism heightened by a stately, slightly stylised formality. The effect is not "distancing"; rather it suggests commitment to a text that is both a brilliant entertainment and an act of moral subversion. The actors both impersonate their characters and comment on them; but the comment, which is a matter of voice tone and precise physical gesture, has none of the dry, patronising self-importance of pseudo-Brechtian detachment.

Orgon (Brontis Jodorowsky) is a family tyrant whose clothes suggest both a conservative Islamic cleric and an old-fashioned Levantine businessman; his bearing reminds you of those arrogant European academics who like to see intellectual matters organised like a command economy. Orgon is often played, quite wrongly, as an irascible but gullible elderly booby; Jodorowsky presents him as a sober, methodical fool whose dogmatic morality has been profoundly corrupted. His brother-in-law Cléante (Duccio Bellugi Vannuccini) is usually played with an air of placid, avuncular wisdom; here he is full of the impatience of a reasonable man who has been tried to the limit.

Valère (Martial Jacques), who is engaged to Orgon's daughter, is a pompous young romantic; more to the point, he is a westernised youth in European clothes and with a thoroughly European sense of self-importance. Dorine, the maid, in a breathtakingly subtle and inventive performance by Juliana Carneiro da Cunha, is played as a shrewd, alert Muslim woman, fully versed in the temperamental ways of the young and the dimwitted ways of their elders: a quiet, ironically humorous wheeler-dealer. This is a real Muslim household. People fetch and carry; linen is being folded; as soon as Orgon arrives home, his coffee is served on a low table. The dialogue is slow and measured but grippingly rhythmical: these people like the sound of their own and each other's voices, and they suggest a sense of a basically kindly, protective culture.

Why this setting? Why portray Christian corruption and hypocrisy in an Islamic context? The answer comes with the appearance of Tartuffe. He is played by Shahrokh Meshkin Ghalam as a youngish fundamentalist cleric, both smug and fierce, basilisk-eyed, stiff-backed and already inclined to portliness. (Here you recall Dorine's description of his eating habits.) He exudes a sinister sense of power, and you realise at once that one of his ploys is to set himself up as someone to be placated. You realise, too, that Orgon is as interested in Tartuffe's air of power as in his aura of sanctity. There is something brutish about Tartuffe; and it is this sense of diabolical force, this hunger for power, which can be so attractive to tired, open societies.

Mnouchkine has, in other words, sensed something in Molière's play that goes beyond Christian religious bigotry and hypocrisy. In her hands it becomes a myth, like the stories of Oedipus or Troy, Hamlet or Faust, a narrative that can take on both timeless and topical significance in a new setting. As far as I can tell, she has not interfered with the text; and yet, quite unexpectedly, the Christian references not only fit easily into an Islamic atmosphere: they give it a new admonitory significance. A peaceful hybrid civilisation is invaded by Tartuffe with the ruthless sense of power that goes with all fundamentalism.

Not all power is fundamentalist, but fundamentalism is always about power: it is its aim, its tool, its justification and its essence. The great dictatorships of Hitler, Stalin or Mao were all fundamentalist. They were also puritanical in principle, and yet many of their leaders were gourmandisers or lechers, just like Tartuffe: think of Goering's greed and drug addiction or the womanising of Goebbels, Beria and Mao; think of Lenin, Trotsky and Stalin seizing large noble estates for their personal use within weeks of the October Revolution. All such fundamentalism (its latest examples have been the fatwa against Rushdie, the massacre of 29 Palestinians praying in a mosque, and the murder of Yitzhak Rabin) justifies its power lust by claiming it to be either necessary or divine, or both.

And so, when Ghalam's Tartuffe arrives with five sinister minders, preceded by the offstage roar of a fundamentalist mob, you are in the past, the present and a possible future all at once. Theatre at this level is a moral force, both public and private. Tartuffe's attempted seduction of Orgon's wife is sometimes played as almost farcical: you can gloat over the pseudo-saint getting randy while wondering if it could really happen. Ghalam leaves you in no such doubt. He is a hungry man, a member of a new master race. His sensuality is methodical but unbridled. I have never before felt, during this scene, that Tartuffe was such a predator. Ghalam has made immediate the brutish side of all fundamentalism.

It so happens that at the Odéon Théâtre de l'Europe there is another production of *Tartuffe* which, in its conventional way, puts Mnouchkine's achievement neatly in perspective. It is not that Benno Besson's production is dressed in 17th-century costumes: it is its pedestrian dreariness that boggles the mind and this despite the fact that it goes at a tremendous lick. Mnouchkine's production takes four hours, which is extremely long but never feels like it, such is her control of rhythm and pace. Besson's rushes by in just over two hours, and the main results are that you get little sense of character, and that nobody on stage seems to have any time to think.

The comedy in Mnouchkine is cruel and psychologically revealing, like all Moliérean comedy, but it is unostentatious. It is not done for its own sake. Her one crude touch, the comic device of Dorine pouring pots of water over people to calm them down, is too often repeated; but it is as nothing compared to Besson's notions of comedy, which consist in making actors run round in circles, possibly to signify puzzlement or panic, and in making Tartuffe recite his speeches all on one note, without punctuation, a device which demonstrates the actor's breath control but which also robs Tartuffe of character and Molière's verse of both humour and drive.

Besson's actors speak impeccable French, but not always clearly and mostly without real feeling. Mnouchkine's speak in a variety of accents: Arab, Polish, Italian, French, Hispanic, but always with clarity and a sense of character. Like Peter Brook's multi-ethnic company, these people give the play a sense of universality. We all live with a Tartuffe in our house. This is the difference between mere theatre and the true theatre of the world.

Tartuffe in Rehearsal

V. TOPORKOV

Stanislavsky Works with *Tartuffe*[†]

As the years passed Konstantin Sergeyevich became increasingly con-
cerned about the future of the theatre. He was particularly disturbed
by this question towards the end of his life. He maintained that there
was a direct and indissoluble link between the salvation and subse-
quent development of the theatre and the cultivation of the actor's
skill. Whenever a complaint was made about the delayed presenta-
tion of plays at the Moscow Art Theatre, Stanislavsky would say: "The
theatre should be closed for three years and devote itself to study.
When you have mastered the acting technique which I am constantly
telling you about, it will be possible to present plays in two or three
weeks."

Konstantin Sergeyevich used every rehearsal and meeting to prop-
agate his ideas. It was at this time that he conceived the idea of a new
method of working with the actor, which subsequently became
known as "the method of physical action."

It is impossible in a short essay to give a detailed account of this
method. In general, it is a perfectly logical extension and develop-
ment of the experience accumulated by Stanislavsky during the long
years of his activity.

He himself formulated the essence of the new method in the fol-
lowing words: "When we say 'physical actions,' we deceive the actor.
They are really psycho-physical actions, and we call them physical in
order to avoid excessive philosophizing, for physical actions are com-
pletely concrete and easy to grasp. The basis of our art is precision of
action, the concrete execution of action in a given play. If I know
exactly the line of my actions, their logic, this serves me as a score,
while the moment of creation lies in the manner in which I will exe-
cute them today, here, before a given audience."

[†] From *Chetyre ocherka o K.S. Stanislavskom* (Four Essays on K. S. Stanislavsky), (Sovetskaya
Rossiya, Moscow, 1963), pp. 34–39. Translated by James B. Woodward.

He wished to test all this in practice and pass it on to a group of actors, even if they were few in number, who would continue with his method, develop it further and put it into practice. This required a great deal of time and the organization of special sessions, which it was difficult to combine with the productive work of the theatre. But Stanislavsky attached the greatest importance to the project and arranged for a group of actors to be freed from all work and placed at his disposal, so that he could work with them and conduct his "seminar" without a time-limit.

Stanislavsky selected Molière's play *Tartuffe*. Before work began, he gathered together the group of chosen participants (including the present writer) and addressed them as follows: "If you are interested merely in gaining from this enterprise the opportunity to play a new role, then I will disillusion you in advance. I am not preparing to put on a play and directors' laurels do not interest me. My major concern is to pass on to you the knowledge which I have accumulated in the course of my life. I ask you to tell me honestly whether you wish to study. I will have more respect for an honest confession than hypocritical conformity. I warn you, however, that without such studies you will come to a dead-end in your art."

Everyone responded enthusiastically to Konstantin Sergeyevich's appeal. One actress even offered to bring detailed notes on all Stanislavsky's rehearsals which she had collected since the foundation of the Theatre. "That is quite unnecessary," said Konstantin Sergeyevich. "Do not look back. The old has been exhausted. Let us continue to search for ways of developing our realistic art in order to save the theatre from stagnation and defend it against the whims which have become fashionable today with directors."

After coming to an agreement with us, Konstantin Sergeyevich set to work. He announced first of all: "We are about to perform a sublime comedy by Molière, but please do not think about the genre of the play in the early stages, for this leads to superficial portrayal. In order to convey the profundity of this magnificent comedy, we must first of all consider carefully its essential meaning. Do not think about the comic situations of the characters; consider rather the tragedy in the house of Orgon. If the audience does not mock Orgon at the height of the comedy—when he crawls from beneath the table—but is sympathetic towards him, it will be a triumph for you. Orgon is not an entertaining fool; he is a blind, gullible man who is deceived by a clever rogue. The playwright has skillfully developed the comic situations in the play itself and they will show themselves without undue efforts on your part."

Stanislavsky revealed to us an abundance of new ways in which the creative nature of an actor could be displayed. Even though all these methods, which were reflected subsequently in his works, have been studied by many people in the theatre, one still hears on occasion such questions as: "Tell me, how much time does Stanislavsky set apart for work at the desk?" Or: "At which rehearsal does Stanislavsky suggest that work begin on the author's text?" If these people had seen the rehearsals of *Tartuffe*, they would not ask such questions. Stanislavsky's working methods cannot be fitted into any dogma. Each time they were new, unexpected, sometimes unbelievable, but always clear in their purpose and essentially understandable.

I remember him addressing me as follows: "Vasily Osipovich, tell me about your encounter with Tartuffe in the church. Tell me how Tartuffe was praying. . . . Remind me, please, how Molière describes it. . . ." I began timidly: "He prayed not far from me, kneeling from beginning to end, now moved by tender emotion, now filled with holy fire. He sighed and groaned and raised his eyes reverently to heaven. . . . He bowed and kissed the ground and beat his breast with all his strength."[1] Stanislavsky replied: "Is it not true that Orgon was so impressed by this prayer that he took Tartuffe to be a saint and almost Christ Himself? Somehow I found this difficult to believe while I was listening to your lifeless intonations." He turned to Kedrov who was playing the part of Tartuffe: "Mikhail Nikolaevich, do you have any idea of how you should pray in order to make such an impression?"

"Yes . . . of course. . . ."

"Then try it. . . ."

"What?"

"Pray. But pray in such a way as to make a powerful impression on all of us as we stand here, living people, at this very moment. Do whatever you like spontaneously. Sum up your courage and act. I am thinking of introducing a new term for such occasions: 'nakhalin.'[2] Hurl yourself into it as if it were cold water. . . . Do whatever you like, however improbable it seems. . . . Fear nothing. . . . We will forgive you everything, even coarseness. . . ."

Encouraged by Konstantin Sergeyevich, Kedrov began to perform this strange task, at first timidly but then with increasing boldness and confidence. He must be given his due; towards the end of the exercise he became so daring and inventive that he really did make a powerful impression on us all. Konstantin Sergeyevich was very satisfied and laughed a great deal. He said: "Now do you see, Vasily Osipovich, how Tartuffe can pray? Now you have a concrete idea. But that is by no means sufficient. You must develop these ideas further.

---

1. The translation is from the Russian, rather than from Molière's French text [translator's note].

2. The neologism is formed from the Russian noun *nakhal* which means an "impudent" or "brazen fellow." Stanislavsky evidently means by it an actor engaged in the type of bold, spontaneous acting which here he calls on Kedrov to display [translator's note].

Let your visions expand endlessly. Do not be afraid to change them at every rehearsal."

The exercise which I have described took place "on bare ground," as we say, before the period of desk-work and study of the text. Moreover, it not only forms a legitimate beginning to work on a play; it may also be used in the final stage. This actually happened.

We were performing a stormy scene in Orgon's family. The head of the family wants to make his daughter sign a marriage contract with Tartuffe. The daughter and all the relatives are horrified and oppose it in every way. They argue and try to convince Orgon that he should give up his ghastly scheme. We improvised at rehearsals, rarely keeping to the text and mostly using our own words. After seeing our work Konstantin Sergeyevich asked as though in surprise: "Are you sure that that is how it really happened? Consider carefully what is taking place: the father has lost his reason and wishes to commit a crime—to marry his daughter, a fifteen-year old girl, to an obvious bandit, a runaway convict, and to persuade her to sign the marriage contract. What a commotion must inevitably result! In addition, you must take the French temperament into account. . . . Its main feature is its furious rhythm."

Konstantin Sergeyevich sat us all down on chairs and asked us to go through the whole scene without getting up from our seats and giving special emphasis to the rhythm. The result was complete failure. He began to teach us rhythm. He went through a number of exercises and demonstrated himself how it was possible to be active and experience a constant and intense rhythm in a sitting position and almost without movement. "Rhythm," he said, "must be felt by the eyes and legs in readiness for action."

The exercise fascinated us and entering into it we did not notice how we began to ignore our cues and act the scene. We also failed to notice how we leapt up from our chairs one after another and first of all dashed across the room and attempted to tear the contract from Orgon's hands. We did not notice how we rushed out of the room into the corridor and continued to play the scene, how we left Stanislavsky alone in the study and transferred the action to the corridor and the other rooms in the apartment, and how we then returned improvising all the time on the same theme. For some reason I finished up with no shoes on—evidently I had thrown them at the odious relatives.

Konstantin Sergeyevich seemed to be satisfied, and suddenly he called out in the middle of the scene: "Stop! . . . You see how well it's going. Such is the turbulent rhythm of the scandals which Tartuffe creates in the house of Orgon. And note what excellent and unexpected *mises-en-scène* have been obtained. It would be difficult to invent such situations. Moreover, do not forget about the rhythm of speech. You are playing Frenchmen. Their emotions are strong and their thoughts are as clear as the stroke of a pen; explanation is unnecessary. They flow rapidly and easily. Thoughts are conveyed in complete sentences. This is complicated by the verse form of the play. Take note of this for future reference. Not one of you has really mastered the art of reading and has a conception of the rhythm or metre of verse. The rhythm of verse must live in the actor both when he is speaking and when he is silent. You must charge yourselves with rhythm for the whole play and then you may make pauses between words and phrases. They will enter naturally into the required rhythm."

Stanislavsky did not restrict himself to working with us. At the same time he endeavoured to work on acting technique with a group of directors. Throughout this work he constantly jotted down his observations and thoughts in a note-book.

"You must understand," he repeatedly told us, "that someone has to concern himself about keeping alive the tender shoots of great and genuine art. At present they are being stunted by misguided searchings and trends which are threatening the foundations of great realistic art, but they are not strong enough to destroy it completely. Formalism is a temporary phenomenon; we must wait for it to pass. In the meantime, however, we must not be idle; we must work. We have a great responsibility. This is our sacred obligation, our duty to art. We are working for the future."

These were the great tasks which Stanislavsky set when he worked with us on Molière's *Tartuffe*.

LOUIS JOUVET

Molière and the Classical Comedy: Extracts of Louis Jouvet's Classes at the Conservatory (1939–40)

Class of 29 November 1939

Tartuffe

Act II, scene 3

Dorine, Hélène
Mariane, Nadia

[Hélène has never worked on the scene and does not know it. Nadia, who is playing Mariane, often makes mistakes, hesitates, doesn't succeed in giving a correct reading. They perform the whole scene.]

Louis Jouvet (to Nadia): You, I have nothing to say to you. * * * You've never seen that scene? It doesn't interest you? Have you read *Tartuffe*? (She has read it.) Yes, you have read it . . . but you don't know it. There are plays that you should know. You should know *Tartuffe*.

(to Hélène, whose memory often faltered, at the beginning.) You've learned it too fast. It's impossible to understand what you say. The fact that you can't be understood proves that the feeling has not entered into you. If you really had the feeling along with the intention of what you're saying, you'd be clearly understood. In your case, it's not a defect of speech; your voice is clear, you articulate well, but given that you don't feel what you say, you seem to mumble; it gives the impression of being mumbled.

Hélène: I wasn't able to work on it aloud.

L.J. (violently): That is a thing you cannot do, that ought not to be done. Even someone with a lot of training who learns a text without speaking it aloud will find some surprises. Because the instrument is not being used. The instrument must be used. A scene like this one should be rehearsed with all the dialogue.

The feeling of the scene is not there, the situation is not there. What is this character feeling? Explain that to me.

† From *Molière et la Comedie Classique*. © Editions Gallimard, Paris, 1965. Translated with permission. Louis Jouvet, the great French actor and director, gave a course for actors at the National Conservatory of Dramatic Art from November 1939 to December 1940. A stenographer took notes of what was said by Jouvet and his students, and the transcript of those notes was later published, without any additions or corrections. Translated by Virginia Scott.

Hélène: Dorine can't understand how Mariane can let herself be bossed by her father. If that had happened to her, she wouldn't have acted like Mariane . . .

L.J.: Any other feeling?

Hélène: She's making fun of Mariane.

L.J.: Yes, and what else?

Michel: This is taking a great liberty, on the part of a servant toward her mistress . . .

L.J.: Mariane is a young girl. In this house, where people suffer under the weight of authority, an intimacy has been born between her and Dorine.

Michel: Dorine is like Lisette and all those characters.

L.J.: Lisette is a soubrette; Dorine is something more. I'll explain that to you another time, it's not the issue today. I'm asking what the character feels. *The personality of Dorine is indicated, from the beginning,* when Mme Pernelle says to her: "You are, my dear, a serving girl, a little too mouthy, and very impertinent: and you have an opinion about everything."

That's the character, one of those people who speak out loud and clear; someone who says what she thinks. That's indicated at the very beginning.

There's something else in the scene that you must have in your mind in order to play it right.

Nadia: Dorine absolutely wants Mariane to marry Valère.

L.J.: That's not it.

Nadia: She can't stand Tartuffe?

L.J.: That's it. *That's why she's so angry, she detests Tartuffe.* The idea that the daughter of the house should be given to him in marriage has her beside herself. She makes fun of Mariane, *but her mockery is aimed especially at Tartuffe.* It's very clear in the passage where she paints his portrait. (Paraphrasing) "What a splendid fellow, M. Tartuffe, you'll see! With his red ears and his florid complexion. He'll take you to the puppet show, what a gent, etc. etc."

All the derision for Tartuffe is in that!

The beginning of the scene is very precise. "Tell me, have you lost the power of speech? Do I have to play your role? So, are you struck dumb? How can you let him propose this ridiculous plan. . . ."

You went too fast. (L.J. acts the beginning of the scene again.) *She's in a bad humor, she's indignant, all that is clear.* And when she says: "Let your father marry him, let Orgon marry his Tartuffe!" There's something enormous in that. And then: "But let's be reasonable, let's discuss, let's examine the business. Valère has asked for your hand. That's clear? And you love him. Good, then no more stuttering. And the two of you are both mad about each other? You both want to be married?" "Certainly," says the little twit. "Well then, if you love him, if he loves you!"—

"It makes me crazy to hear someone talk that way." That's to the audience. And then she declares: "Marry Monsieur Tartuffe, he's handsome, he's noble (in his own district), he's rich . . . not a trifling proposition." And that's the beginning of putting Tartuffe in the can. It's a funny bit. Mariane says, "Oh, please, stop talking like that!" * * * "No, a daughter has to obey her father. You'll meet the bailiff's wife and the tax-collector's, too." . . . She amuses herself describing the little town. It's a comic scene; a lot of animation under all that, you have to show that.

"You have to be punished . . ."—In the end, you are too stupid.— And it's then that she looks at her and all the great love she has for Mariane reappears. And suddenly Valère enters: "But here's Valère, your lover." And all the incomprehension and misunderstanding begins again. The scene is not hard to play, but it has *to be played with the heart and with humor.* * * *

Dorine must not be too cunning. What's wrong with most of Molière's servants, or rather with the actresses who play them, is that they add on clever bits. They crook their little fingers, they wink at the audience. There's this very stupid side to the soubrettes; although they are also *characters full of heart, full of good sense, and very sane.* They speak naturally. Their happiness and their good sense come from the heart. But they shouldn't be played "witty," it's irritating. * * *

Michel: Is there a tradition for the character of Tartuffe, I mean his physical aspect? Because I saw at the Comédie-Française a print of Tartuffe from 50 years ago: a skinny character . . .

L.J.: There is no tradition in the theatre. There is a corrupt "tradition" as in everything.

Tartuffe, in the troupe of Molière, was played by Du Croisy who was a *jeune premier.*[1] Now, *Tartuffe* has become an anticlerical play, the anticlericalism that existed just before the separation of Church and State [1905]. At that time there were newspapers that specialized in anticlericalism, that published every morning portraits of parish priests who were potbellied, moonfaced, with rolls of fat, repugnant. That's when Tartuffe became a repellant-looking character and has stayed that way. The last actors who played him are Silvain, who was very potbellied, very fat, very repugnant and Coquelin who played him as a pig, with various bits I'll tell you about later. . . . It's a little too soon now. * * * There was Gémier, then Paul Mounet. They played Tartuffe as a criminal who had escaped from the galleys, who still had the brand on his shoulder, and who had come to Paris to make his fortune, a kind of gangster of the times.

But that's not it at all. He's a swindler who thinks: There are people who live from professions that are not professions, who live off

1. Leading man.

women, who live by fawning on people with money, * * * or who take up collections on the street for Chinese babies or wounded soldiers and live off that.

Tartuffe is a swindler, a scrounger (as Jules Renard says) who says to himself: Really that man Orgon is too easy; he wants to be virtuous, he wants to do good; when a man has that degree of obsession, he can certainly be had. *The blindness of a man with an obsession,* whether it's postage stamps or autographs, is so great that when you skillfully encourage his obsession, he won't resist; you can make him believe anything. That's the whole theatre of Molière: men blinded by passion. In the blindness of their passion, their good sense evaporates. * * *

Since the time of Molière, Tartuffe has become part of "religion," or rather the politics of religion. The critics, the politicians have said: It was the genius of Molière that he foresaw anticlericalism! If you study *Tartuffe* from Molière's time to ours, you will see what's been said about the play in each epoch, and that it becomes the reflection of antireligious thought in each epoch. * * * And that still exists.

Now, he's played as lewd. If you show me a Tartuffe like that, I'll leave, thinking "you must really take me for an imbecile."

When an error is imposed to this point, what to do? The very word "Tartuffe" is applied to the hypocrite, to the man who unctuously rubs his hands together. . . . What can be done against such a tradition?

Michel: Go squarely for the opposite.

L.J.: Yes, but when you do that you have to be successful. When you rejuvenate *Tartuffe,* you have to find *a charming young man, very intelligent, very disturbing;* and you have to feel scandalized, shocked, during the scene with Elmire and Tartuffe. There is no declaration of love, on any stage, that is as sophisticated, as charming as that of Tartuffe and Elmire. You must feel, from the beginning of the play, that this is a *dangerous man but you must not hate him.* But, in all the productions of *Tartuffe,* from the beginning of the play he is smothered in hatred. No. *He is charming, disturbing.* There is the meeting with Elmire. This meeting must create a feeling of unease, of danger. Elmire is a young woman * * * a charming woman [and turning toward the girls in the class], barely older than you.

Then comes this shocking scene where we see that Tartuffe is stalking Elmire, trying to arouse her. That goes on until the second scene where Orgon is under the table. There is no more daring scene in the whole theatre than that one, where the husband is under the table, not believing his eyes nor his ears, and where Tartuffe pursues his endgame. That has, sexually, something very daring. * * * It's a shocking scene; the idea of this husband who hears everything, of this wife who feels both aroused and hunted, who coughs desperately. Her decency is at stake; it's a tragic scene.

It's usually played with such idiocy, such stupidity, such lack of danger, that it's disgusting, nauseating.

Michel: And at the end, when Tartuffe is unveiled; The house is mine. That's when we see how hard he is.

L.J. (speaking forcefully): "You're the one who must leave, you who speak as if he were the master; the house belongs to me. I'll make you know that." No, that's very Victor Hugo, very stupid. *Tartuffe should say that clearly and with perfect tranquility.* Like a stone dropped in the water. * * *

And in the middle of all this, there's Dorine, a charming person. *She is not one of those fat women with double chins and a big bottom, who dominate their young mistresses.*

Hélène: Yes, the servants in Molière are always fat, that's why I didn't think I could play one of them.

Class of 20 December 1939

Act I, Scene 1

Dorine, Hélène
Mme Pernelle, Claudia
Damis, Michel
Mariane, Irène
Cléante, Jacky

[Hélène knows her lines. As the others perform rather badly (they have not rehearsed together), the scene gives the impression of a muddled debate. The scene finished, they all stop, arms dangling, not knowing what to think.]

Louis Jouvet: Well! After that, I have to ask your opinion. I don't know what you think of it. I don't think anything of it.

Claudia: I'm the one who . . . [She had the most lines.]

L.J.: I don't know what you showed us.

Claudia: We didn't rehearse.

L.J.: That's not the issue. You are future actors. When one rehearses a text for the first time, at the least one should make it understandable, especially if it's a question, as it is here, of a text that you should know. I understood nothing, even though I know the scene well. [To Hélène.] Supposing that an amnesty is granted to your comrades, I should at least have understood you. But I didn't understand a word you said. For two reasons: first, you spoke too fast; second, you continually faced Mme Pernelle, while turning your back on us. When we saw your face, in profile, we could see that you were laughing; your face was lit up, filled with amazement at the malicious things you dared to say. But I heard nothing. I asked myself why you were in the scene.

This first scene of *Tartuffe* is exposition; everything must be clear from the beginning. You played the scene for Dorine; *Dorine, in the circumstances, keeps her distance;* she doesn't answer Mme Pernelle directly; one does not *answer* the grandmother directly. *She directs her answer to Cléante;* she speaks her first reply to him. So when someone is speaking to several other persons, there is always one among them who goes further. That's what Dorine does. *She seizes the moment to get her word in.* You have not given us even once the feeling of doing that. * * *

Hélène: Is Dorine angry during this scene?

L.J.: No, she's not angry.

Hélène: You've had me work on several of Dorine's scenes. The first time she was light-hearted, in a good mood. But then she was angry, wasn't she? . . .

L.J.: This is the beginning of the play. * * * *The attitude of Dorine,* at this moment, is not as playful, as daring as you showed us. *If you give Dorine that freedom, from the beginning of the first act, she'll appear to be a daughter of the house: she is nothing but the suivante.*[2] If you give her this "tone" from the first scene, I ask myself what she will become later. * * *

Look at the text, pay attention to what you say, what you do, the relationships among the characters, and you will discover the dramatic situation.

This is an old lady who comes to reprimand people who are more or less her children, or her heirs, and among whom the servant has a word to say, with some freedom, but without addressing Mme Pernelle directly.

Since *this beginning is an exposition, a convention,* it must be clear. But, what you did was not at all clear, we didn't see what happened, we were not informed about the play. *This first scene must fix us on what is going to happen;* it must interest. What you did didn't engage our interest.

What are you working on, aside from that?

Hélène: From Racine's *Esther*. Esther's prayer.

L.J.: Boring. [He thinks about Dorine.] You should be able to play Dorine. It's too bad you don't feel that.

Hélène: No. I don't like this character at all.

L.J.: You see. In the profession that we practice, we sometimes play characters that we don't like. *We are the servants of the characters; we must like them,* since one runs the risk of playing them, even when one does not like them.

---

2. A kind of lady's maid or upper servant.

A character of the classical theatre must be liked. The profession of actor means learning to like, learning to practice that sympathy that is at the base of social and human relations. To the extent you do not like Dorine, you will not play her well. It's not so difficult to learn to like someone, it's a matter of a little indulgence, a little good will. That's how you penetrate a character, with solicitude, constant affection; and little by little you will discover the character. But if you pick up your text and say: "I don't like Dorine, I don't understand," you will never succeed.

Actors have different attitudes toward roles they have to interpret; they say: "I don't like this role" or "Oh, that! That's easy!" There are some who read the role and who say, "Oh, I see exactly how that works." That's a very bad attitude. Even in life, as you grow, you will see, with your friends, whom you think you know very well, that you haven't entirely understood them; you will say: "I would not have believed that of him." . . . What is interesting in humanity, said Montaigne, is its diversity. One can never know all the diversity of men. And that leads you to understand *that no character in the theatre is simple.*

You must be very circumspect before the characters, very reserved. Some fling themselves on the emotions of a character like a seal on pieces of bread; they plunge into feelings. You must move much more slowly than that. *It needs long, daily acquaintance.* It's at the moment you really "feel" the character that you know it.

What talent is, it is this penetration of the character; 200 or 300 performances of the character, that's not a long acquaintance; and one does not finally play it well until one has played it a long time. If one has rehearsed also for a long time, one will play it well from the first performance.

Some great actresses have made their debuts in the role of Dorine. You must bring to the work that you do for this role as much seriousness as if you were going to play it. You must perform well, in your mind, all of Dorine's scenes.

Hélène: Yes, all right.

L.J.: Now, say to me: the first scene is so and so, the second is . . . etc.

Hélène: The first scene is with Mme Pernelle; the second is "And Tartuffe?"; the third is the one that I learned: "Have you lost the power of speech?" After . . . I forget.

L.J.: You see, your character is part of the action, she has very characteristic scenes. You try to go through the whole role now, because I ask you to, but you've never thought about it before.

When you learn a rôle, you must see the whole play, know how the character behaves, the succession of scenes that she has. The whole will charge your imagination, help you find the character. Learn a scene, come and play it like that, that's not enough. You have to live with characters, love them. That's the only way to draw something out of a character; otherwise, our profession could be practiced by anyone.

Michel: Do you think one could play a scene like that first one of Dorine's without having rehearsed all the characters?

L.J.: Obviously, that's hard; one is always obliged to adjust what one does to the responses of the others. However, if Hélène had been thinking about her character, she would not have made the mistakes she made.

Michel: If she had worked with Mme Pernelle, she would have been able to find the tone of the scene.

L.J.: Her first response is not to Mme Pernelle; and all the rest of her interventions in the piece were not at all as indicated.

Claudia [Mme Pernelle]: Yes . . . the first time the voices of the others surprise you.

L.J.: When you play in an ensemble, in which you have a part, even before a rehearsal with the others, you know your part. It doesn't matter which clarinetist, which bassoonist, anyone who knows his business a little, has the right tempo; he comes in at the right moment. The leader of the orchestra can make certain adaptations, but the musician has learned his part.

Nadia: But they are professionals.

L.J.: Exactly. Why did Hélène make such nonsense out of her role? It's not that I revealed things that were so immensely deep; she could have found them on her own. She came with her natural good humor, she whispered her lines, no one could understand them, they corresponded to nothing, to no feelings. She has not thought about the scene. Isn't that it, you haven't explored it?

Hélène: Dorine ought to respond rat-a-tat-tat . . .

L.J.: Exactly wrong. *She does not "respond."*

Hélène: I imagined it. I didn't do it at all the way I imagined it. I have no feeling for the character.

L.J.: And why?

Hélène: . . .

L.J.: There is an art in acting a play. This art includes a number of details that you are here to learn, that I am here to teach, to try to get you to understand. * * * If a there is a character that you have no feeling for, a scene that you do not understand, come tell me; that would be better than to play a scene that means nothing. We will talk about it, and you will not work blindly. * * *

Hélène: I'm sure that if I had been able to do it again, I would have done it much better.

L.J.: You knew your lines in an ensemble scene where everyone else was stumbling; you should not have stumbled like the others; then we could see that you were prepared since you had the advantage over them of having learned your lines. But you stammered like the others. If you had had the feeling of the scene and of your character, you would have been able to give the impression that your comrades were in your way, but you followed the herd.

What is important for the actor, his essential quality, is *his attitude in his work,* how he behaves. *The classical character is someone who exists much more than you.* You must not, as you do, step into the character's shoes without thinking. The character has *a dramatic existence much greater than yours.* [To Hélène.] To become Dorine, you have to think about it seriously. You glance at the text and speak it; you think that's all there is. Unbelievably superficial. Not the theatre! * * *

For the actor, everything depends on his attitude toward the character and toward the audience; his attitude toward himself, that is, perhaps, more difficult. That is composed of many things. *To play a character is to lend oneself to someone else.* You have to obey the character; and you know it's already difficult to obey yourself. You have to know how to lend yourself to the audience, but not too much.

The profession of actor, which does not require great intellectual faculties, nonetheless demands an interior intelligence, an intuition, a subtlety and refinement.

If an actress is simply an animal that is led onto the stage, well coiffed, well dressed, with a beautiful voice . . . no. An actress, that's someone with an interior life.

That attitude of the actor toward himself, toward his profession, his audience, his character *makes up a discipline.* When you are going to play a character, you adopt a regimen. To prepare to play Phaedra, for six months you have to force yourself to embrace a certain intellectual regimen; and that is how, often, without your being aware of it, *the character has an influence on the interpreter.* * * *

It's hard enough to observe in life; we don't have the habit of doing so; I speak, you listen; you could, however, not really be listening. . . . You know, *people who have an attentive attitude, and who are thinking of something else?* The faculty of attention in a theatre creates an accumulation of sensibilities that is an element favorable to the actor. It's no more mysterious than the waves of electric current. It exists. * * *

Michel: I think that this contradicts what you said before, that if you rehearse a character for a long time you'll play it well. I think you should say: by dint of playing it, you will play it well.

L.J.: You haven't understood. What is difficult for an actor, for a director, is *the art of rehearsing.* A play that is well-rehearsed, that's a play easy to perform. Ordinarily, you don't rehearse. What you think is a rehearsal is a group of people who arrive at different times. The text is recited; an unexpected incident occurs, someone brings a message. It's ended. People congratulate each other: "you were very good, absolutely remarkable." These friendly meetings go on for a certain time, until the day when the director decides that it's time to perform it.

A rehearsal is much more than that: to be the character, to become it, that is, to feel him deeply; and when this character is deeply felt, when you have an intimate belief, that's been tested, when you could say of the character what he would do outside of the circumstances where he finds himself, when you can speak of him like an old friend, when you can say to someone: "Oh! no he would certainly not do that!" Then you know the character. *And when you know him well, substitute yourself for him, execute him.* That's something else, however.

To believe yourself the character, to be him, put him on the stage. It's a place of a special magic, where everything is transformed. When marble is wanted for the set, if you use real marble it will look like papier-mâché; you need paper if you want marble. The translation of feelings is the same. Sometimes you must have another than the one you want to show. It's the trick of the trade as in painting or sculpture. *Emotion is sometimes translated in roundabout ways.*

To spend time with a character, know it, become it, to finally find the means to execute this character; add to that, the actor always has this great problem of being both the piano and the pianist, the instrument and the instrumentalist; and you will have an idea of the difficulties of our art.

Essays

NANCY SENIOR

Translators' Choices in *Tartuffe*[†]

Translators make choices at every point, some explicit and some implicit, some made at the beginning and others arising in the course of translation. The sum of these decisions can make for very different versions of the same work.[1] In this paper treating twelve twentieth-century English versions of Molière's *Tartuffe*, I will first make some remarks on the kinds of choices made by the translators. Then I will look in detail at how they deal with a few short passages, chosen to illustrate aspects of seventeenth-century French language, religion and everyday life. The eight prose translations included here are by Stanley Appelbaum, Haskell M. Block, David Edney, Miles Malleson, Renée Waldinger, A. R. Waller, and John Wood, as well as one, published in the Modern Library series, where the name of the translator is not given. The four verse translations are by Morris Bishop, Donald Frame, Christopher Hampton and Richard Wilbur. I have not included versions that are very free adaptations.

The Kinds of Choices

Any translator of Molière, and indeed any literary translator, must choose where he or she stands on the continuum between, on the one hand, bringing the work to the public, and on the other hand bringing the public to the work.[2] Should the reader or theatre audience

---

[†] From *TTR: Traduction, Terminologie, Rédaction* 14.1 (2001): 39–62. Reprinted by permission of the author.

1. Ideally, different translations of a work should be considered in their entirety, particularly when the object is to evaluate their relative merits. Since this procedure is cumbersome when more than two or three versions are considered, and since this study aims to illustrate some general points about choices rather than to judge the translations as a whole, only short passages will be compared.

2. In an essay first published in 1813, Friedrich Schleiermacher characterizes the two approaches in extreme terms. He sees only two roads open to the translator: "Either the translator leaves the author in peace, as much as possible, and moves the reader towards him: or he leaves the reader in peace, as much as possible, and leads the author to him." (Schleiermacher, 1977, p. 75)

be expected to make an effort to understand the play and its time, or should the play be adapted to appeal to the taste of the public? Each translation will bring a different answer, as will each production of a play.

A theatrical text has of course two possible destinations. It can be performed, with each production supplying a different interpretation. It can also be read with no intention of putting it on stage, in which case the reader's imagination supplies an individual interpretation, including a vision of the characters, their relations, and the overall meaning of the play. In effect, the play might be compared to a novel consisting of dialogue, stage directions, and in some cases more or less copious notes. In this way theatrical texts reach a public which does not have access to stage performances for geographical, financial or other reasons. Although different aims of translating a play are not mutually exclusive, a translator will probably have one uppermost in mind: is the play to be performed, will it most often be read, will the translation accompany the original text as an aid to the reader? Hampton and Malleson refer to specific productions of their texts; Wilbur mentions audiences' reactions to his (frequently-performed) verse translations; Edney gives alternate versions of the officer's speech in the final scene, depending on whether the director chooses a seventeenth-century setting or a modern one. On the other hand, the manner of presenting Appelbaum's and Waller's English texts makes visible their relation to the original French on facing pages, and allows the reader to pass easily from one to the other.[3]

Many factors other than purely literary ones may affect translations, particularly when a play is to be performed (as is so often the case for Molière, who always wrote for the stage). Susan Bassnett criticizes "the link between theatre translation and crude economic concerns" which sometimes leads to questionable practices.[4] As one might expect, the "crude economic concerns" she mentions are not cited to justify such practices; rather, a more respectable explanation is given. "It is principally among English language translators, directors and impresarios that we find the use of the notion of 'performability' as a criterion essential to the translation process." (Bassnett, 1991, p. 102) Bassnett argues that assumptions about the relation of the text and performance on which this notion is based are "often

3. In the introduction, Appelbaum acknowledges a tension between two goals: to provide a translation that is "literal, in English prose, line for line," and "to offer an acting version" without copyright entanglements. (p. xiii)

4. Bassnett describes the contemporary British policy, as practiced by the National Theatre, in which "translators are commissioned to produce what are termed 'literal' translations and the text is then handed over to a well-known (and most often monolingual) playwright with an established reputation so that larger audiences will be attracted into the theatre. The translation is then credited to that playwright, who also receives the bulk of the income." (Bassnett, 1991, p. 101)

oversimplistic and based on a concept of theatre that is extremely restricted." (p. 103) Traditions of performance vary from one time and place to another, and there are "enormous differences in rehearsal convention, in performance convention and in audience expectation." There is no such thing as a universal "performability," and the concept should not be used to prove that changes must be made in order to make a play accessible to audiences. Bassnett's argument can be used by those who think the public should come some distance to meet the work, rather than having the work come to meet the expectations of the public.

Neal A. Peacock shows more sympathy than does Bassnett with steps taken to obtain what he calls "theatrically successful solutions to the problem of translating Molière for the English stage." (Peacock, 1994, p. 83) He groups translators (or adapters) into three categories: conservationists, who wish to preserve all the features of the seventeenth-century structure, though in a renewed form; modernisers, who "have upgraded certain aspects for the modern age"; and post-modernisers, who "have knocked down and rebuilt the main structure but have reused some of the original materials." (p. 84) According to Peacock, Malleson subjected Molière's texts to "the theatrical emendations appropriate to the English stage," keeping the French setting and plot but having the characters speak in "a modern idiom." (p. 85) Peacock considers Malleson to be halfway between conservationist and moderniser. Peacock's language is revealing: the word "upgrade" seems to imply that modern versions are superior to the original work, and the expression "emendations appropriate to the English stage" suggests that a translator who departs from the rhythms of the original is doing the author a favour. According to Peacock, Malleson's *Tartuffe*, dating from 1950, is even now a source for adapters who do not read the original French play. One may guess that their use of this version, already quite different from Molière in phrasing, will give an adaptation far from the original in many respects.

A translation of Molière may be intended to last for years, or, as Bassnett and Peacock point out, it may be aimed specifically at a particular production. The text of *Tartuffe* gives various indications about the title character, not all of which are compatible and coherent. Is Tartuffe a buffoon, a vulgar sensualist, a convincing con man, a menacing force of evil, a man trying but failing to lead a godly life? Does he fall in love with Elmire, or is he a habitual seducer? Is Elmire flirtatious, or just calm and clever? Does she enjoy Tartuffe's attempt to seduce her, is it painful for her, is she tempted or disgusted? Molière's text moves from comedy at the beginning to disturbing final acts. Should comedy be emphasized, at the expense of the serious material underneath? What kind of comedy should it be? How subtle or crude? A translator can emphasize one aspect of the action and characters, or keep many possibilities open.

French theatre has a long history of different interpretations for this play, as Roger Planchon observes: "When I decided to stage *Tartuffe* I studied all the previous productions. That's when I realized that there is no such thing as tradition." (Quoted by Carmody, 1993, p. 56)[5] In the twentieth century serious interpretations, including notably those of Planchon, have been predominant.[6] A modern sensibility often finds dark elements where seventeenth-century directors and audiences may have seen the opposite. In the final scene, the officer arresting Tartuffe announces that the King knows everything and reads all hearts. This flattery of Louis XIV was presumably meant to be reassuring at the time, and to win royal support in the controversy raised by the play. (See Salomon, 1962, Ch. 1 and 2.) Today it can sound considerably less benign. Planchon's staging, building on the invasion of private life, showed the terrifying power of a police state by means of a massive show of force in the arrest. In contrast, the North American tradition of playing *Tartuffe* tends toward broad, often farcical comedy, to the point that spectators may wonder how anyone could be taken in by such an obvious impostor.[7] When the play is performed for the broadest laughs, much of the content is lost; character study disappears and menace is removed. Copley's remark about adaptations could apply as well to some stagings: "Molière has largely disappeared in the process; he has been transformed from a dramatic poet into an expert purveyor of near-farce." (Copley 1960, p. 116)

What Language to Use

The question of setting must be considered not only by the director of a performance, but also by the translator. To what extent is the audience supposed to see the play as set in a particular time and place? Should it be fully of its time, should it be timeless, or of the

5. Salomon's *Tartuffe devant l'opinion française* confirms Planchon's remark. At times in the eighteenth and nineteenth centuries, interpretations tended toward the indecent, no doubt to the delight of a certain part of the public but to the dismay of others. Napoleon congratulated Mademoiselle Mars because, unlike some of her predecessors, she played Elmire as "une honnête femme," for "les gens de goût." (Salomon, 1962, p. 138) In 1825, Stendhal notes that "l'on rit fort peu au *Tartuffe*," though "on a plusieurs fois souri et applaudi de plaisir." (Quoted by Salomon, 1962, p. 140)

6. At the Planchon production, my first experience of the play on stage, I was surprised that there were no laughs at all. The Comédie Française version in 1997 was also serious. Both productions explored the nature of Orgon's attachment to Tartuffe. In Planchon, the implicitly homosexual element was brought out, though without any overt homoerotic acts. In the 1997 Comédie Française version, a broken-hearted Orgon embraces Tartuffe before the latter is led off by the arresting officers.

7. Edney relates how a festival adjudicator, baffled by a restrained production of *Tartuffe*, remarked sarcastically to the cast: "I have always wondered what it would be like to see *The Mikado* done seriously." (Edney, 1998, p. 61)

translator's own time? If the setting is specifically Molière's time, how much information should be given to help the present-day public understand things that people of Molière's time knew immediately? The language of translation will be chosen as a result of that choice. It can either keep some strangeness, some feeling of the foreign origin of the text; or else it can aim for fluency, for a "naturalness" that gives the impression the work was written in the target language.[8] The translator could in theory use language of the time the play was written. This option in its pure form is practically never chosen, for writing authentic-sounding seventeenth-century English is a daunting task, and the result would probably not be appreciated by the public. A commonly adopted middle way is to use modern English while avoiding anachronisms as much as possible, so that obviously recent words and references do not break the illusion. At the other extreme, especially for purposes of comedy, a translator may use deliberate anachronisms. (See Simon, 1976.)

In the case of a verse play, the choice between verse and prose in the target language is probably the first definite decision to be made. Other considerations such as those discussed above no doubt underlie the decision; but only the question of verse or prose must receive an explicit answer before one can put pen to paper or fingers to keyboard. Frame writes in an introduction to his translations that since "rhyme affects what Molière says as well as the way he says it," it is worth while to use it in English as well. (Frame, 1967, p. xiv) In English as well as in the French original, rhythm and rhyme can create surprising and memorable lines. As Wilbur points out, Molière's lines are arranged in intricate patterns of balancing half-lines, lines, couplet, quatrains and sestets. "There is no question that words, when dancing within such patterns, are not their prosaic selves, but have a wholly different meaning." (Wilbur 1958, pp. x–xi. See also Waldinger, 1999.) Some other translators consider that prose is more suitable for the twentieth century stage. At about the same time Wilbur finds verse essential, Block argues that "the language of present-day prose is much closer to [Molière's] idiom than that of verse" (Block 1958, p. xii), and Hampton says that the ingenuity demanded for rhymed translations "cannot avoid drawing attention

---

8. Berman, referring to Schleiermacher's two poles, says that a translator who chooses the foreign work as exclusive master "runs the risk of appearing to be a foreigner, a traitor in the eyes of his kin"; if on the other hand he settles for a conventional adaptation, "he will have satisfied the least demanding part of the public, sure enough, but he will have irrevocably betrayed the foreign work as well as, of course, the very essence of translation." (Berman, 1992, pp. 3–4) According to Venuti, a translated text is judged acceptable by most publishers, reviewers and readers when it reads fluently, when it gives the appearance "that the translation is not in fact a translation, but the 'original.'" The translator's invisibility is "a weird self-annihilation, a way of conceiving and practicing translation that undoubtedly reinforces its marginal status in Anglo-American culture." (Venuti, 1995, p. 1 and p. 8)

to itself, somewhat at the expense of the line of the play as a whole."
(Hampton 1984, p. 8)

Translators of French classical theatre usually maintain a high
level of decorum, corresponding to the *bienséances* required at the
time. The restrictions on what could be said certainly did not make
for dull comedies. Molière is often earthy but not obscene. In many
plays he suggests improper things, and allows the audience to com-
plete the thought. In *L'École des femmes,* a great deal is made of the
fact that Horace has taken something from the innocent Agnès. The
audience, along with her jealous suitor Arnolphe, can imagine things
other than the ribbon that Horace has in fact stolen. Certain English
versions of Molière take a different approach, using openly obscene
language, with corresponding staging.[9] Molière's wit is replaced by
crudeness, perhaps because the translator or director thinks that oth-
erwise a modern audience will not understand the jokes.

One challenge to translators is to deal with word play, which may
not survive the passage into another language. In Act I, sc. 2 of
Tartuffe, when Cléante refers to Madame Pernelle as "cette bonne
femme," the servant Dorine remarks:

> Ah! certes, c'est dommage
> Qu'elle ne vous ouît tenir un tel langage:
> Elle vous dirait qu'elle vous trouve bon,
> Et qu'elle n'est point d'âge à lui donner ce nom.

The adjective *bon* is taken in several senses here, including uncom-
plimentary ones as well as the obvious favourable meaning. The 1694
Dictionnaire de l'Académie Française mentions that "un bon homme"
can mean "Un vieillard, homme avancé en âge," as well as "Simple,
idiot." Cléante's reference to Madame Pernelle may be polite; on the
other hand, it may refer to her age or to her limited intellectual
capacities. Dorine then uses it in yet another sense; according to the
Dictionnaire, "On dit aussi d'Un homme, Il a esté bon, pour dire,
qu'Il a fait ou dit quelque conte, soit avec esprit, soit par sottise."
According to Dorine then, if Madame Pernelle heard Cléante call her
a *bonne femme,* she would object to the slighting reference to her age,
and would say that he was being silly. None of the translators quite
manage to replace all the word play by an equivalent one, though
most transmit the general idea of the exchange and some do have

---

9. Ranjit Bolt's translation of *L'École des femmes* in Peter Hall's production (London, 1997)
was apparently quite successful; it pleased many members of the public and was praised
by some critics. However, having seen the production, I sympathize with one reviewer's
view that it was a great disappointment, with a translation "heavy-handed and awash with
contemporary vulgarities," and acting done in an "over-the-top farcical style." (Urban
Desires)

Dorine make humorous remarks. Waldinger simply uses "old," both for Cléante's expression "this old lady," and for Dorine's reply: "she would soon tell you that you have some nerve and that she is not old enough to be called that." Edney introduces another adjective: "What a strange, old lady!" Dorine takes up both: " 'Strange' she might not like, but 'old' would really have her up in arms." Bishop has Cléante say "that good woman," to which Dorine replies that Madame Pernelle would say she is "not old enough yet to be good"—a clever remark, but perhaps not one that the prudish Madame Pernelle would make. Hampton's Cléante exclaims: "Silly old . . . ," and his Dorine remarks: "I know / she'd tell you you're the one who's being silly / and that no one would ever call her old." With Wilbur, Cléante begins a remark about "How that old lady . . . ," but is interrupted by Dorine's observation: "She'd thank you for the *lady*, but I'm sure / She'd find the *old* a little premature."

Everyday Life Then and Now

* * *

One of the funniest scenes in the play, the first one in which Orgon appears (Act I, sc. 4), presents a number of questions to the translator. The scene has been prepared by the various characters' comments about Orgon's infatuation with Tartuffe, and it confirms all that has been said. It gives information about Tartuffe himself, who has not yet been seen; the man's sensuality is revealed, in contrast with what has previously been said about his severity towards others.[1] When Orgon, just returned from a trip, inquires what has happened in his absence, Dorine informs him that his wife Elmire has been ill. After each description of Elmire's suffering, Orgon asks: "Et Tartuffe?" Each time, Dorine tells him that Tartuffe has been well: he has eaten heartily, drunk copiously, and slept well. Orgon replies each time: "Le pauvre homme!" In the last of the exchanges, Dorine says that Elmire finally agreed to be bled, and felt better afterwards. Orgon asks the same question:

> Orgon: Et Tartuffe?
> Dorine: Il reprit courage comme il faut
> Et contre tous les maux fortifiant son âme,
> Pour réparer le sang qu'avait perdu Madame,
> But, à son déjeuner, quatre grands coups de vin.
> Orgon: Le pauvre homme!

1. It may well be that Molière has Dorine exaggerate for comic effect. When Tartuffe appears in Act III, he does not appear as clumsily obvious as Dorine's remarks suggest.

Translation of this passage raises a number of questions concerning everyday life, including how to deal with words having several meanings, and words whose meanings have changed since the seventeenth century. Tartuffe drank to fortify "son âme," a term that may refer simply to oneself, or the soul (appropriate in the context of this play). It is translated as "his soul" (Appelbaum, Block, Waldinger, Frame), "his spirit" (Bishop), "himself" (Edney, Hampton, Modern Library, Waller, Wood), "his cheerfulness" (Bishop). The line is omitted by Malleson. Against what was he fortifying his *âme*? It could be "all ills" (Appelbaum, Waller), "all evils" (Block), "disease" (Edney), "all harm" (Modern Library), "the worst that might happen" (Wood), "trouble" (Bishop), "the blows of fate" (Hampton). The expression is replaced by a different formulation, "at any cost," by Wilbur and Frame. The latter two verse translators, working independently, came to the same solution because of the need for a rhyme with "lost."

> Wilbur: To keep his cheerfulness at any cost
>   And make up for the blood *Madame* had lost
>   He drank, at lunch, four beakers full of port.
>
> Frame: And, girding up his soul at any cost
>   To make up for the blood Madame had lost
>   He downed at breakfast four great drafts of wine.

Few of the translators managed to capture Dorine's ironic use of religious terminology to describe Tartuffe's self-indulgent behaviour.

* * *

Tartuffe drank "quatre grands coups de vin." How much was that? *Un coup* is not an exact measurement. Several translators choose "draughts" (or the variant spelling, "drafts"): "big draughts" (Appelbaum), "great drafts" (Frame), "large draughts" (Modern Library). For others, he drank four "glasses": "large glasses" (Block), "big glasses" (Edney), "glasses full of wine" (Bishop). Waller has him drink "four large bumpers," Bolt writes "several stoups," Wood has "good swigs" (a colourful word, but "three or four good swigs of wine" is not necessarily a large quantity), Hampton gives "tumblersful" (which suggests a large amount), and Wilbur writes "four beakers full of port."[2]

Orgon's repeated exclamation "le pauvre homme," following Dorine's reports on Tartuffe's hearty appetite, is the chief source of laughs in the scene. Even today the adjective *pauvre* has a double meaning in French, expressing either pity or affection. Orgon could

---

2. When I asked a number of people "What is a beaker?," everyone said it was a piece of laboratory glassware, except for a British-born chemist who mentioned a container similar to a tankard. This odd result is no doubt skewed because the chemist knew the context in which the word was used.

have used it in either sense in speaking of Elmire, in view of her illness. However, ignoring the news of his wife, he expresses his attachment to Tartuffe by this word. At the same time the audience thinks of the other meaning, clearly not applicable to Tartuffe. The English translator cannot have it both ways; he or she must choose "dear" or "poor." Either Orgon says something in English that makes sense but is not very comic aside from the repetition, or else his exclamation is wildly inappropriate and thus funny. None of the translators find a way to have Orgon mean the remark one way while the audience takes it in another way. All of them, with one exception, use "poor." Edney has considered the two possibilities; while in his article he mentions the expression "Poor man," in his own translation he writes "Dear man!"

Language Sacred and Salacious

The scene in which Tartuffe tries to seduce Elmire (Act III, sc. 3) presents another kind of challenge to translators, for Tartuffe uses religious terminology to speak of sensual desire. The scene must have been deliciously shocking to some members of the audience and truly horrifying to others. Its power depends on the widespread and ancient practice of using erotic language in speaking of religion. The love poems in the *Song of Solomon* were interpreted in Jewish tradition as an expression of God's love for Israel. Christian commentators applied the same approach to the work, assuming the love to be that of Christ for the Church. (See Reese, 1993.) Over the centuries, writers such as John of the Cross have continued to use the language of human love to express love of God.[3] The image of a nun as the bride of Christ is still used today in the Catholic Church.[4] In the other direction, the language of religion was used in the literature of courtly love, where the lover's devotion to the lady was of a quasi-religious nature.

Many seventeenth-century religious writers presented the austere practices of religious devotion in terms of pleasure. One of the most eminent of these was François de Sales, whose extremely influential *Introduction à la vie dévote* was published in 1608. According to him, "la dévotion est le vrai sucre spirituel, qui ôte de l'amertume aux

---

3. The sixteenth-century Spanish mystic John of the Cross carries on this tradition in his well-known poem "The Dark Night," in which the soul steals out of the house for a secret meeting with her beloved. The last stanza reads: "Quedéme y olvidéme, / el rostro recliné sobre el Amado; / cesó todo, y dejéme, / dejando mi cuidado / entre les azucenas olvidada." ("I stayed, myself forgotten, / My countenance against my love reclined; / All ceased, and self forsaken / I left my care behind / Among the lilies, unremembered.") (Brenan, 1973, pp. 146–147)

4. The metaphor occasionally comes to popular culture; the Belgian nun "Soeur Sourire" sang: "Mets ton joli jupon mon âme / J'ai rendez-vous, Seigneur, avec vous." Sister Luc-Gabrielle's record became popular not only in Europe but in North America as well. She won a Grammy award in 1963 for the song "Dominique," and appeared on the Ed Sullivan show in 1964. (See Infoplease.)

mortifications et la nuisance aux consolations." (Sales, 1804, Pre-
mière Partie, Ch. II) A prayer states: "Et vous, ô mon Dieu, mon
Sauveur, vous serez dorénavant le seul objet de mes pensées; [. . .]
vous serez les délices de mon cœur et la suavité de mes affections."
(Première Partie, Ch. X) Devout people are like happy birds in the
air of divinity, "qui les environne de toutes parts de plaisirs incroy-
ables." (Première Partie, Ch. XVI)

Tartuffe's attempt to seduce Elmire must be seen in the light of this
back-and-forth movement between sensual and mystic impulses and
the expression of one in terms of the other. In his declaration, he
assures her:

> Que si vous contemplez d'une âme un peu bénigne
> Les tribulations de votre esclave indigne
> S'il faut que vos bontés veuillent me consoler,
> Et jusqu'à mon néant daignent se ravaler,
> J'aurai toujours pour vous, ô suave merveille,
> Une dévotion à nulle autre pareille.

While this may seem like ordinary language to a modern audience, in
seventeenth-century France it was highly charged in both a religious
and an erotic sense. Tartuffe speaks of the possibility that "vos bontés
veuillent me consoler." While the singular "votre bonté" would prob-
ably mean simply "your goodness" or "your kindness," the plural sug-
gests "vos faveurs."[5] These *bontés* are meant to console him. While *la
consolation* is often used in the ordinary sense of "soulagement que
l'on donne à l'affliction, à la douleur, au desplaisir de quelqu'un" (*Dic-
tionnaire de l'Académie*), it is often used in a religious sense. The same
dictionary gives as examples for this meaning: "Dieu est toute sa con-
solation." "Dieu est le consolateur de nos ames, le consolateur des
malheureux, des affligez. L'Eglise appelle le saint Esprit Le consola-
teur, l'Esprit consolateur." Tartuffe asks Elmire, in consoling him, to
condescend "jusqu'à mon néant." In addition to its meaning of "noth-
ing," as in mathematics, *néant* can refer to the unworthiness of the
sinner before God. According to the *Dictionnaire*, "les creatures se
sentent tousjours du neant dont elles sont sorties."

Tartuffe addresses Elmire as "suave merveille." The adjective *suave*
may not be recognized today as a religious one even in French, and the
English word borrowed from French is even further from the
seventeenth-century meaning.[6] As we have seen above, François de

---

5. A little earlier in the scene, Elmire has thanked Tartuffe for praying for her health; she says
she is grateful for "toutes ces bontés," using the term in a moral and religious sense. Later,
in Act IV sc. 5, Tartuffe demands that Elmire provide "un peu de vos faveurs" to prove to him
the "charmantes bontés que vous avez pour moi." Clearly, he is not asking for her prayers.
6. The *Petit Larousse* defines the adjective *suave* as: "D'une douceur agréable, exquis," and
gives as examples of usage, "Parfum, musique suave."

Sales often uses the word to speak of the sweetness of religious devo-
tion. The *Dictionnaire de l'Académie* defines *suave* as "Qui est doux &
agreable, il n'a guere d'usage qu'en parlant des odeurs." *Suavité* is "La
douceur d'une odeur. [. . .] Il signifie en termes de spiritualité, Cer-
taine douceur qui se fait sentir à l'ame, quand Dieu la favorise. Durant
l'oraison il sent des suavitez merveilleuses." On the other hand, a *mer-
veille* is simply a "Chose rare, & qui cause de l'admiration," such as the
seven wonders of the world. In translating the expression "suave mer-
veille," one obviously cannot use the borrowed word *suave*, since its
meaning is inappropriate. The entire expression is omitted by Frame,
Malleson and Wilbur. It is translated without religious connotations by
Appelbaum ("sweet wonder") and Hampton ("delicious prodigy"). A
number of translators use the noun *miracle* to restore some of the lost
meaning of the adjective: "lovely miracle" (Bishop), "delicate miracle"
(Block), "miracle of nature" (Edney), "miracle of sweetness" (Modern
Library), "sweet miracle" (Waldinger), "miracle of loveliness" (Wood).

Tartuffe promises Elmire "une dévotion à nulle autre pareille."
Dévotion is "Pieté, attachement au service de Dieu," according to the
Dictionnaire de l'Académie. Even today it retains the same meaning;
the *Petit Robert* defines it as "attachement sincère à la religion et à ses
pratiques." The *Robert & Collins Senior* offers the English equivalent
"devoutness, religious devotion." The cognate English word refers
only secondarily to religious practice; the primary meaning is attach-
ment, as in devotion to duty or to family. For the French *dévotion*, all
the translators use the English "devotion." In the combination
"Immeasurable worship and devotion," Bishop restores religion by an
additional noun. Frame omits the language of spirituality entirely:

> A bit of sympathy is all I crave
> For the distress of your unworthy slave.
> If your kindness, Madame, should ever deign
> To condescend to me, and end my pain,
> Nothing would be as constant and as true
> As the devotion I shall have for you.

Hampton omits most of it as well:

> If you could bring yourself to show some favour
> to your unworthy servant's tribulations,
> if you would deign to stoop down to my level
> and out of kindness offer me relief,
> delicious prodigy, I guarantee
> my eternal, unparalleled devotion.

Wilbur keeps a religious flavour:

> And if, in your great goodness, you will deign
> To look upon your slave, and ease his pain,—

> If, in compassion for my soul's distress,
> You'll stoop to comfort my unworthiness,
> I'll raise to you, in thanks for that sweet manna,
> An endless hymn, an infinite hosanna.

The use of "manna" and "hosanna" recall biblical language, though "hosanna," a public exclamation of praise, is inappropriate in a declaration of illicit love where Tartuffe later promises complete secrecy. The translator's clever rhyme reduces the character's cleverness and the menace that he represents for the family.

*   *   *

In the second seduction scene (Act IV, sc. 5), where Orgon, hidden under a table, hears for himself the proof of Tartuffe's treachery, Tartuffe uses less religious language. The tension here comes less from a contradiction between his words and his intentions, than from suspense about what is going to happen next. While the scene can be very funny, it has a more serious aspect because of Elmire's distress. As I mentioned earlier, Elmire's character can be played in different ways. In some interpretations she finds her dealings with Tartuffe unpleasant but necessary, while in others she enjoys flirting with him. A translator may tend to one or the other of these views. In addition, the rendering of as little as a half-line may make a difference in the way the audience sees her. When Tartuffe demands that Elmire prove her feelings towards him by "un peu de vos faveurs," Orgon still remains hidden, and Elmire coughs loudly to signal that it is high time to reveal himself. The coughing is so obvious that Tartuffe remarks:

Tartuffe:	Vous toussez fort, Madame.
Elmire:	Oui, je suis au supplice.
Tartuffe:	Vous plaît-il un morceau de ce jus de réglisse?
Elmire:	C'est un rhume obstiné, sans doute; et je vois bien Que tous les jus du monde ici ne feront rien.
Tartuffe:	Cela certes est fâcheux.
Elmire:	Oui, plus qu'on ne peut dire.

Elmire's remarks "je suis au supplice" and "plus qu'on ne peut dire" indicate clearly that she is suffering. Not only is her cold "obstinée," as she says two lines later, but her husband is so as well. While Tartuffe takes the first of her remarks, "Oui, je suis au supplice," to refer to the cough, the audience understands that she is calling on Orgon to end the situation. In the wording chosen by some translators, Elmire refers to the source of her distress as "it," which logically would mean the cough: "Yes, it is very bad" (Block), "It tortures me" (Bishop), "Yes, it racks me" (Waller), "Yes, yes. It's bad indeed" (Wilbur). Other translators avoid the pronoun "it," so that the remark can equally indicate other causes of suffering, understood immediately by the audience if not by the slow-acting Orgon: "Yes, I'm in torture" (Appelbaum), "Yes, I am in agony" (Edney), "Yes, I am very much tormented" (Modern Library), "Yes, I am very uncomfortable" (Waldinger), "Yes! I'm in great distress" (Wood). Even if the rhythm is sometimes heavy, these versions retain the double meaning which is essential to the passage; they thus express her distress, and contribute to the portrayal of her as "une honnête femme" at the mercy of an evil man.

Conclusion

Earlier in this article I mentioned some questions that a translator must answer explicitly or implicitly, the most general one being whether to bring the work to the public or the public to the work. According to some people, the criterion of "performability"—criticized by Bassnett, accepted by Peacock—must be met in translations of dramatic works to be used on stage. In some of the passages from *Tartuffe* quoted above, concessions can be made to changing times without too much damage. Adapting or explaining matters of everyday life, for example, does not touch the heart of the play. The translators studied here describe the amount of wine drunk by Tartuffe in various ways, some more colourful than others. * * * In other cases, it is impossible to retain everything that is in the French text. None of the translators quite manages to capture *cette bonne femme*, and all of them lose the double meaning, and thus much of the comic effect, of *le pauvre homme.*[7] In the latter case, Orgon's repetition of the expression, whether it be "Poor man!" or "Dear man!," still conveys his infatuation with Tartuffe.

One of the most difficult challenges is to capture the religious language and references which were so shocking at the time of the play's first appearance, and which are still powerful today to the reader or spectator who understands them. In the passage quoted from the first seduction scene, some of the translators retain this crucial element, while others omit it almost entirely.[8] Tartuffe becomes simply ridiculous, without the danger or scandal of the original.

7. Copley points out that Malleson's addition of "chips of explanatory dialogue" to Molière's phrases ("Poor man! He was haggard enough when I first saw him." "Poor man! Maybe you should have let him sleep") loses the economy of the original and upsets the balance. Still, Copley prefers Malleson's dramatic effectiveness to certain accurate translations of Molière that are almost impossible to speak. (Copley, 1960, pp. 120–121) Since, as Peacock says, Malleson's version is used as a base for adaptors, one wonders how much of Molière is left in the twice-removed product.

8. The limitations of comparing very short passages are evident here. A six-line extract is not enough to see how the translators have communicated religious content and connotations; they could have compensated for losses in one place by the way they treat other parts. In this case, Tartuffe's speech or even the entire scene could be considered as a suitable unit of comparison. A look at the entire scene shows that while most of the translators successfully communicate explicit religious references, they do not use a language suffused with religious imagery or connotations to the point of making up for the sort of loss shown in the lines quoted.

The language of seventeenth-century French religious devotion, as we have seen, includes many common lexical items having a specialized meaning. Tartuffe masters this language perfectly, and uses it to serve his lechery and greed; he increases his crimes by hiding them under cover of the sacred. In a double borrowing, words such as *suave, bonté* or *consolation* move from the neutral register to the sacred, and in Tartuffe's speech, to the obscene. Such a complex set of relations is difficult to capture in another language, and yet if a translation loses this aspect, the work loses much of its force.

The challenge may in some ways be compared to translating a sociolect, that is, the language of a particular social group. In this play, there is no question of non-standard grammar or constructions; the language of devotion expresses ideology more than regional origin or social class.[9] What subset of the target language can best render this aspect of the source text? If historical accuracy is the translator's main aim, the language of Catholic devotion in English would probably be used. If one wishes a dynamic equivalent, to use Nida's terminology, the vocabulary of another religious group might be chosen. If a translator aims to show the universality of the theme—after all, religious frauds are as common in our time as they were in Molière's, and they are found in religions both traditional and new—he or she may prefer to use a more general pious language. The application desired for a particular performance can be made by means of staging. Stage sets, costumes and acting can evoke many different contexts in which an opportunist takes advantage of the gullible, or an oppressive regime threatens the integrity of private and family life.[1] Anne-Françoise Benhamou warns of the danger of attempting a too-precise parallel with contemporary situations in translating great theatrical texts: "La traduction doit conserver, évidemment, le 'feuilletage' du texte, et ne pas réduire à une seule possibilité de représentation un texte qui en offre plusieurs." How, otherwise, can one play (with) a text that already supplies all its interpretation? (Benhamou, 1990, p. 13)

---

9. A. Chapdelaine and G. Lane-Mercier write of the dichotomy between "la langue officielle, correcte, non marquée et des langages 'illégitimes,' incorrects, marqués," where the contrast between the two types represents the social hierarchy. (Chapdelaine and Lane-Mercier, 1994, p. 8) In the case of *Tartuffe*, the language, although correct, is marked; and the translator of the play, like the translator of a non-standard sociolect, must attempt "la reconstruction sémiotique et rhétorique" (Ibid., p. 10) of the author's use of the language of a particular group.

1. This applies of course to productions in the original language as well. In 1995, Ariane Mnouchkine set the play in North Africa in the context of Islamic fundamentalism. When questioned about this, she replied: "Je reste persuadée que la pièce a été écrite exactement dans ce contexte. [. . .] Donc, si j'avais vécu dans le sud des États-Unis, j'en aurais sans doute fait un pasteur protestant intégriste, mais je ne voyais pas l'intérêt de jouer ça en cols de dentelle." (Mnouchkine, 2000)

In the remarks above, I have assumed that the public recognizes religious language—an assumption that perhaps cannot be justified. Every teacher of literature has had to explain religious references so that they will not be missed by many students. It can no longer be taken for granted that readers will catch the biblical references that are so important in English literature. In *Tartuffe*, the power to shock came from seeing a hypocrite manipulating the language of the sacred for evil ends. Since for many members of the public today, religious language is often no longer even recognized, and if recognized, often not held sacred, it is a real challenge to translate at the same time the comedy, the scandal and the menace of the play.

According to Antoine Berman, "Il faut retraduire parce que les traductions vieillissent, et parce qu'aucune n'est *la* traduction."[2] (Berman, 1990, p. 1) André Topia analyzes the reason for this different fate: the original has a network of organic interactions with its time, language and culture, which the translation cannot have.[3] (Topia, 1990, p. 46) *Tartuffe* more than most literary works has both deep roots in its time and potential applications to specific situations in other times. In the words of Ariane Mnouchkine, it is "une fontaine de jouvence." (Mnouchkine, 2000) For these reasons it will no doubt continue to attract translators, who will make choices based on their understanding of the work, their talents and the purpose for which they undertake the translation.

References

Edition of the French text of *Tartuffe*:
Théâtre de Molière (1961). Collection Internationale, Garden City, New York, Doubleday.

Translations of *Tartuffe*:
Appelbaum, Stanley, trans. (1998). *Tartuffe and The Bourgeois Gentilhomme*. Mineola, New York, Dover Publications, Inc.
Bishop, Morris, trans. (1957). *Eight Plays by Molière*. New York, the Modern Library.
Block, Haskell M., trans. (1958). *Tartuffe*. Northbrook, Illinois, AHM Publishing Corporation.
Edney, David, trans. (1997). *Tartuffe*. Saskatoon, University of Saskatchewan.

2. Berman makes an exception for what he calls "les grandes traductions" such as the Vulgate, Luther's Bible, the Authorized Version of the Bible in English, and specific literary translations such as Schlegel's Shakespeare. (Berman, 1990, p. 2)
3. As later generations constantly renew their view of the period, says Topia, their perspective on the work will change as well, and new translations will be needed. "Ainsi, alors que cette œuvre ne cesse de se ré-ajuster à l'intérieur d'une configuration toujours en mouvement, la traduction ne 'bouge' pas." (Topia, 1990, p. 46)

Frame, Donald, trans. (1967). *Tartuffe and Other Plays*. New York, New American Library.

Hampton, Christopher, trans. (1984). *Molière's Tartuffe or The Impostor*. London, Faber and Faber.

Malleson, Miles, trans. (1950, 1978). *Tartuffe*. London, Samuel French.

Plays by Molière (no date). Introduction by Waldo Frank. New York, Modern Library.

Waldinger, Renée, trans. (1959). *Tartuffe*. Woodbury, N.Y., Barron's Educational Series.

Waller, A. R., trans. (1926). *The Plays of Molière*, vol. IV. Edinburgh, John Grant.

Wilbur, Richard, trans. (1963). *Tartuffe*. New York, Harcourt, Brace & World.

Wood, John, trans. (1959). *The Misanthrope and Other Plays*. London, Penguin Books.

Other sources:

Bassnett, Susan (1991). "Translation for the Theatre: The Case Against Performability," *TTR*, vol. IV, no. 1.

Benhamou, Anne-Françoise (1990). "Quel langage pour le théâtre?" (À propos de quelques traductions d'*Othello*), in *Retraduire*, pp. 9–31.

Berman, Antoine (1992). *The Experience of the Foreign: Culture and Translation in Romantic Germany*. Tr. by S. Heyvaert. Albany, State University of New York, 1992.

———— (1990). "La retraduction comme espace de la traduction," in *Retraduire*, pp. 1–7.

Bishop, Morris, trans. (1958), *Molière, The Misanthrope*. London, Faber and Faber.

Brenan, Gerald (1973). *St. John of the Cross, his Life and Poetry. With a Translation of his Poetry by Lynda Nicholson*. Cambridge, Cambridge Unversity Press.

Carmody, Jim (1993). *Rereading Molière. Mise en Scène from Antoine to Vitez*. Ann Arbor, The University of Michigan Press.

Chapdelaine, Annick and Gillian LANE-MERCIER (1994). "Traduire les sociolectes: définitions, problématiques, enjeux," *TTR*, vol. VII, no. 2, pp. 7–10.

Copley, J. (1960). "On Translating Molière into English," *Durham University Journal*, no. 52 (New Series 21), pp. 116–124.

Dictionnaire de l'Académie Française (1694). ARTFL Project, University of Chicago, www.lib.uchicago.edu/efts/ARTFL/projects/dicos/.

Edney, David (1998). "Molière in North America: Problems of Translation and Adaptation," *Modern Drama*, no. 41, pp. 60–76.

Infoplease. www.infoplease.com/ipa/A0150546.html.

Mnouchkine, Ariane (2000). Interview in *Périphéries*, http://www
.peripheries.net/g-mnchk.htm.

Nida, Eugene (1964). *Toward a Science of Translating*. Leiden, E. J.
Brill.

Oliver, Raymond (1975). "Verse Translation and Richard Wilbur,"
The Southern Review, no. 11, pp. 318–330.

Peacock, Noël A. (1994). "Translating Molière for the English
Stage," *Nottingham French Studies*, vol. 33, no. 1, pp. 83–91.

Reese, James M. (1993). "Song of Solomon," in Metzger, Bruce M.
and Coogan, Michael D., eds., *The Oxford Companion to the
Bible*. New York, Oxford, Oxford University Press.

Retraduire (1990). *Palimpsestes* 4, Paris, Publications de la Sorbonne
Nouvelle.

Sales, François de (1804). *Introduction à la vie dévote*. Paris, Société
typographique.

Salomon, Herman Prins (1962). *Tartuffe devant l'opinion française*.
Paris, Presses Universitaires de France.

Schleiermacher, Friedrich (1977). "On the Different Methods of
Translating," in Lefevere, André. *Translating Literature: The Ger-
man tradition from Luther to Rosenzweig*. Assen, Amsterdam, Van
Gorcum, pp. 66–89.

Simon, John (1976). "Translation or Adaptation?," in Weiner, Dora B.
and Keylor, William, eds. *From Parnassus: Essays in Honor of
Jacques Barzun*. New York, Harper and Row, pp. 147–157.

Topia, André (1990). "*Finnegans Wake*: la traduction parasitée. Étude
de trois traductions des dernières pages de *Finnegans Wake*," in
Retraduire, pp. 45–61.

Urban Desires / Performance, Tuesday June 24 (1997?), www
.urbandesires.com/3.5/performance/london_theater/docs/ltj_24
.html.

Venuti, Lawrence (1995). *The Translator's Invisibility: A History of
Translation*. London, Routledge.

Waldinger, Albert (1999). "A Certain Slant of Light: Richard Wilbur
as Translator of French," *META*, vol. 44, no. 2.

EMANUEL S. CHILL

Tartuffe, Religion, and Courtly Culture[†]

The famous Company of the Holy Sacrament, a secret organization of priests and laymen, is now widely recognized as having been a leading participant in the social action of the French Counter Reformation.[1] Founded toward the close of the 1620's by followers of Cardinal Pierre de Bérulle, the Company (known to its victims and critics as the *cabale des dévots*) enlisted prominent nobles, magistrates and officials, as well as religious figures, in a vast campaign against the "evils of the age." As the power of the central government declined during the 1640's the *dévots* extended their network of provincial branches to most of the kingdom and promoted systematic projects for charitable assistance, for religious observance, and for the repression of various forms of lower-class indiscipline and disorder. During the 1650's the Company covertly prepared the way for the condemnation of Jansenism (despite a significant rigorist tendency within its own membership). However, the spread of the Jansenist controversy, which sapped the strength of the whole religious movement, also exposed the Company to the criticism of an increasingly unsympathetic public opinion. As religious feelings waned the *dévots* were investigated, ridiculed, and attacked as meddling, conspiratorial vigilantes. Finally, having aroused the suspicions of Mazarin, the Company was officially suppressed in 1660. For some years thereafter a small group of *"anciens"* continued to meet, covertly and intermittently, but it would appear that by 1666 this remnant of the main Company was extinct. Nevertheless, during this very period of decline, the die-hard *dévots* and their friends came into sharp and memorable conflict with the new and rising literary culture of *cour et ville*.

Toward the middle of 1664 it might have seemed to the inner circle of *dévots* that the barrage of official persecution had passed. Mazarin

---

[†] From *French Historical Studies* 3.2: 151–83. Copyright 1963, the Society of French Historical Studies. All rights reserved. Used by permission of the publisher, Duke University Press.

1. The basic document on the Company is the *Annales de la Compagnie du Saint-Sacrement* . . . (Bibliothèque Nationale, ms. No. 14,489, *fonds français*). I refer to the published edition by H. Beauchet-Filleau, *Annales de la Compagnie du St-Sacrement par le Comte René de Voyer d'Argenson* (Marseille, 1900). A comparison of Beauchet-Filleau's edition with a microfilm copy of the original manuscript has revealed only minor discrepancies.

   Since the rediscovery of the *cabale des dévots* in the late nineteenth century a number of articles have appeared and there are numerous references to it in modern literature on the period. The basic study of the Company's inner history and program remains Raoul Allier's *La Compagnie du très Saint-Sacrement de l'autel: La cabale des dévots* (Paris, 1902). (Since the publication of the *Annales* a few volumes of other documents have appeared—mainly correspondence.) A useful bibliography will be found in the *Dictionnaire de Spiritualité Ascétique et Mystique* under the article "Compagnie du Saint-Sacrement—I. Histoire" by Eugène Levesque (Vol. II, cols. 1304–5).

was dead and the Queen Mother still exercised great influence on behalf of the *"gens de bien"* at court. A letter to the Company of Grenoble spoke of the "reestablishment" of the central group (June 17, 1664), and the *Annales* of the main group noted that in July much was done in accordance with the Company's "spirit."[2] Indeed, the Company of the Holy Sacrament had achieved its last success—the suppression after its initial performance of Molière's *Tartuffe*.

The vehement campaign mounted by the *dévots* against Molière is probably unequaled in the history of literature. The polemics and intrigues conducted by the Company of the Holy Sacrament and its allies kept him from a successful staging of *Tartuffe* until 1669, three years after the disappearance of the central group. Partly to overcome criticism, partly to confound his enemies, Molière had reworked and expanded his play between 1664 and 1669. *Don Juan*, written in 1665 and suppressed as a result of *dévot* pressure, belongs to the political history of *Tartuffe*, for it bristled with sharp rejoinders to the "cabal." But Molière's counterattacks involved more than polemical asides. The comedies of the mid-1660's marked a new stage in Molière's artistic development, in which his work becomes more realistic, serious, and problematical. *Tartuffe*, besides castigating bigotry, embodied moral attitudes which found a natural habitat in the royal court of the 1660's and which challenged the whole *dévot* way of life.[3]

The *dévots* had probably been aware of Molière as an enemy of religion for some years before 1664. A prominent member of the Company, the Prince de Conti, once an enthusiast of the "comedy,"[4] had supported Molière's company the provinces; but after his conversion in 1655–56 the Prince became a zealous censor of "disorders," withdrew his patronage and probably secured the expulsion of Molière's troupe from Lyon. Through Conti the Holy Sacrament undoubtedly learned of Molière's arrival in Paris in 1658. Molière's first Parisian triumphs came in the years when the Company was under official attack and its records rudimentary: thus it is understandable that the *Annales* do not mention the irreverent *École des Femmes* (1663), despite the *dévots'* almost indubitable participation in the attacks on that play. It is also probable that the Company learned of *Tartuffe* while it was being written, toward the close of 1663.[5] At any rate, on April 17, 1664, nearly a month before the first

2. *Annales*, pp. 231–33; Allier, *Cabale*, pp. 383, 411–12.
3. For the interpretation of Molière as a spokesman of courtly culture I am indebted to the brilliant work of P. Bénichou, *Morales du grand siècle* (Paris, 1948).
4. The generic term for all stage works in the seventeenth century.
5. J. Cairncross, *New Light on Molière* (Geneva, 1956), pp. 8–12. This writer agrees with A. Adam that the prominent magistrate who tried to interdict *L'École* may have been Guillaume de Lamoignon, a sympathizer and former member of the Company. "The accusation of impiety was everywhere in the polemic of 1663" (Adams, *Histoire de la littérature française au xvii* siècle, III, 304).

performance, the inner circle of the Holy Sacrament decided to "secure the suppression of the evil comedy *Tartuffe*. Each agreed to speak about it to such of his friends as had any credit at court . . ."[6]

The *dévots* were unable to prevent the staging of the comedy at Versailles on May 12. Given as part of a series of royal spectacles known as *Les Plaisirs de l'Isle enchantée*, this first *Tartuffe* was judged "*fort divertissante*" by the king and his court. Unfortunately its text does not survive, nor does there appear to have been any substantial comment from the first audience on the actual content of the play. This silence is itself remarkable, for the audience, which was a brilliant one and included such literary connoisseurs as Bussy-Rabutin and Marigny, had not stinted its comments on other parts of the royal entertainment.[7] There can be little doubt that the apparently cool reception accorded the first *Tartuffe* resulted from discretion rather than indifference. Amusing and spirited, the comedy must have been bold enough to make the well-disposed audience catch its breath: better say little and write nothing before the outraged *dévots* have spoken, for everyone knows that they are still powerful and that they influence the Queen Mother.

Unquestionably the *dévots* found the play highly offensive. It was probably stronger, in the obvious sense, than the version which we have. Certainly there must be substantial differences between the two and it is clear that the original three-act play does not survive integrally in the present five-acter. Although the various reconstructions of the first *Tartuffe* are of necessity highly conjectural, it has been persuasively argued that the original play was a broad farce in which a low-comedy bigot was presented as the dupe of an equally vulgar confidence man. It is likely, moreover, that this petty crook, the first Tartuffe, was portrayed as a *fourbe en soutane*, a priest.[8] But whatever

6. *Annales*, p. 231.
7. D. Mornet says there were three contemporary descriptions (*Histoire de la littérature française classique* [Paris, 1947], p. 210).
8. These notions were developed by Jules Lemaître ("Les Deux Tartuffe" 1896, in *Les Contemporains* [Paris, n.d.], VII, 338–61) and Gustave Charlier ("Le Premier Tartuffe," *Académie Royale de Langue et de Littérature Françaises*, 1923, pp. 25–61; "Autour du Premier 'Tartuffe'," *ibid.*, 1929, pp. 91–110).

    Charlier has propounded a cogent explanation of the reworking of *Tartuffe* which accounts for certain anomalies within the extant version through a reconstruction of the first. If the original villain was given holy orders (and thus a kind of social *passe partout*), then he might well have been a vulgar gourmandizing scoundrel (e.g., lines 234–35) and the dupe a low-comedy buffoon. The *dévots*' outrage at such overt anti-clericalism led to the introduction of a spokesman of "true" religion (Cléante) and the laicization of Tartuffe. Therefore, in *L'Imposteur* (the second version) the villain's hold on his victim must depend, not on external marks of priesthood, but on his own talents as a confidence man— on his own powers. To make these powers socially convincing, his social rank must be raised. Although Orgon's family is also given more resource and respectability, it is no match for the enhanced villain, who must be disposed of by a *deus ex machina*.

    Charlier suggests, therefore, an evolution from a low-comedy farce to the present realistic satirical comedy of character.

    Without any remnant of the original text such ideas remain pure conjecture. However, since the first *Tartuffe* is of obvious interest to the history of literature and to the study of

the play's actual content, it is clear that the surviving remnant of the Company was moved to exert great pressure against *Tartuffe*, and that its "excitation" resulted in the royal prohibition of its public performance. During the meeting of May 27, 1664, "It was reported that the king, thoroughly informed by M. de Péréfixe, archbishop of Paris, of the bad effects which the comedy *Tartuffe* might produce, prohibited it absolutely."[9] The whole literary world of Paris was aware of the forces mobilized to overcome the king's predilection for Molière's comedies.

> When Molière wrote his *Tartuffe*, he recited the first three acts to the King. This work pleased the King, who spoke of it too favorably not to arouse the jealousy of Molière's enemies, and above all the *cabale des dévots*. M. de Péréfixe, archbishop of Paris, placed himself at their head and spoke to the King against this comedy. The King, pressed on it on several occasions, told Molière that the *dévots*, who were implacable people, must not be irritated, and that therefore he must not perform his *Tartuffe* in public.[1]

Even after the ban on public performance (which was to remain in force for three years) Molière continued to feel the *dévots'* fury. In August 1664, Pierre Roullé, *curé* of St.-Barthélemy, published a venomous personal attack in which he condemned *Tartuffe* as an outrage of true religion and its author as an infidel worthy of the stake.[2]

Since Molière's pride and pocket had been hurt, he tried to come to grips with his invisible opponents in his next comedy, *Don Juan*, which portrayed piety as a fool rather than a bigot. After a few successful performances in the Palais Royal, this play was withdrawn, probably at the suggestion of the king.[3] Before long, an author describing himself as the Sieur de Rochemont launched a polemic against the irreligion of *Don Juan* which included an attack on

---

literary creation, other modern scholars have attempted its reconstruction (see, e.g., J. Cairncross, op. cit., where the literature is also reviewed). Although the results have been of unedifying diversity (and the resulting discussions doubtless oversanguine), tacit agreement is at least revealed on a number of points:

(1) No one now maintains that the original play was merely the first three acts of the present version (as contemporary sources seem to suggest).

(2) The play we have includes the first three acts only in reworked form, with the probable laicization of Tartuffe and the addition of other new materials, specifically the *deus ex machina*.

(3) Modern authorities (with the explicit exception of G. Michaut, *Les Luttes de Molière* [Paris, 1925], pp. 100–106], however they reconstruct the direction and extent of the changes between the first and final versions, agree that the Company of the Holy Sacrament played a major part in forcing the evolution.

9. *Annales*, p. 232.

1. "Mémoires de Brossette sur Boileau Despréaux," in A. Laverdet (ed.), *Correspondance entre Boileau Despréaux et Brossette* (Paris, 1858), p. 563.

2. *Le roi glorieux au monde, ou Louis XIV le plus glorieux de tous les rois du monde.* This very rare brochure is summarized by E. Despois and P. Mesnard (eds.), *Oeuvres de Molière* (Paris, 1873–1900), IV, 282–86.

3. And never again performed in Molière's lifetime (Michaut, *Les luttes de Molière*, p. 174).

Tartuffe. "Rochemont" was especially concerned about the ambiguous effect created by a hypocritical villain:

> The hypocrite and the *dévot* have the same appearance and are one thing to the public; it is only the inner life which distinguishes them; and in order "to avoid equivocation and remove anything that might confound good with evil," it is necessary to show what the *dévot* does secretly, as well as the hypocrite.[4]

The effect of these criticisms became apparent in Molière's revision of the original *Tartuffe*. His object was twofold: to turn the force of the religious attacks by strategic mollifications and changes, and thus secure permission for a public staging; and to reply to his attackers, whom he had begun to identify with the *cabale des dévots*.[5] In his second *Placet* he wrote that he had

> disguised the character with the decoration of a man of the world; I had been willing to give him a small hat, long hair, a large ruff, a sword, and lace over all his habit, . . . to soften the [play] in several places, and to carefully remove anything which I thought capable of furnishing the shadow of a pretext to the celebrated originals of the portrait I wanted to draw: . . .[6]

But besides laicizing the hypocrite, Molière also pointed out that he had removed any grounds for mistaking his postures for true religion. His allusion was to the figure of Cléante who, if he had appeared in the original play at all, bore little resemblance to the dispassionate *raisonneur* of the second and third versions.[7] It is more than likely that the change was disingenuous. Cléante's function is ostensibly apologetic: he condemns Tartuffe in the name of true religion; however, his religion is the cool and reasonable piety of *honnêteté* and the *juste milieu*, doctrines unappealing if not repugnant to the adorers of the hidden god of the Holy Sacrament. The stoic sage, like the laicized

---

4. *Observations sur le Festin de Pierre* (as reproduced in Despois and Mesnard (eds.), op. cit., V, 223.

5. He would probably have been correct in the cases of the two individuals I have cited.

   "Rochemont" may have been the Jansenist Barbier d'Aucour; but whether or not he was, it seems probable that he was in touch with the Company, for his eulogy of the pious labors of the "great prince" reads like a catalogue of the Company's good works (Despois and Mesnard, op. cit., V, 231).

   Certain parts of Pierre Roullé's diatribe, *Le roi glorieux au monde*, which argues proposals close to the hearts of the confreres of the Holy Sacrament, suggest that he too may have been party to the "secret," and that if not an actual member of the Holy Sacrament, he may have been "excited" by one to indite his furious screed. At any rate someone must have given him an eyewitness account of the performance at Versailles since it is most unlikely that a parish priest of his stamp would have attended personally (see F. Baumal, *Tartuffe et ses avatars* [Paris, 1925], p. 203). Roullé himself, a doctor of the Sorbonne, "was completely devoted to the Jesuits, although he had been one of the numerous supporters of the *Fréquente Communion*." (G. Hermant, quoted in Ch. Urbain and E. Levesque, *L'Eglise et le théâtre: Bossuet* [Paris, 1930], p. 25n.).

6. Second "Placet," *Oeuvres*, ed. Despois and Mesnard, IV, 392.

7. Michaut, *Les Luttes de Molière*, p. 81.

Tartuffe, deflected the thrust of the play without weakening its force; and while the orthodox fury may have been baffled, it was not abated by Molière's apparent concessions. Moreover, his desire to stage *Tartuffe* did not prevent him from including polemical references to the "cabal" in the revised version of the play as well as in *Don Juan*.[8]

Louis XIV's fondness for comedy, his desire to settle accounts with the censorious *dévots*, the death of Anne of Austria (Jan. 20, 1666), and the extinction of the Paris circle of the Holy Sacrament enabled Molière to win the king's informal consent in the spring of 1667 for a public staging of the revised and expanded *Tartuffe*. On August 5, 1667, this five-act version, called *L' Imposteur*, with the name Panulphe substituted for Tartuffe, was given at the Palais Royal.

By that time, unfortunately, the king had departed for the siege of Lille. In his absence the police of Paris devolved on the first president of the Parlement, Lamoignon. Guillaume de Lamoignon, once a member of the Company of the Holy Sacrament, had naturally severed his ties with the officially suppressed group, but he remained a sympathizer. This most powerful *dévot* saw, like everyone else, that *L'Imposteur* was a disguised version of the "*méchante comédie*" which had angered his former confreres in 1664, and that its irreligion was, if anything, greater than that of the original. Thus on August 6, Lamoignon ordered the theater closed and prohibited further performances. An archiepiscopal interdiction followed in five days.

Lamoignon's prohibition remained in force for nearly two years. Although the king continued to support Molière, he apparently hesitated to affront *dévot* opinion until 1669. It was not until February 9 of that year that *Tartuffe* was finally presented in the version we have today. This play, probably bolder than *L'Imposteur*, was a prodigious success and enjoyed a first run of twenty-eight performances.[9]

Although the central Company had been defunct for nearly two years when Lamoignon closed *L'Imposteur*, the first president's action was faithful to the Holy Sacrament's spirit of rigorous piety. Molière, however, probably unaware of Lamoignon's connection with the cabal, and hoping to have the interdict lifted, managed to obtain an interview with him. The *dévot* magistrate remained adamant and made it clear that Molière's offense had been fundamental.

> Sir, I am much impressed by your merit; I know that you are not only an excellent actor, but also a very clever man [and that] you do honor to your profession and to France . . . ; however, with all the good will I have for you, I cannot allow you to perform your comedy. I am persuaded that it is very pleasant and very instructive, but it is not proper for comedians to instruct

8. *Tartuffe*, I, 5; *Le Festin de Pierre*, V, 2. Also in his second "Placet," op. cit., IV, 392.
9. Michaut, op. cit., p. 53.

men in questions of Christian ethics and of religion: It is not for the theater to preach the gospel.[1]

Molière tried to show the innocence of his play but he was cut short by the first president: "Sir, you will observe that it is nearly noon; I will be late for Mass if I remain any longer."

Probably as a result of the *dévots'* attacks Molière had introduced a more or less abstract moral position into his comedy in the person of Cléante. This position was the basis of his own defense of *Tartuffe* in which he adopted the idea suggested by Scudéry, Aubignac, and others[2] that comedy was capable of improving morals through the depiction and castigation of vice.[3] Lamoignon apparently took account of such arguments, condemning *Tartuffe* not only for the impieties which it contained but for its representation of "true" religion as well.

The first president's reaction was not unique, and it reflected the Jansenist condemnation of the theater as formulated by Nicole. In his *Traité de la comédie*[4] Nicole held that all theatrical representations were inherently vicious since their effectiveness and success depended on the power of moving the spectator by arousing his passions. Truly Christian subjects such as humility, silence, etc., were incapable of such representation,[5] for "comedy" spoke only the language of the passions. The good intentions of the dramatist could not redeem his work's essential concupiscence and, indeed, served only to disguise it. Nicole's argument was directed at the defenders of the theater, and especially those who argued for its moral function; he pointed out that the edifying dramas, those which were free of the obvious impurities, exalted the pagan virtues such as pride and ambition—that is, they praised sin.[6] The more serious the writer, the more dangerous his play.

These attitudes apparently dominated the Holy Sacrament in its last years. The drama is not only a vehicle of disorders, of lewdness and profanity—it is in itself a grave disorder, inherently immoral and un-Christian. Lamoignon's rebuff to Molière reverberates in the

1. "Mémoires de Brossette . . . ," op. cit., p. 565.
2. C. Urbain and E. Levesque, op. cit., pp. 13, 17.
3. Especially his preface to *Tartuffe* (1669), in which he gives a little history of the moral function of the theater and argues for the reforming power of ridicule: "If the use of comedy is to correct the vices of men, I cannot see by what reason any should be privileged. In a state this has much more dangerous consequences than all others; . . . To expose vices to the ridicule of society is to strike a great blow at them. One suffers reprehension easily, but one does not suffer raillery" (*Oeuvres*, IV, 377).
4. First written in 1659 and later expanded. I use the version which appears in the *Essais de Morale* (Paris, 1713), III, 183–223.
5. Ibid., III, 198–99.
6. "However if one considers the comedies of those who have most affected this apparent decency, one will find that they have not avoided the representation of completely indecent objects, in order to paint others as criminal and hardly less contagious. All of their plays are nothing but lively representations of the passions, of pride, jealousy, vengeance, and principally of that Roman virtue which is nothing else than a furious love of oneself. The more they color these vices with an image of grandeur and generosity, the more they render them dangerous . . ." (ibid., III, 198).

writings of two other important members of the Company of the Holy Sacrament, the Prince de Conti and Bossuet; and there can be little doubt that the scandal of *Tartuffe* was the catalyst of their ideas on the theater.

During the campaign against Moliére, Conti, who was well acquainted with his plays, was occupied in writing a *Traité de la Comédie et des Spectacles*. Conti's little book was published posthumously in 1666.[7] Not without intellectual merit, it suggests not only the influence of rigorist morality but a wide acquaintance with the theater. The *Traité* concludes with a stricture similar to Lamoignon's— namely, that comedy has no business teaching morals. Its defenders claim that the theater can instruct and edify; however, the theater is based on the exploitation of the spectator's passions, while true morality aims at their repression. The test case of the moral efficacy of the theater is the drama with a Christian theme. Conti points out that there have been few *comédies saintes*; but (he asks) even in the most famous of these, Corneille's *Polyeucte*, is it the Christian martyrdom which really moves or is it the *human* passions of the pagan characters?

> God did not choose the theater for the glorification of his martyrs: he did not choose it for the instruction of those whom he calls to participate in his heritage. But as the great bishop says,

> To change their ways, and to regulate their reason,
> Christians have the Church and not the theater.[8]

The "great bishop" was Antoine Godeau, former libertine, poetaster, and habitué of the Hôtel de Rambouillet, who had like Conti himself, become a member of the Company of the Holy Sacrament after abandoning the vain things of the world.

Bossuet, an active participant in the Company during the 1650's, gave wholehearted support to the campaign against Molière. His later writings on the theater show how seriously he regarded *Tartuffe*[9] and suggest the influence of Conti and Nicole. Bossuet's condemnation, like theirs, is based on a psychological analysis:

> The first principle guiding the work of tragic and comic poets is that it is necessary to interest the spectator, and if an author

---

7. I use the version in *Sammlung Französische Neudrucke*, ed. K. Vollmöller (Heilbron, 1881), Vol. II. Roullé's tract against Molière had been suppressed because of its violence and Molière's rebuttal. The members of the Company had probably seen this privately circulated reply (the first "Placet," August or September 1664) through their connections at court. Recognizing the futility and danger of a war of words with such a man, they resolved, on September 14, 1664, "to exhort an individual of capacity to write nothing against the comedy *Tartuffe*, and it was said that it was better to forget than attack it for fear of arousing the author to defend it" (*Annales*, p. 235). The "individual of capacity" may very well have been Conti.

8. Op. cit., pp. 18–19. Conti took these verses from the sonnet "Sur la Comedie" (*Poësies Chrestiennes d'Ant. Godeau* [Paris, 1660], p. 464).

9. Especially Chapter III of his *Maximes et Réflexions sur la Comédie*. This work, together with his letter to Caffaro (1694), is reprinted in Urbain and Levesque, op. cit.

or actor of a tragedy does not know how to excite and move him through the passion which he wants to express, what will greet him but coldness and boredom . . . [1]

The fact that open indecency has been driven from the stage, or that prostitution has been replaced by marriage, cannot overcome the fundamentally vicious tendency of the theater:

. . . the licit, far from forbidding its opposite, provokes it; . . . that which comes of reflection cannot suppress the urgings of instinct . . . [because] of the propensity of the human heart to corruption.[2]

As for the instructions of the theater, its touch is too light, and there is nothing less serious, since in it man all at once makes a game of his vices and an amusement of his virtue.[3]

The root-and-branch condemnations of the theater formulated among the *dévots* in the 1660's were reactions to the special political and cultural circumstances of that decade. Of course, members had always been enjoined not to attend comedies or other spectacles;[4] but Molière was the first and only playwright specifically named in the *Annales*. The fact is that down to the 1650's the *dévots*, faithful to their vocation of practical moral reform, worried mainly about traditional and popular types of disorder. In the theater this led them to the denunciation of jugglers, mountebanks, and *comedians* (a term which probably referred to *farceurs*). Thus the Holy Sacrament's repressive zeal was turned against the popular "license" of the Pont Neuf and the St.-Germain fair but apparently not against the Hôtel de Bourgogne and other fixed theaters. To some degree the Company may even have tacitly approved the steady elevation of the moral tone and language of the theater which began with Corneille's first plays. Richelieu's support of playwrights contributed to this change,[5] as did the emergence of a literate, socially exclusive public. The purification of the stage involved, in Paris at least, the near-extinction of the popular theater, with its ribaldry and violence on stage and parterre. Since the *dévots* had hastened the decline of the popular theater, they inadvertently promoted the vogue and dominance of "fashionable" comedy among the upper classes during the first years of Louis XIV's personal rule. Such amusement, like aristocratic libertinage, had been at least tolerated by the Holy Sacrament during the high tide of its influence in the 1640's and '50's.[6]

1. Urbain and Levesque, op. cit., p. 176.
2. Ibid., p. 187.
3. Ibid., pp. 275–76.
4. *Annales*, p. 255.
5. See M. Barras, *The Stage Controversy in France from Corneille to Rousseau* (New York, 1933), p. 54.
6. The passion for the theater of Anne of Austria, also a good friend of the Company, was well known in the 1640's, and she was twice reproved for it by the curé of St.-Germain

Had the *dévots* not tacitly accepted the upper-class theater, their good relations with the Jesuits during those decades would have been impossible, for the Jesuits included play-acting—often of a rather worldly sort—as a regular part of the curriculum of their colleges. Moreovor the *dévots'* disregard of the upper-class theater probably reflected their confidence of the imminent Christianization of the whole society. Since the French playwrights were moving toward more decent and refined expression their work could be safely ignored and might even one day serve as an instrument of religion. Thus, during the 1640's Antoine Godeau, a prominent ecclesiastical member of the company (who was later to manifest Jansenist sympathies and—as noted above—disapproval of upper-class theater) looked forward to the replacement of profane by religious subjects:

> The French muses have never been so modest, and I believe that very soon they will be entirely Christian. Already the theater, where they so often forgot their character of virgins, is being purified and there is reason to hope that soon a stage scene could as well be set on the banks of the Jordan as on the banks of the Tiber or of the Tagus.[7]

This confidence was gone by the 1660's. Not only had the development of religious drama during the previous decades proved disappointing,[8] but far more important was the fact that the unity and prestige of the religious movement itself had been gravely threatened by the Jansenist crisis—that the widening polemics tended to isolate the *dévot* as a generic bigot, intriguer, vigilante—a veritable type, neither strictly Jansenist nor Jesuit, but embodying traits of both extremes. The Company of the Holy Sacrament was indeed linked with the Jesuits and Port Royal—with the former through its actual recruitment as well as its propagandistic zeal and political docility; with the latter by virtue of a strain of moral rigorism among certain of the members. The Jansenists rejected systematic religious propaganda and social action in a world they saw without faith or grace. Truculent and vocal, this rejection was the rear-guardism of the strictly orthodox at the close of the "age of saints." Within the Company of the Holy Sacrament a group of "Jansenizers" shared these attitudes covertly or half-consciously. They regretted the doctrinal asperity of the Port

---

l'Auxerrois. However, some of the bishops secured a judgment from the Sorbonne which held that comedy, if decent, was morally indifferent (Urbain and Levesque, op. cit., pp. 15–16).

Desmarets de Saint-Sorlin, who was at least an agent of the Company in the pursuit of the "Son of Man," Simon Morin, attacked the Jansenists in the 1660's. In reply Nicole wrote his *Imaginaires* (1664–65) and *Visionnaires* (1666–68), the latter title referring to Desmaret's own play of 1640.

7. Antoine Godeau, "Discours" in *Poësies Chrestiennes* (Paris, 1646), p. 11. Godeau's sonnet condemning the moral pretensions of the theater (see above p. 131 and n. 8) appeared for the first time in the 1660 edition of this work.

8. M. E. Pascoe, *Les drames religieux du milieu du xviie siècle* (Paris, n.d.), pp. 192–97.

Royalists and sought to suppress open religious conflict; but they preserved a decided sympathy or nostalgia for the rigors and élans of the devout 1630's and '40's. At the same time the Company of the Holy Sacrament largely abandoned—through necessity, it is true—what Port Royal rejected in principle: the far-reaching social action of discipline and propaganda which had also marked the heroic period of the Counter Reformation. Thus the Company of the Holy Sacrament came to renounce, as did the Jansenists, the serious effort at a Christian infiltration of society. In the 1650's the idea of the rechristianization of society by coteries of patrician zealots could not be practically tolerated by the increasingly assertive and powerful government. This government, cool to the old leadership of the Counter Reformation, tended to favor the Jesuits—supple conformists, largely purged of their old regicidal tendencies. The Jesuitry *à la Louis Quatorze*, pliant to power and rewarded by that power, had to act as if (and indeed probably believe that) the cause of Christianity was prospering—despite the irreligion of the royal court and the increasingly worldly tone of high society. Tacitly the typical *dévot* of the 1650's and '60's shared this acceptance of the new facts of political life; certainly he will not become doctrinally and morally intransigent; but on the other hand the *dévots* will not celebrate the new order or ignore its threat to their religion.

The *dévots* seem to have resolved this difficult situation by somehow cleaving to the ideal of a church-dominated society while implicitly conceding the everyday world to religious indifference. In effect a defensive line was drawn between Christianity and the "world," between serious and vain things. To hold during the 1660's with Lamoignon and Conti that the theater must not teach morals, and to base this restriction, as the latter did, on the inherent immorality of *all* dramatic art, was to grant (however grudgingly) the existence of a theater which merely amused. But while the rear guard of ascetic Christianity was forced to accept the existence of a polite society increasingly indifferent to its values and even, from its point of view, unregenerate, it could not tolerate that this world should have a seriousness of its own, distinct from Christian seriousness. The real danger of plays which claim to teach morals is not so much that the claim is false but that their morals are.[9]

Tartuffe was such a play par excellence. To the *dévots* it represented not merely a deviation from order; Molière's impiety had the magnitude of moral rebellion. Behind the castigation of hypocrisy they

9. Thus Bossuet's merciless irony against Molière's "discourses in which this rigorous censor of the great canons, this grave reformer of the bearing and expression of our *précieuses* displays . . . in the fullest light the advantages of an infamous tolerance among husbands and solicits wives to shameful vengeances against their jealous spouses. He has shown our age the fruit which it can expect from the ethic of the theater, which attacks only the ridiculous while allowing the world all its corruption" (*Maximes et Réflexions sur la comédie*, in Urbain and Levesque, op. cit., p. 184).

must have sensed not only criticism, but a view of things quite alien to their own vision of moral and social order—an alternative expressed with a coherence and conviction of which the contemporary philosophical libertines and amateurs of science were incapable. If only the worldly confined themselves to the world, to vain and trivial things; if only they could amuse without pretending to instruct.

There can be no doubt that in their own way the *dévots* grasped the cultural importance of *Tartuffe* and the adjacent plays. The Jansenizing savant Adrien Baillet, a protégé of the Lamoignons, held that "M. de Molière is one of the most dangerous enemies which the age or the world has raised up against the Church of Jesus Christ . . ."[1]

The Company's leaders attacked Molière's impiety and rebellion with unusual venom. More than a generation after the event, the count D'Argenson, compiler of the *Annales*, recalled with regret the ultimate failure to suppress *Tartuffe*:

> Although the [presentation of] the comedy was through its efforts delayed for a rather long time . . . finally the evil spirit of the world triumphed for the libertine author of that work, despite all the efforts and all the resistance of solid piety.[2]

Indeed the "spirit of the world," evil or not, did triumph. Corneille's Christian drama *Polyeucte* belonged to the passing "age of saints," the high-tide of the Counter Reformation. Racine's *Esther* would have its day only after Louis XIV's reign had passed its zenith of achievement and confidence. But the 1660's were dominated by the comedies of Molière. To the *dévots* his vogue meant that the world was once again asserting itself against the Faith, that impiety was encroaching on the hard-won conquests of the true religion. Less gingerly than modern critics in their approach to literature, the *dévots* had no hesitation in ascribing irreligious motives to Molière. D'Argenson could not restrain his satisfaction over the thought that Molière "was doubtless punished for all his impieties by a most unhappy end. For in playing *Le Malade Imaginaire* he died suddenly in the theater, almost in the view of all the spectators, without spiritual or temporal aid."[3] Years after Molière's death Bossuet too attacked the author of *Tartuffe* as a paragon of impiety.

> Posterity will perhaps know the end of this poet comedian, who in playing his *Malade Imaginaire* . . . suffered the last attack of the malady of which he died a few hours later, passing from the pleasantries of the theater, among which he gave up almost his last breath, to the tribunal of the one who says: Sorrow to you who laugh, for you shall weep.[4]

1. *Jugements des savants* (Amsterdam, 1725), IV, 305.
2. *Annales*, pp. 231–32.
3. Ibid.
4. Urbain and Levesque, op. cit., p. 184.

These religious criticisms underline the cultural importance of Molière's œuvre of the 1660's. But the hatred and vituperation which the *dévots* concentrated on the single figure of Molière[5] also points up the fact that *Tartuffe*—with a secular, dechristianizing tendency hard to ignore in any age—was drawn from the life of the time. This life, the lay piety of the Counter Reformation and of the devout upper classes, was encompassed by the Company of the Holy Sacrament. Molière's castigation of bigotry, his praise of earthly happiness, were effected at the expense of *its* adherents, *its* works. The struggle between the *dévots* and Molière was in this sense political. The moral force of Molière's comedies depended on a realistic depiction of vice. In dramatizing the fevered, ascetic bigotry of the passing generation's religious life Molière had incidentally caught the *cabale des dévots* in a net of ridicule.

A favorite occupation of Molière critics, in his time as in ours, has been the search for a unique personal model of Tartuffe. Although Molière himself insisted that his victim was a group, and referred to a "cabal" and to "originals,"[6] a persistent curiosity has unearthed a number of different and more or less plausible life models of the hypocrite. A mere listing of these models weakens the case for any one of them and suggests that Tartuffe was a real composite. On the other hand, the enumeration of Molière's alleged real-life victims, the "hypocritical" *dévots* of the day, has the virtue of disclosing the links between them as well as their common milieu.

Michaut has culled a list of these supposed victims from contemporary memoirs.[7] Madame de Sévigné, Lenet, Saint-Simon all pointed to the Abbé Roquette, who became Bishop of Autun in 1667. Tallemant des Réaux held that Molière intended an admirer of Ninon de l'Enclos, a "great hypocrite," the Abbé de Pons, while an anonymous pamphleteer spoke with assurance of Desmarets de Saint-Sorlin, intendant of the Duchess de Richelieu, writer of mystical treatises and also a dramatist. Rapin and Deslions, Jesuit and Jansenist respectively, suggested the names of the baron de Renty, the marquis de Fénelon,[8] the Count d'Albon, and the Count de Brancas.

5. "If the purpose of comedy is to correct men in diverting them, the purpose of Molière is to corrupt them in making them laugh, just like those serpents whose lethal bites spread a false joy on the faces of those who are attacked" (Rochemont, *Observations* . . . , quoted in *Oeuvres de Molière*, V, 221).
   "A man, or rather a demon incarnate clothed as a man, the most notable infidel and libertine there ever was . . . He deserves . . . the extreme penalty, . . . the stake" (P. Roullé, *Le roi glorieux au monde* . . . , quoted in *Œuvres de Molière*, IV, 283).
6. Thus in his first "Placet" he speaks of "the Tartuffes" as "the originals who finally had the copy suppressed, . . ." (*Œuvres*, IV, 387–88), and in the second of "the people whom I pain in my comedy," of their "means," their "party" (ibid., IV, 393). The preface to the first edition referred to "Hypocrites" (ibid., IV, 373).
7. *Les luttes de Molière*, pp. 91–92.
8. A pious contemporary biographer of Fénelon's daughter recalled that he was said to belong to "the cabal of the faction of *dévots* who were then regarded as seditious and dangerous

This list could doubtless be extended by a more exhaustive search. However its significance is already clear enough: with the exception of the Abbé de Pons, every one of those mentioned had been either a member or a trusted agent of the Company of the Holy Sacrament.[9] The Abbé Roquette had been a follower of Conti (who was himself suggested as the prototype at least once[1]). Desmarets, author of extravagant religious dramas, flourished within its milieu (Mme. d'Aiguillon, Guillaume de Lamoignon) and served as the Company's *agent provocateur* in the pursuit of the illuminist Simon Morin. Renty, Fénelon, and Albon were not only members but belonged to the ruling central committee.

In our own time two studies have been devoted to establishing the real-life model of Tartuffe, and in each case convincing evidence has been produced to show important connections between the proposed model and the Company—although in neither case are these connections essential to the conclusion. Francis Baumal maintains that not only *Tartuffe* but also Scarron's novel *Les hypocrites* (probably Molière's main *literary* source) were both inspired by the character and doings of one Cretenet, a Lyon barber and false *dévot*, who attracted a fervent band of followers as a lay spiritual director and evangelizer of the countryside.[2] These interests were typical of the *dévots*; and through his missionary activity Cretenet won the support of J. J. Olier, one of the most famous leaders of the cabal.[3] According to Paul Emard, *Tartuffe* was based on a family situation—complete with cuckold, clerical intruder and scolding mother-in-law—which Molière easily could have observed in the rue St.-Thomas-du-Louvre where he lived.[4] All three moved in the *dévot* milieu, and the confidence man and his dupe were probably both members of the Company.[5] The remarkable resemblances between this menage and the *plot* of *Tartuffe* assume their proper significance, however, when the characters of the play, particularly the protagonist, are compared with their supposed models. From this it is clear that the Ansse-Patrocle

---

people. When the comedy *Tartuffe* appeared someone said to the author that he would have done much better to give his false *dévot* a sword rather than a soutane: M. de Fénelon was indicated" (quoted in R. Allier, "Le problème du 'Tartuffe,'" *Revue de Genève*, No. 7, Jan., 1921, p. 12).

9. The fact that most of the individuals thought by contemporaries to have served as models for Tartuffe belonged to the Holy Sacrament is noted by A. Rébelliau, "Deux ennemis de la compagnie du Saint-Sacrement," *Revue des Deux Mondes*, October 1909, pp. 910, 912.

1. By Cosnac, bishop of Vence. See Allier, *Cabale*, p. 396.

2. Francis Baumal, *Tartuffe et ses Avatars* (Paris, 1925), p. 182.

3. Ibid., pp. 52–59.

4. P. Emard, *Tartuffe: sa vie—son milieu et la comédie de Molière* (Paris, 1932), p. 187. Besides Baumal and Emard there is R. Derche, "Encore un modèle possible de Tartuffe: Henri-Marie Boudon, grand archdiacre d'Evreux (1624–1702)," *Revue d'histoire littéraire de la France*, April–June 1951, pp. 129–53. Boudon was associated with the "Aa" of Paris and the Hermitage of Caen, both closely linked with the Company of the Holy Sacrament.

5. P. Emard, op. cit., pp. 119–24, 205–206.

menage described by Emard may very likely have provided important elements of the *situation*, but little of the *substance* of the comedy.

What emerges from a consideration of all of these more or less plausible originals is a vivid appreciation of Molière's power of social observation—a power which created a genuine theatrical composite of the *dévot* types of his time.[6] *Tartuffe* was built on an unusual awareness of what was currently plausible in religious circles, a true sense for the gestures and idioms of upper-class piety. If the comic treatment of this style was to succeed with the alert audiences of the court and the Palais Royal it would have to be based on a concrete and convincing average of their own experience. As a comic writer, therefore, and also as polemicist who expanded and deepened his work in the course of the controversy, Molière cast his net wide. What he could not fully know was that the fragments of reality—which so greatly encouraged his contemporaries to search for the "victim"—had nearly all belonged to the Company of the Holy Sacrament.

The figure of the hypocrite as it emerges in the final version of *Tartuffe* is a powerful evocation of the "cabal." Originally portrayed, in all probability, as a cleric, then as a gentleman, the villain of the present play is neither and both. The Tartuffe we know wears semiclerical dress and is priest-like without being a priest.[7] He is austere without being unworldly; he has hauteur and finesse. Tartuffe is, in fact, a lay director of conscience, a readily recognizable Counter Reformation type which had been given social currency by leaders of the Company of the Holy Sacrament and which Moliére's audiences would naturally have identified with the cabal.

The theology espoused by this lay director probably confirmed his connection with the cabal. Tartuffe's "doctrine" is neither Jesuit nor Jansenist, but a pastiche of maxims such as an average *dévot* might have drawn from a whole range of "spiritual" writings, including both "relaxed" and "austere" sentiments.[8] Molière lampooned both, and the force of his attack fell not on the Jesuits or Jansenists as such, but rather on the way of life exposed and endangered by the religious vendetta of the 1650's—the dead-center piety of the Counter Reformation. This piety was the special cause of the Company of the Holy Sacrament, which hoped for a practical reconciliation of all zealous

6. One of these was Mme. Pernelle, Orgon's mother. A sympathetic contemporary witness remarked that in her description of other people "she succeeds so well in all these different character sketches that the spectator, removing from each of them that which she adds herself, that is to say, the ridiculous austerity of the past by which she judges the attitude and conduct of today, knows those people better than she herself does, . . ." ("Lettre sur l'Imposteur," in Molière, *Oeuvres*, IV, 532).

7. In Molière's day the soutane was not peculiar to the clergy. The bar and the lower reaches of the magistrature were given to similar dress, and one would expect to find lay members of the Holy Sacrament wearing a somber, priestly kind of habit without imposture.

8. E.g., lines 933–36, 1241–48, 1485–97, 1502–1506 for relaxed, and lines 860–62, 1074–80, 1095–1100 for austere tendencies.

Catholics against "disorder." As the religious movement waned in the late 1650's, the surviving groups of *dévots*—unable to make their inner peace with the rising generation of statists and libertine courtiers, but at the same time unwilling to oppose the new establishment (in the manner of Port Royal)—came to represent the irretrievable fervors and fanaticisms of the 1630's, and tended, therefore, to identify themselves with the cause of "religion" as such. Religion meant, of course, their grand design of social regeneration: incense and ashes, public discipline, ostentatious ceremonial, and private mortification, the regimentation of beggars and prostitutes, the campaign against décolletage, the promotion of lay direction and of a patriarchal family and economic morality. Translated into everyday life, this vision of order is at least recognizable in the outrageous religion of Tartuffe and Orgon.[9]

Outrageous as it was, this religion and the relation between dupe and villain which it allowed, did not violate the probabilities of everyday life. *Tartuffe* is not a farce. Although it contains low-comedy passages, these are mainly in the first acts, that is, the "older" ones which probably contain most of the material from the first version; moreover, *Tartuffe* is much less broad than Molière's earlier comedies. Given the social prestige and authority of lay directors of conscience, given Tartuffe's aristocratic bearing, his suavity and unction the successful invasion of Orgon's household is not implausible: Molière offered his public something more substantial than the conventionalized hypocrite of the Italian comedy.[1] From his first entrance the villain advertises his piety in the very tropes and formulas popularized by the Company of the Holy Sacrament in its perennial campaign for moral order and *bonne police*:

> Laurent, serrez ma haire avec ma discipline,
> Et priez que toujours le ciel vous illumine.
> Si l'on vient pour me voir, je vais aux prisonniers
> Des aumônes que j'ai partager les deniers.[2]

> [Laurent, lock up my scourge and hair shirt, too.
> And pray that our Lord's grace will shine on you.
> If anyone wants me, I've gone to share
> My alms at prison with the inmates there.]

It would have been almost as difficult for the first audiences as for Orgon to have dismissed this figure as a clown or conventional comic

---

9. Allier interprets Molière's attack on the cabal in this light (*Cabale*, pp. 389–96). Michaut's argument that the Company of the Holy Sacrament was not specifically intended by Molière (*Luttes*, pp. 94–104) does not necessarily run counter to this idea.
1. D. Mornet, *Histoire de la littérature française classique*, p. 266.
2. Act III, Sc. 2.

type. On the other hand, Orgon is, indeed, taken in; but the con-
temporary literature of domestic piety—so copiously reproduced by
Bremond[3]—will show that his infatuation, while exaggerated, was
not incredible:

> On le voit entêté
> Il l'appelle son frère, et l'aime dans son âme
> Cent fois plus qu'il ne fait mère, fils, fille et femme.
> Enfin il en est fou; c'est son tout, son héros;
> Il l'admire à tous coups, le cite à tout propos;
> Ses moindres actions lui semblent des miracles,
> Et tous les mots qu'il dit sont pour lui des oracles.[4]

> [And so he worships this imposter who
> He calls "brother" and loves more than one—
> This charlatan—more than daughter, wife, son.
> So this fake hears all our master's dreams,
> And all his secrets. His every thought, it seems,
> Is poured out to Tartuffe, like he's his priest!]

These oracles teach austerity and renunciation:

> Qui suit bien ses leçons goût une paix profonde,
> Et comme du fumier regarde tout le monde.
> Oui, je deviens tout autre avec son entretien;
> Il m'enseigne à n'avoir affection pour rien,
> De toutes amitiés il détache mon âme;
> Et je verras mourir frère, enfants, mère et femme,
> Que je m'en soucierais autant que de cela.[5]

> [Behold him. Let him teach you profound peace.
> When first we met, I felt my troubles cease.
> Yes, I was changed after I talked with him.
> I saw my wants and needs as just a whim!
> Everything that's written, all that's sung,
> The world, and you and me, well, it's all dung!
> Yes, it's crap! And isn't that a wonder!
> The real world—It's just some spell we're under!
> He's taught me to love nothing or no one!
> Mother, father, wife, daughter, son—
> They could die right now, I'd feel no pain.]

Despite such transports, Orgon himself is not a complete carica-
ture. He is a sober bourgeois paterfamilias, anchored in the matter

3. H. Bremond, *Histoire littéraire du sentiment religieux en France*, esp. Vol. IX, *La vie chré-
tienne sous l'ancien régime*, and Vol. X, *La prière et les prières de l'ancien régime*.
4. *Tartuffe*, I, 2.
5. Ibid., I, 5.

of fact—a man of substance, risen above or removed by a generation from trade (which has apparently left its mark on his scolding mother). During the Fronde he had gained the reputation

> d'homme sage
> Et pour servir son prince il montra du courage.

> [In the troubled times, he backed the prince,
> And that took courage. We haven't seen it since.]

Together with this solidity and piety goes an irascible and violent temper. One moment he kneels before Tartuffe; the next he turns on his son.

> Ah! tu résistes gueux, et lui dis des injures?
> Un baton! Un baton! (*To Tartuffe*) Ne me retenez pas.[6]

> [What? You refuse? Someone get me a rod!
> A stick! Something!
> [*To* Tartuffe]
>   Don't hold me.

Undoubtedly this veneer of pious serenity on a base of quotidian coarseness produces an extremely funny character. The role suggests heaviness, a corpulent solidity: Orgon is a bastion of the comic. For all this, such a man could have been readily taken as an agent of the cabal, perhaps a moral vigilante, perhaps a member of one of the Holy Sacrament's Parisian outworks, the "parochial companies of charity." Orgon's victimization does not, after all, result from a stage type's gullibility. It is a seizure, the effect or symptom of a malady. This malady is a social contagion, the religion of incense and ashes. Propagated among all classes by the Company of the Holy Sacrament, its fervid, docile orthodoxy took root among the solid *bon bourgeoisie* of Paris, the *rentiers* and landlords—Orgon's class. It is the phrases and formulas of this religion which certify the sinister lay director and allow him to dominate the family. Orgon's household is the natural habitat of the false *dévot*.

In *Tartuffe* this domestic environment is hardly less important than the character of the man who exploits it. Molière's mastery of this concrete situation distinguished his play from preceding treatments of hypocrisy. The religious hypocrite had appeared in Boccaccio and Aretino, and in the seventeenth century, when false devotion was considered a vice of the times, the subject became very common. In Molière's day stories about hypocrites of religion were already something of a literary tradition. Undoubtedly Molière appropriated materials from

---

6. Ibid., III, 6.

this tradition;[7] but the unprecedented furor provoked by *his* treatment of religious hypocrisy suggests, by itself, that he also transcended it.

In itself the delineation of a false *dévot* is not necessarily irreligious or subversive. What is required is a socially approved religious style and the free movement of "strangers" who can conceal their motives by assuming that style. Because of the writer's piety (or prudence), or the force of literary convention, or both, the victim and his religion are ordinarily treated rather abstractly: the *situation* is stable, unquestioned, and indeed unimportant—a kind of back-drop against which the intrigue is played out. The focus of interest is the exploiter rather than the persons and values exploited. Hypocrisy is depicted through the stratagems and machinations of the villain; but that this species of fraud might have a necessary social and religious basis need not even be suggested.[8] Thus in the tradition which Molière received, the imposter tended toward a fixed type, while the story was at best either a morality or a farce, devoid of concreteness of milieu and characterization. The traditional interest in the false *dévot* lay in the fascination of the double standard, in the distinction between mask and motive—in the *fact* of hypocrisy, as conveyed in asides, overheard conversations, exposures, and denunciations.

It is not, of course, this simple treatment of hypocrisy which makes the figure of Tartuffe so memorable. As "Rochemont" and La Bruyère respectively pointed out, he is neither a typical (recognizable) nor a perfect imposter[9] (nor need he be the latter, given the situation in Orgon's household). Tartuffe's special virtues are not cunning and deception but energy, will, virtuosity. Clearly what interests Molière is not the techniques of fraud but the human conditions which make it possible and profitable: on the one hand, the powers, desires, destiny of a hypocrite of the time; on the other, the particular illusions and fixations of a rather ordinary *homme de bien*. The villain may have his virtues, and the victim may after all have his vices.

Molière's realism, seen in the symbiosis of villain and victim, the dramatic interaction of Orgon's coarse sadism and Tartuffe's nuanced villainy, was probably an important ingredient of his public success, and certainly of his continuing troubles with the *dévots*. *Tartuffe* delighted and shocked because it questioned what was given and unquestionable, the virtues of the victim—and thus, implicitly, the moral value of *sincerely* professed ascetic Christianity.

7. Michaut lists a number of these works (*Luttes*, pp. 87–90), although according to him it is certain that the idea (whatever that may be) of *Tartuffe* was suggested by Scarron's novel *Les Hypocrites* (ibid., p. 3).

8. "It seems indeed that neither Aretino, Regnier, Scarron, nor Sorel, whatever their religious opinions may have been, had a really polemical objective, anti-Christian, or, if one may risk the anachronism, 'anticlerical' aims. But it does not follow from this that Molière did not have them" (Michaut, *Luttes*, p. 92).

9. "Observations sur le Festin de Pierre," in Molière, *Œuvres*, V, 223; *Onuphre*, No. 24 of "De la mode," *Œuvres de la Bruyère*, ed. G. Servois (Paris, 1865–78), II, 154–59.

Molière's heterodoxy is, as I have suggested, already present in the "explainer" Cléante—a role which was expanded and altered (or perhaps even newly introduced) after the first public performance, ostensibly to contrast true religion with the combination of stupidity and villainy which emerged from the dramatic situation itself. It is, of course, clear that to the champions of the Counter Reformation Cléante's rational, moralizing piety could hardly have sounded better than virtuous paganism.[1] The "true" religion which he expounds is in fact a religion of decency (*honnêteté*), in which anathemas are reserved for bad taste and extremism, for the exaggerated conduct of snobs, social climbers, pedants, and bigots. Bayle, at once skeptical and religious, was in a particularly good position to see this.

> Many people in Paris say very seriously that Molière has done more by himself to correct the faults of the Court and the City than all the preachers together: and I believe that they are right, provided that they refer only to certain qualities which do not constitute a crime as much as they do a false taste, or a stupid infatuation as you would describe the humor of Prudes, *Précieux*, of those who exaggerate styles, who elevate themselves to Marquis, who speak incessantly of their nobility, who always have some poem of their own making to show people, etc. These are the disorders which Molière's comedies have diminished a little.[2]

Cléante is a typical *honnête homme*, an exemplar of decorum, balance, and good sense. Traveling in the sphere of the generally valid, and universal, he is (unlike his plebeian counterpart, the *railleuse* maidservant Dorine) detached from the humdrum world of the particular, and we know nothing of his profession, income, interests, or even his physique. In his imperturbable composure he represents a program—an order of conduct and social relations which greatly appealed to the new aristocratic-bourgeois literary public of the 1660's. This public, the audiences of *la cour et la ville*,[3] received Cléante as an exemplary figure, a model of good form. But Cléante's success in this didactic function required that his antagonist, Tartuffe, be a flesh-and-blood actuality, a fully believable villain. If classical comedy became a kind of school of *honnêteté* in the 1660's,

---

1. Voltaire's reaction is of some interest and carries perhaps an unintended irony: "Today many people regard this play, which was once found so scandalous, as a lesson in ethics. It may be boldly stated that the discourses of Cléante, in which true and enlightened virtue is opposed to the imbecile devotion of Orgon, are . . . the most powerful and elegant sermon which we have in our language; . . ." ("Sommaire du 'Tartuffe'," quoted in Molière, *Oeuvres*, IV, 369).
2. Bayle, *Oeuvres Diverses* (The Hague, 1737), I, 40.
3. I have relied on E. Auerbach's suggestive essay "La cour et la ville," in *Vier Untersuchungen zur Geschichte der französischen Bildung* (Bern, 1951), pp. 12–50, in discussing Molière's public.

this was because it presented, along with its exemplifications of good sense and *bon ton*, a socially veracious depiction of vice and extremism built on the audience's own experience.

This evocative power the figure of Tartuffe had (and still has). Molière took great pains with him, creating an extraordinarily concrete representation of the *dévot*. Certainly Tartuffe with his transcendent malevolence is the center of interest. Exposed and denounced, he cannot be humiliated. Parading under an impervious egoism, evil maintains a composed and unflinching integrity before outraged common sense. Each unmasking reveals new and unsuspected heights of effrontery and depths of intrigue. What begins as the gluttony and transparent fraud of a petty crook, ends with the inscrutable designs and contemptuous bravado of an accomplished Machiavellian. If Tartuffe is betrayed by his vices, it is at least clear that such a character will learn nothing from the "facts" (as we must assume a comic figure would) for he *is* his vices. Frustrated in his desire for Elmire, for Orgon's legacy, his very defeats carry him beyond the level of household intrigue. The first unmasking is thwarted by telling the "simple truth"—the supreme hypocrisy. The second merely provides the occasion for playing the trump and coolly turning Orgon out of his own house. To the very end Tartuffe retains, almost as a question of honor, the obvious grimace of virtue. This grimace produces not deception but awe (although now virtue is civic rather than religious):

> Oui, je sais quels secours j'en ai pu recevoir;
> Mais l'intérêt du Prince est mon premier devoir;
> De ce devoir sacré la juste violence
> Etouffe dans mon coeur toute reconnaissance,
> Et je sacrifierais à de si puissants noeuds
> Ami, femme, parents, et moi-même avec eux.[4]

> [I know that there were things you did for me.
> But my duty to our monarch stifles
> Memory, so your past gifts are trifles.
> My obligations to him are so rife,
> That I would give up family, friends, and life.]

This unfathomable character has no equal in the play. Damis, Dorine, even Elmire and her charm and good sense, are unable to cut Tartuffe down to size. Nor is Cléante. A declaimer, not a doer, the gentleman sage vindicates *honnêteté* and the *juste milieu*, but his role is purely forensic, not dramatic and actual. Thus the *raisonneur* never catches up with the hypocrite. Lifted above the action by reason-

---

4. *Tartuffe*, V, 7.

ableness itself he remains true to his conception in apostrophizing the vagaries of human nature:

> Les hommes la plupart sont étrangement faits!
> Dans la juste nature on ne les voit jamais.[5]

> [Men are strangely made, most of them.
> The boundaries of reason hem them in.]

The inability of enlightened common sense to overcome credulity and versatile malevolence seems to insure the triumph of Tartuffe. However, to the literate public of the 1660's, which knew nothing of romantic demonism, such an ending with such a hero would have been unthinkable. Thus the preservation of the play's comic form was a necessity for Molière as impresario, if not also as thinker. Tartuffe's invincibility poses the dramatic problem of the last act: since he cannot be defeated on the scene, he must be removed. This deliverance can be effected only by a Higher Power. In the last two acts the family is on the brink of disaster. Damis, gone in search of help, has not returned. Cléante's lucidity and wisdom are of no practical use: *honnêteté*, the reason of ordinary social relations, always necessary, is unfortunately not always sufficient. At odds with the "strange power of religion" and the protean villainy which exploits it, good sense and reasonableness must be rescued and enforced by the Reason which gives no reasons, a *lettre de cachet*. Thus the royal *deus ex machina* intervenes to dissipate the domestic tragedy, carrying off the villain, vindicating common sense, and so restoring order—that is, allowing peaceful domesticity and ordinary happiness to reassert themselves.

To the modern ear, this resolution seems arbitrary and specious; and the closing eulogy of the king is, of course, transparent flattery. Moliére's adulation of royal justice and omniscience reflected his strategy against the invisible cabal and doubtless, also, his recent ascent to the status of royal comedian. However it would be wrong to stress the manipulative and self-interested impulses behind these obeissances to the extent of ignoring Molière's sincerity not only as a courtier[6] but also as a writer. Praise of the royal power of punishment

---

5. Ibid., I, 5.
6. Molière had inherited the office of *tapissier du roi* from his father, and was also considered a friend of the king. His enjoyment of this position was probably not lessened by the hurried production of royal diversions which it imposed. The notion that Molière considered his theatrical responsibilities at court a burden or a necessary evil is a typical distortion of romantic literary criticism; and it is probable that he gave his comedy-ballets and other specifically royal entertainments great care (see Bénichou, op. cit., pp. 161–62). The role of courtier also entailed other satisfactions (besides financial ones): Molière's great triumph over his *dévot* enemies, the staging of *Tartuffe*, would have been impossible without the continued favor of the king. Even during the course of the struggle, this favor had been clearly evident in a royal pension and an official grant of patronage to Molière's company, which became the *troupe du roi* (Aug. 14, 1665) (Michaut, *Luttes*, pp. 47, 52).

"It is foolish to compare Molière to Shakespeare. Shakespeare was not received in Elizabeth's chamber" (Michelet, *Histoire de France* [Paris, 1898], XII, 76).

and correction could be more than a ritual form in the 1660's and probably rang very true for Molière and for most of his public. The monarch embodies a supereminent, public reasonableness which serves the interests of all reasonable men:

> Un prince dont les yeux se font jour dans les cœurs,
> Et que ne peut tromper tout l'art des imposteurs.
> D'un fin discernement sa grande âme pourvue
> Sur les choses toujours jette une droite vue;
> Chez elle jamais rien ne surprend trop d'accès,
> Et sa ferme raison ne tombe en nul excès.
> Il donne aux gens de bien une gloire immortelle,
> Mais sans aveuglement il fait briller ce zèle,
> Et l'amour pour les vrais ne ferme point son cœur
> A tout ce que les faux doivent donner d'horreur.[7]

> [We have a king who sees into mens' hearts,
> And cannot be deceived, so he imparts
> His wisdom, that we can be guided by.
> Imposters fail in everything they try.
> Our king sees things clearly for what they are,
> So hypocrites do not get very far;
> Our king has been endowed with fine discernment,
> So frauds are guaranteed a quick internment.
> He never can be taken by surprise,
> He sees right through imposters and their lies.]

Molière lauds his royal patron not only for exposing fraud but for checking disruptive passions and imposing public order. One response to Tartuffe's villainy would be direct action; and the impulse of the hot-headed Damis is to kill him. However, the sagacious Cléante points out that the times are no longer propitious for head-long violence:

> Voilà tout justement parler en vrai jeune homme
> Modérez, s'il vous plait, ces transports éclatants.
> Nous vivons sous un règne et sommes dans un temps
> Ou par la violence on fait mal ses affaires.[8]

> [Damis, you're talking like a little boy,
> Who's armed. Tantrums are one of your flaws.
> We live in modern times, with things called "laws?"
> Murder is illegal. At least for us.]

Violence is after all but the ultimate form of extremism, and all extremism fares badly with Molière. In the earlier comedies he

7. *Tartuffe*, V, 7.
8. Ibid., V, 2.

exposed the snobbish marquis, the affected *précieuses*—the blind exaggeration and automatism of hypertrophied social forms. *Tartuffe* delineates a third aspect of the old society, the *dévot* life itself. This life, with its bizarre idiom, its exclusiveness and secrecy, is the most tenacious of the follies of the past. Tartuffe's unusual villainy merely makes concrete the remarkable hold of the piety of the Counter Reformation over its victims. The *dévots* saw quite correctly that *Tartuffe* gave little comfort to their "true" religion; and the author of the *Lettre sur L'Imposteur*, a supporter and probably a friend of Molière, in effect admitted as much. Describing Orgon's speechless praise of the hypocrite (*Un homme . . . un homme . . .*), he notes that

> the admiration which our *entêté* has for his bigot, although he does not know what to say to praise him, shows perfectly the truly strange power of religion over the minds of men, which prevents them from reflecting on the faults of those they deem pious.[9]

It is this "power" of religion and the criminality of its agent, Tartuffe, which necessitates the *deus ex machina*—an intervention which only a purist aesthetic could find arbitrary. Moreover, given the mood of the libertine court and the literate public in the 1660's, given the king's encouragement of a certain anticlericalism, it will be seen that the mode of Tartuffe's removal was far from violating contemporary audiences' sense of the real.

The concluding encomium of the king reflects a buoyant confidence, shared by the most advanced spirits of the age, in the liberating and progressive tendencies of the new personal rule—a confidence which had only begun to dissipate around the time of Molière's death. The fact that Molière wrote his greatest comedies in the middle 1660's, that is in the years when he won royal favor and patronage, testifies in itself to the optimism fostered under the new political order. On the other hand, *Tartuffe*, *Les Précieuses Ridicules*, and *L'Ecole des Femmes*, contain, each in its own way, an affirmative response to absolutism and a recognition of the moral possibilities which it opened up. As comedies these works dealt with "light" subjects drawn from private and domestic life; but in an absolutist environment trivial themes like the etiquette of salon and bourgeois household can function as substitutes for "great" ones, can be made to bear the same social weight as heroic subjects. The controversies which raged around Molière suggest that in his time domesticity and the private side of court life had become sources of serious art and, indeed, that questions of everyday life—of taste, of pedantry, of the relations between parents and children, between friends and between the sexes, and of religious behavior—were suffused with social and political meaning.

9. "Lettre sur l'imposteur," in Molière, *Oeuvres*, IV, 537.

Under the absolute monarchy, which claimed a monopoly of culture as well as political authority, questions of etiquette, style, and fad tended to become the most important "public" questions. After the reduction of the *overt* intransigence of the privileged frondeurs, it was in these areas, and especially on the ground of *decorum*, that the monarchy joined the issue with the tenacious defenders of the old order—the literary bluestockings, the aristocratic snobs, the old-fashioned *bons bourgeois*, the censorious and domineering *dévots*.

Molière exposed the private life of this old order for laughs, not reform. But ridicule is a powerful weapon; and his audiences laughed, in the first place, because the ridiculous situations in his plays usually corresponded with serious ones in the real world and were, in effect, comments on that world.[1] The much mooted question of whether Molière wanted to amuse or instruct is badly posed, for it obscures the essential ones of *what* Molière's audiences found amusing, and *how* he chose to amuse them.[2] The realistic satire in *Les Précieuses Ridicules*, *L'Ecole des Femmes*, and *Tartuffe* was based on an unerring sense of the ways of the world, but it also involved notions, indeed, judgments about what is irreducibly important in ordinary life—and hence, implicitly, in society. These judgments, inseparable from Molière's power of social observation, emerge dramatically and effectively, not as program or doctrine. It is true that Molière's public was receptively disposed to an exemplifying literature of *honnêteté*, ready to listen to models of good sense like Cléante. But while Cléante may indeed have been Molière's *philosophical* mouthpiece, ultimately no single character, and least of all Cléante, can speak authoritatively for Molière as comic writer. The audiences of *la cour et la ville* prized the doctrines of good sense and the *juste milieu*, but its taste for the courtly style, its applause of a theatrical royal magnificence, suggest a current of hedonism which went beyond the formal limits of those doctrines.[3] In *Tartuffe*, *honnêteté* belongs to a larger order of values, of greater appeal, one relying less on the moderation and control of the passions than on their pleasurable fulfillment. This kind of happiness cannot be secured by

1. "Until then there was wit and pleasantry in our comedies; but he added a great naïveté, with such live images of the manners of his age and with characters so well marked that the representations seemed less to be comedies than the truth itself" (Perrault, *Les hommes illustres* [Paris, 1701], I, 168–69).
2. Michaut, for example, holds that Molière's only purpose was aesthetic—"*simplement de faire rire les honnêtes gens*" (*Luttes*, p. 114). But who were these "*honnêtes gens*" and what made them laugh?
3. Bénichou, op. cit., pp. 162–72. *La cour et la ville* denotes not merely a cultivated public but has a definite class reference. It is the new public of the 1650's and '60's, which includes not only the great of the court but the near great and the upper bourgeoisie in Paris which aspired to the style of the great. Molière's greatest comedies speak simultaneously to all of these groups as mirrors and models of conduct. *La cour et la ville*, in turn, represents the cultural fusion of the aristocracy and upper middle class, effected by their common assimilation of courtly values and of the mystique of absolutism (Auerbach, art. cit., passim).

reasonableness and moderation alone: since *honnêteté* is no match for the combined force of stupidity and villainy it must be enforced by a Higher Power. The ethic of the *juste milieu* is in fact a means to an end. (Indeed, precisely because it is a means it can be *imposed*.) This end, which justifies not only *honnêteté* but the absolute monarchy itself, is the higher cause of earthly pleasure.

When Molière has done with the demonism of a Tartuffe and the attitudinizing of a Cléante his aesthetic interest is the untrammeling and fulfillment of *human* passions. Perhaps this is also his "program." One of the few things which Molière never takes lightly is pleasure. What makes men happy is not moderation and wisdom but the primary physical enjoyment of life. Wisdom and even common sense are valuable only insofar as they promote the free expression of man's natural powers. Given his deep antipathy to ascetic Christianity and its traditions,[4] it is no wonder that Molière tends to locate these powers in man's animal nature, and chiefly in the sexual impulse. In the *École des Femmes*, where he first verged on irreligious sentiments, as in *Tartuffe*, the denouement produces the defeat of conventional, gerontocratic piety, and the happiness of young lovers.

Ultimately it was Molière's hedonism which set him at odds with the *dévots* and their defenders. To the Christianity of Bérulle and Bossuet the passions are in principle corrupt and their free expression is generic rebellion. Catholic critics from Rochemont to Brunetière have therefore maintained that Molière's libertarian hostility to ascetic Christianity is identical or at least continuous with moral anarchy and social subversion. This idea is polemically inspired[5] and wrong in itself. Molière teaches not rebellion but "adaption to social life and the necessities which it imposes"[6]—social life being understood as centering around a court and a just prince who propagates and enforces courtly values.[7]

The comic form is essential to the representation of these values, and its preservation against the "strange power" demands a countervailing

4. "I doubt that there is such a great perfection in the powers of human nature, and I don't know if it isn't better to correct and calm the passions of men than to want to suppress them entirely" (preface to the edition of 1669, *Œuvres*, IV, 383).
5. As is especially clear in Rochemont's *Observations sur le Festin de Pierre*. This vehement *dévot* held that Molière was not only unworthy of the sacraments, but a menace to society. Conscious of the dramatist's special favor at court, Rochemont points out that while the "greatest and most religious monarch in the world" bends all his efforts to maintain religion, Molière seeks to destroy it. He concludes with a tirade on the political dangers of atheism and an extravagant eulogy of the "invincible monarch, the glory of his age, the ornament of his State, the love of his subjects, the terror of the impious, and the delight of the whole human race" (pp. 226, 227–28, 231–32, of the "Observations," as reproduced in Molière, *Œuvres*, Vol. V).
   Brunetière regarded Molière as a bold continuator of the Renaissance's "revolt of the flesh against the spirit, of nature against discipline . . ." and as a "genius" who points forward to the irreligion of the eighteenth century ("The Philosophy of Molière," in *Brunetière's Essays in French Literature*, sel. and trans. by D. Nichol Smith [New York, 1898] pp. 66–133. See also his *Les époques du théâtre française* [Paris, 1892] pp. 141–42).
6. Michaut, *Luttes*, p. 108.
7. Bénichou, op. cit., pp. 181–82.

"arbitrary" power. Thus a contrivance of plot is used to produce a happy ending in *École des Femmes*. Thus in *Tartuffe* the omnicompetent good sense of the monarch is invoked to support the claims of youth and pleasure against the fatuous sadism of a bourgeois patriarch in league with a nefarious director of conscience. Good Sense (Cléante) indicates that gratitude and respectful obeissance are the due of this awesome but generous deity, and the comedy ends with Orgon's conversion to the new cult:

> Oui, c'est bien dit. Allons à ses pieds avec joie
> Nous louer des bontés que son coeur nous déploie;
> Puis, acquittés un peu de ce premier devoir,
> Aux justes soins d'un autre il nous faudra pourvoir,
> Et par un doux hymen couronner en Valère
> La flamme d'un amant généreux et sincère.

> [Yes, and well said. So come along with me,
> To thank him for his generosity.
> And then once that glorious task is done,
> We'll come back here for yet another one,
> I mean a wedding for which we'll prepare,
> To give my daughter to the good Valère.]

Thus in *Tartuffe*, political obedience is linked to an optimistic view of the human passions. Far from leading to violence and chaos, these passions appear to possess an inherent rationality and their claims suggest an order, both political and moral, especially appropriate to their humane realization. At any rate, natural pleasure does not endanger a society which looks for its values to a magnificent and youthful court. On the other hand, the absolute power which creates this court does not discourage but rather supports and protects the cause of pleasure. Conformism to this order, and to the ranks and values of "good" society, where *agrément* and *honnêteté* are mutually dependent, is the part not only of prudence but of happiness as well.

ROGER W. HERZEL

The Decor of Molière's Stage: The Testimony of Brissart and Chauveau[†]

"The decor of Molière's Stage"—the title seems almost self-contradictory, so prevalent is the concept of the French classical theater as a poor, barren place, prohibited by an austere, puritanical doctrine from indulging in even the most limited forms of scenic display. The rule of unity of place, so it is believed, required that each play have only one setting;[1] and, it is further believed, this single setting could and did serve equally well for all plays of the same type, since the classical emphasis on universality made it meaningless to differentiate one palace or street corner or domestic interior from another. A hundred years ago, no less an authority than Eugène Despois stated the matter with flat finality: "for all plays except those called *pièces à machines*, which the Marais theater specialized in, stage settings were virtually nonexistent."[2] And succeeding generations of scholars have done little to modify this view. Antoine Adam says that "the classical spirit reduces decor to nothing";[3] and Deierkauf-Holsboer dismisses the staging of classical drama in a sentence:

> As soon as they were in possession of a palace, several rooms, a street and some houses, the actors could produce whatever tragedy, tragicomedy or comedy they wished, and the new additions to their repertory were staged without causing them to incur the cost of new scenery.[4]

As we shall see, this accurately describes the state to which French scenic practice had evolved by the very end of the seventeenth century; but does it also apply to the practices of the sixties and seventies in the professional theaters for which Molière and Racine wrote their plays? The prevailing opinion would have us believe that it does, that the classics of the French theater first appeared before an audience in a "classical," universalized, unspecific decor.

This idea, which is extremely well entrenched, possesses two powerful advantages. First, it implies that Racine and Molière belong in an ethereal environment that transcends the crass realities of

† From *PMLA* 93.9 (Oct. 1978): 925–41. Reprinted by permission of the Modern Language Association of America.

1. Eugène Despois, *Le Théâtre français sous Louis XIV* (Paris: Hachette, 1874), p. 130. This gross oversimplification has been corrected by Jacques Schérer, *La Dramaturgie classique en France* (Paris: Nizet, 1950), pp. 149–95.

2. *Le Théâtre français*, p. 130. All translations of excerpts from French texts are mine.

3. "Baroque et préciosité," *Revue des Sciences Humaines*, NS 55–56 (1949), 221.

4. S. Wilma Deierkauf-Holsboer, *L'Histoire de la mise en scène dans le théâtre français à Paris de 1600 à 1673* (Paris: Nizet, 1960), p. 59.

the working theater; by minimizing the importance of the physical production, it exalts the importance of the script, suggesting that the play can be completely understood when considered purely as literature. This notion is very popular among literary critics. Second, the concept of a "classical" decor can be well maintained without the support of evidence—indeed, is nourished by the absence of evidence: if, as this theory maintains, stage settings were virtually nonexistent, it follows naturally that there will be no evidence of these nonexistent settings and, therefore, no point in looking for it.

But some sort of scenic background, however neutral, had to be placed on the stage, and someone had to put it there; and at the Hôtel de Bourgogne this responsibility fell to the *décorateur* Michel Laurent, who in 1678 began to compile a *Mémoire* of the scenic requirements of each play in the repertory.[5] For most of the tragedies his task was simple: a "palais à volonté" was all that was needed for thirty-three of the thirty-eight tragedies by authors other than Racine. But in 1678 the staging of Racine's tragedies was somewhat more varied: the "palais à volonté" sufficed only for *La Thébaide, Britannicus,* and *Mithridate.* For *Alexandre,* "Stage is battlefield tents and pavilions"—a setting that must have been very similar to the one used in the play's original production by Molière's troupe at the Palais-Royal, about which Robinet wrote

> J'y découvris en perspective,
> Agréable & récréative,
> Les pavillons, & campemens,
> Qui pour lui [Alexandre] furent si charmans.[6]

For *Iphigénie,* Laurent specified, "Stage is tents"—perhaps the same ones—"and, at the back, a sea and some ships." The sea and ships were undoubtedly represented by the same painted backdrop that was used for *Andromaque*: "Stage is a palace with columns and, at the back, a sea with some ships." But was the "palace with columns" the same scenery as the "vaulted palace" that was used for *Phèdre*? And was either the same as the "small royal chamber" of *Bérénice* or the "salon in Turkish style" of *Bajazet* (pp. 112–14)? None of these possibilities seems likely, for these entries were simply Laurent's notes to himself, and their only purpose was to list the articles that needed to be pulled out of storage for each performance; calling the same scenery by different names would have been confusing and pointless. When a "palais à volonté" would suffice, that is what Laurent wrote down; when he wrote something more specific, the fact suggests that a specific decor, different from the decor for other plays, was called for.

---

5. *Le Mémoire de Mahelot, Laurent et d'autres décorateurs de l'Hôtel de Bourgogne et de la Comédie-Française au XVII⁰ siècle,* ed. Henry Carrington Lancaster (Paris: Champion, 1920).

6. Quoted in Claude and François Parfaict, *Histoire du théâtre françois depuis son origine jusqu'à présent* (Paris, 1745–49; rpt. New York: Burt Franklin, 1968), ix, 389.

Unfortunately, Laurent gives us only enough information to arouse our curiosity, not to satisfy it. In order to form any clear idea of what the original settings for Racine's plays looked like, we would need to compare Laurent's terse notations agaist some visual record of the performances; and there is none. The engravings that appeared as frontispieces in seventeenth-century editions of the plays are entirely imaginative, as Raymond Picard has pointed out, and have nothing to do with the tragedies as they appeared in performance; indeed, the illustrator often chose as his subject some event that does not even occur onstage, such as the spectacular death of Hippolyte in *Phèdre*.[7] But when Chauveau and other illustrators of the period turned to comedy, they found that the performances themselves provided excellent ideas for expressive pictures—such as Orgon emerging from under the table to confront Tartuffe—and they copied these scenes, and the stage on which they were played, with the realism appropriate to the comic genre.[8]

Thus the stage of Molière can be studied in a way that the stage of Racine cannot, for we have available to us both written and icono-graphic documentation for the scenic environment of his plays. Five of these plays were in the repertory of the Hôtel de Bourgogne in 1678, performed, no doubt, in settings much like those used by Molière's troupe at the Palais-Royal and the Hôtel Guénégaud. Laurent made entries in his *Mémoire* for these five plays; and in 1680, when the troupe of the Hôtel de Bourgogne was absorbed into the Guénégaud troupe, Laurent retained his position and made notations of the scenery that was in stock for the rest of Molière's plays. These notations, brief and sometimes cryptic as they are, form a useful supplement to the illustrations in seventeenth-century editions of Molière's plays.

No complete edition of Molière's works appeared during his lifetime; but after his death La Grange, Molière's loyal friend and the main-stay of his troupe, undertook this project with the help of another friend, Vivot, and in 1682 the eight small volumes of the *Œuvres de Monsieur de Molière* appeared. This edition included not only most of the previously unpublished writings but also a short biography and a playlet honoring Molière's memory by the actor Brécourt. More important, it also included thirty engravings, drawn by Pierre Brissart and copperplated by Jean Sauvé, that served as frontispieces to the

7. "Racine and Chauveau," *Journal of the Warburg and Courtauld Institutes*, 14 (1951), 262–66.
8. See Picard, p. 263, n. 1. Book illustrations for a third dramatic category, the machine play, were realistic in a different sense. Since the primary attraction of these plays was the scenery itself, the illustrations aimed at reproducing the "magical" illusions as convincingly as possible and were drawn from the ideal eyepoint in the center of the auditorium. As a result, it is rather difficult in these drawings to pick out the separate components of the decor. But this subservience to the illusion is precisely what the illustrators of Molière avoided.

plays.[9] There is reason to believe that Molière himself, near the end of his life, had contemplated some such illustrated edition of his works but had abandoned the idea because of the cost.[1] In many ways, however, this was a memorial edition, and the expense was not spared.

Most of Molière's plays had been published in individual volumes during his lifetime, and several had gone through many editions, both authorized and pirated. But only six had been illustrated: *L'Ecole des maris* (1st ed., 1661) and *L'Amour médecin* (1st ed., 1666), both with unsigned frontispieces by François Chauveau; *L'Ecole des femmes* (1st ed., 1663, and 1665 ed.), with a frontispiece signed with Chauveau's initials; *Le Misanthrope* (1st ed., 1667) and *Le Médecin malgré lui* (1st ed., 1667), both with frontispieces by the same unknown artist; and *Le Tartuffe* (2nd ed., 1669, and 1673 ed.), with a frontispiece attributed to Chauveau. * * *

All of Chauveau's drawings were used, with more or less modification, in the edition of 1682. The frontispiece for *L'Ecole des femmes* was copied almost perfectly: only the absence of the signature in the later version and a slightly different treatment of the tree and one of the houses in the background make it possible to distinguish between the two illustrations. For *L'Ecole des maris* and *L'Amour médecin*, Brissart copied the general disposition of characters and scenery (reversing left and right for *L'Amour médecin*) but updated the costumes and suppressed almost all the detail of the scenic background. Both jobs are hasty and crude, and neither is signed. The reworking of Chauveau's engraving of *Tartuffe* shows more care and bears the signatures of both Brissart and Sauvé. The face of Orgon is redrawn, apparently in order to resemble Brissart's memory of Molière, who had always played that role; this figure is recognizable in almost all Brissart's drawings.

Brissart felt free to disregard the two frontispieces by unknown hands in the first editions of *Le Misanthrope* and *Le Médecin malgré lui*. For the former play, he chose the same scene to illustrate, but gave it a completely new treatment; for the latter, he illustrated an entirely different scene.

These, then, are the illustrations of Molière's plays that were drawn during or shortly after his lifetime. Taken together with Laurent's notations and the information about staging that can be gleaned from the scripts themselves, they make it possible to reconstruct at least in part the decor for each of Molière's major plays. And furthermore, they shed unexpected light on Molière as a man of the theater, for they reveal that

9. The tricentennial of Molière's death has made Brissart's frontispieces much more widely available than before: the edition of 1682 has been reissued in facsimile (Geneva: Minkoff, 1973), and most of the engravings have also been reproduced in Sylvie Chevalley's *Molière en son temps* (Geneva: Minkoff, 1973).
1. Eugène Despois and Paul Mesnard, *Notice bibliographique*, Vol. XI of *Œuvres de Molière* (Paris: Hachette, 1873–1900), pp. 40, 71. All quotations from Molière are from this edition, and translations are mine.

his conception and management of the visual environment for his plays changed over the brief span of his career in a fashion that reflected and supported his development as an actor and as a playwright.

Molière began his writing career as an author of farce, with two early playlets, *La Jalousie du Barbouillé* and *Le Médecin volant*, which were not included in editions of his works until the nineteenth century. No doubt there were other farces, but they have not survived. His first full-length play, and the first play in the 1682 edition, is *L'Etourdi ou Les Contretemps*; it is typical of his early work in that it is dominated by the tricks of the ingenious servant Mascarille—played, naturally, by Molière. The action of this play, like that of countless French farces and *commedia dell'arte* scenarios, takes place in a street before two houses—a location that has no particular identity of its own: a no-man's-land where anything can happen, any character can wander on, any encounter can take place; in short, the perfect environment for a quick-witted schemer like Mascarille to display his skills.

Brissart's frontispiece to this play (Fig. 1) gives us a partial view of a very simple set. A sturdy angle wing, containing a practical door and second-story window, represents one of the houses. The front surface of the wing, parallel to the front edge of the stage, lies outside the boundary of the picture, as does the second house on the other side of the stage. The front and side surfaces of the wings form an angle greater than ninety degrees, so that the two side surfaces converge as they recede. A backdrop is painted to represent a rural landscape. We can glimpse the line where the backdrop

Fig. 1. *L'Etourdi ou Les Contretemps*. Brissart, 1682.

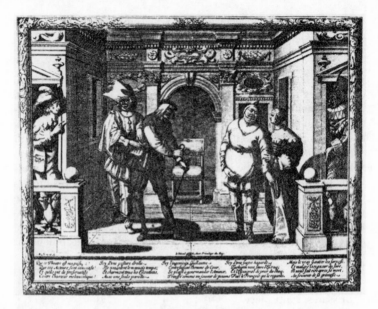

Fig. 2. Farce players at the Hôtel de Bourgogne. Abraham Bosse, c. 1630. (Courtesy Bibliothèque Nationale, Paris.)

meets the stage floor, and from that line we can calculate that there is a substantial distance from the backdrop to the upstage edge of the wing—more than enough to allow entrances and exits. Presumably there is also room for the actors to pass on the downstage side of the front surface of the wing.

There is little that is novel about this arrangement of the stage: like the character Mascarille and like the dramatic situations he creates, the set has an honorable ancestry on both the French side and the Italian. It can be viewed as a low-budget version of the "comic scene" Serlio had proposed more than a century earlier, which the *comme-dia* troupes had simplified and adapted to their own purposes * * *; in Molière's set the perspective effect is de-emphasized. Alternatively, we can see Molière's set as a more decorative version of the standard native farce setting, which was already in use in the 1580s, as a drawing in the *Recueil Fossard* attests * * *, though it is more familiar to us from Bosse's engraving of about 1630 (Fig. 2).[2] From both these sources Molière inherited the basic stage arrangement that served him well in seven of his first nine comedies.

2. Bosse's engraving is compared to the sketches of Mahelot by Gaston Louis Malécot, "A propos d'une estampe d'Abraham Bosse et de l'Hôtel de Bourgogne," *Modern Language Notes*, 48 (1933), 279–83.

But while the settings continued to be dominated by the farce tra-
dition, the style and subject matter of the plays began to change in a
way that the farce setting would ultimately be unable to accommodate.
Molière's role, and consequently the center of the comic plot, changed
from Mascarille the comic manipulator to Sganarelle the comic
victim—first in *Sganarelle ou Le Cocu imaginaire*, then in *L'Ecole des
maris*. Chauveau's frontispiece to the first edition of the latter (Fig. 3)
is the earliest illustration we have for a Molière play, and in many ways
it is the best. In general, the arrangement of the stage for this play is
the same as for *L'Etourdi*, with the interesting exception that the back-
drop, representing a prospect of trees, is framed by an open archway
several feet downstage.[3] Between the archway and the backdrop, the
floor is painted in foreshortened squares to enhance the illusion of dis-
tance. Downstage of the archway, the stage floor is simple planks; even
the nails are not neglected. The stage is illuminated by two chande-
liers, which are ordinarily not shown in these drawings.

None of these drawings shows what to our eyes would be the most
disconcerting visual element of Molière's stage: the presence on the
stage of spectators, seated in straw-bottomed chairs at either side,
downstage of the wings. These were notoriously rude and unruly
young men whom we would regard as an unmitigated nuisance, and
no doubt the actors who had to share the stage with them felt the
same way; but for better or worse they were part of the spectacle,
and in *L'Ecole des maris* Molière used them as a way of defining in
visual terms the degree to which the principal characters in the play
were ridiculous. The play begins with Sganarelle arguing with his el-
derly brother Ariste about styles of dress. Ariste, with slight absurd-
ity, insists on dressing indistinguishably from the young dandies
sitting a few feet away from him, who could be his grandsons. But
Sganarelle insists on dressing in the style of an earlier generation;
his position is even more absurd than Ariste's and is hostile to the
audience to boot. Thus when Valère, Sganarelle's young, fashionable
rival for the love of Isabelle, appears on stage, his suitability is imme-
diately ratified by the visual harmony between him and the members
of the audience who serve as frame to the stage picture.

Over the years the young dandies continued to display the latest
trends in fashion—indeed, that was their principal reason for
choosing to sit on the stage—and Valère's costume continued to
keep pace with theirs. Thus in 1682 Brissart shows Valère dressed
much differently from the way he had been twenty-one years ear-
lier; but Sganarelle's antiquated costume is in every detail the same
(Fig. 4).

---

3. Figs. 3 and 5 are discussed, and ground plans based on them are provided, by Pierre Son-
rel, *Traité de scénographie* (Paris: Librairie Théâtrale, 1956), pp. 59–60.

LESCOLE
DES
MARIS.

Fig. 3. *L'Ecole des maris*. Chauveau, 1661. (Courtesy of the William Andrews Clark Memorial Library, University of California, Los Angeles.)

The presence of spectators on stage also had the effect of greatly narrowing the acting area. We cannot be sure, however, that it was quite so constricted as it would appear in Chauveau's drawings for *L'Ecole des maris* and *L'Ecole des femmes* (Fig. 5).

* * *

However, we need not carry the idea of artistic license so far as to doubt the credibility of these drawings as records of stage decor. The essential accuracy of Chauveau's frontispiece for *L'Ecole des femmes* is confirmed by Laurent's entry for this play in his *Mémoire*: "Stage is two houses in front and the rest is a city square" (p. 119).

Fig. 4. *L'Ecole des maris*. Brissart, 1682.

The "two houses in front" is a common entry in this document, but the "city square" is not, and the implication is strong that Laurent was listing a backdrop that belonged uniquely to this play. Thus the setting that Chauveau drew in 1663 was still in use fifteen years later.

Now *L'Etourdi ou Les Contretemps, L'Ecole des maris,* and *L'Ecole des femmes* could, if necessary, have all been staged in one and the same setting; but Deierkauf-Holsboer is clearly wrong in believing that this was in fact the practice of Molière's troupe. All three plays have modest, simple, and inexpensive settings that conform to the same general ground plan; but each play has a setting distinctively its own—formal and conventional for *L'Ecole des maris*, for example, and more particularized and homelike for *L'Ecole des femmes*.

So very homelike, in fact, that the exterior location ceases to be an entirely appropriate environment for the play. Some aspects of the action—the chance encounters, the long-lost fathers—could only occur in the traditional farce setting of the public street; but other

F·C· fec.

· L'ESCOLE DES FEMMES ·

Fig. 5. *L'Ecole des femmes*. Chauveau, 1663. (By permission of Houghton Library, Harvard University.)

moments in the play belong in the privacy of an interior, most notably the scene between Arnolphe and Agnès that Chauveau has chosen to illustrate (III.ii). The inappropriateness of the street setting for this scene did not escape the notice of Molière's rivals, one of whom remarked derisively that there must not be much carriage traffic in the streets of that neighborhood of Paris.[4]

L'Ecole des femmes is a transitional work in Molière's career as a playwright and as an actor. Though rooted in the traditions of *Le Cocu imaginaire* and *L'Ecole des maris*, it is also the first of the great character comedies—the forerunner of *Tartuffe* and *Le Misanthrope*. In the same way, Molière's role of Arnolphe looks both backward to the Sganarelles and, more important, forward to Orgon and Alceste. The weight of tradition kept this play situated in the public street, but that was clearly an environment that Molière had now outgrown, and most of his mature full-length comedies are situated in that most private of places, the domestic interior of a French bourgeois family.

Molière had already taken a step in that direction with the one-act play *Les Précieuses ridicules* (1659), his first major success in Paris and an intriguing blend of satire and farce. The foolish girls of the title could scarcely be expected to expose themselves to Molière's satire in a Serlian public square, and so Molière placed the action in their home. But the agent who exposes their folly is very much a creature of the street: the clever servant Mascarille (played by Molière), disguised for the occasion as a marquis. His first entrance is perhaps the most striking, and certainly the most extraordinary, in all of Molière: he is carried in, bumping and swaying dangerously, in a sedan chair, through a door that the porters complain is too narrow. The intrusion of the street into the salon could scarcely have been more discordant if he had ridden a horse onstage.

Mascarille is an impostor who penetrates an environment where he does not belong and gains acceptance by using a disguise; at the end of the play his disguise is stripped away and he is driven off the stage. With allowances for the vast differences in tone, exactly the same statement can be applied to *Tartuffe*; it is crucial to both plays that the stage appear to be a place where some characters belong and others do not— where entrances and exits are not mere random wanderings through a public square but actions expressing the ebb and flow of power among contending characters. Two recent studies of *Tartuffe* have stressed the symbolic importance of the setting. One points out that

> Tartuffe's whole act is an *intrusion*; with all the force that the compound word "housebreaker" wrings out of the word "house," it

---

4. Donneau de Visé, *Zélinde* (Paris, 1663), Sc. iii. Quoted by Ch. L. Livet, "Molière illustré: Les Primitifs," *Le Livre*, 7 (1885), 40. The problem was not a new one. Cf. *Dépit amoureux* II.i.341–47; Pierre Corneille, *Examen de La Galerie du Palais*.

calls up the solid walls, the privacy, the inward familial reality it breaches. The very nature of Molière's design defines the proper setting for it. . . . The full reality of domestic existence descends upon the action, anchoring comedy in the here and now.[5]

And it is around the house itself that the struggle ultimately revolves: the play's darkest moment comes when Tartuffe reveals that he has the power to turn Orgon and his family out of doors. "When a bourgeois like Orgon loses his house, he loses his identity. The bourgeois in Moliere considers his house, his wife, and his children as property. . . . His house is particularly dear to him, however, since his status depends on it, a bourgeois being by definition a person who owns property in the city."[6]

The play resolves itself, then, into the most basic conflict of all, the animal struggle for the control of territory; and from the audience's point of view, that territory is precisely coextensive with the visible portion of the Palais-Royal stage.

In *Le Misanthrope*, the territorial struggle is more veiled, more amusing, and, if anything, more pervasive and more important to the economy of the play. The stage represents Célimène's salon; and it seems to be not Célimène herself but access to Célimène that is the prize for which the men in the play compete. * * * Célimène, in her newfound freedom as a young widow, chooses to turn her domestic interior into a meeting ground as open of access as any public street, while Alceste wishes to return it to its customary function as a private preserve that only the most privileged—that is to say, Alceste himself—can penetrate. * * *

In these two plays, then, the location or territory, and the stage setting that represented it, served in an entirely novel way as the emblem of the internal life of the characters. But in concrete terms there was nothing novel about the way this emblem was constructed: the interior settings for *Tartuffe* and *Le Misanthrope*, like the exterior settings for *L'Etourdi* and *L'Ecole des femmes*, consisted of a simple pair of angle wings set four or five feet downstage from a painted backdrop. This arrangement provided four points of entry to the acting area, upstage and downstage of the wing on each side. In the exterior settings, these four passages were supplemented by those invariable and vital elements of farce decor, practical doors and windows in the wings; but for most plays with interior locations these extra passages were not required, and wings without openings were less costly to build. Aside from this minor difference and the addition of a ceiling cloth, the settings for these two plays consisted of the familiar plantation of the familiar components, now painted to represent inside rather than outside walls.

5. Marcel Gutwirth, "*Tartuffe* and the Mysteries," *PMLA*, 92 (1977), 35.
6. Quentin M. Hope, "Place and Setting in *Tartuffe*," *PMLA*, 89 (1974), 48.

The change, although a simple one, constituted a sharp break with the scenic conventions that had governed French comedy up to that time, and it was made possible because Molière and his troupe had the use of the Palais-Royal, the only public theater in Paris with a permanent proscenium arch. This unique feature served a practical purpose in masking the downstage edge of the ceiling cloth; more generally, it gave visual reinforcement to the new convention that the stage represented a completely enclosed, small-scale, and precisely limited space, of which one boundary was the transparent proscenium plane. The theaters that were in operation when Molière arrived in Paris, the Hôtel de Bourgogne and the Marais, were governed by an entirely different set of scenic conventions. There was no sharp dividing line between stage and auditorium; spectators on the stage were a nuisance, but they were not considered trespassers. Audience and actors were presumed to inhabit the same space, and that space was generally defined as public, exterior, and capable of indefinite extension past the edge of the stage into the auditorium. In these circumstances there was nothing natural about the idea of situating a comedy in a totally enclosed space, particularly on the limited scale of familiar domestic architecture. Interiors were occasionally represented, but in general they were the site of only part of the action, and the scenery representing them composed only part of the stage picture. Even on the rare occasions when an interior setting filled the entire stage, it was represented as being open to the sky: over the heads of the actors hung the same cloud borders that were used for the more common exterior locations.[7]

Thus when Molière set a full-length comedy in one fully enclosed unchanging interior location, he was breaking with tradition; and he was using the proscenium to set off the decor in a way that anticipated the later development of scenic realism. But the decor itself was not particularly realistic, for its various components had the basic shape and arrangement, not of a room, but of the street that they were originally designed to represent. * * *

When Brissart came to the task of providing a frontispiece for *Le Tartuffe ou L'Imposteur* (Fig. 6), he did precisely what he had done for *L'Ecole des maris*, already discussed, and also for *L'Amour médecin*: he worked from Chauveau's drawing rather than from a performance, devoting most of his care to the human figures and their costumes and contenting himself with a sketchy and much simplified version of the scenic background. The result, inevitably, is that the background looks not like a stage setting but like an actual room, in

7. Pierre Corneille, *Examen d'Andromède*. Cf. Schérer, p. 193.

Fig. 6. *Le Tartuffe ou L'Imposteur.* Brissart, 1682.

which the side and back walls have identical projecting moldings that meet in a perfect mitered corner. The same treatment of the moldings can be seen in Brissart's frontispiece to *Dom Garcie de Navarre* (not reproduced here), which was not drawn from performance for the excellent reason that the play had not been performed in the past eighteen years; in both drawings the resemblance of the scenic background to an actual room reveals that, for different reasons, Brissart was not drawing the play in its stage decor.

But when Brissart draws an interior that is not put together like a room in real life—when he draws side and back walls that do not meet in proper corners or are in some other way mismatched—we can be sure that he is attempting to convey the way the stage looked during a performance of the play. Such mismatching can be seen in the frontispieces for the two one-act satires with interior locations that preceded *Tartuffe*: in *Les Précieuses ridicules* (Fig. 7)[8] the trim at the top of the wing comes to a dead end rather than continuing around the corner, and in *La Critique de l'Ecole des femmes* (Fig. 8) the pilasters on the backdrop, which are clearly not three-dimensional, have no relation to the adjacent edge of the wings.

8. The prosperous bourgeoisie had decorated their rooms in the style shown since the 1630s, with tapestries covering the walls and with mirrors and portraits hung on top of the tapestries. See André Blum, *Abraham Bosse et la société française au dix-septième siècle* (Paris: Albert Morancé, 1924), Pls. 10, 12, 13, 14, 17; *L'Œuvre gravé d'Abraham Bosse*, ed. André Blum (Paris: Albert Morancé, 1924), Pls. 5, 11, 18, 20, 21, 28, 32, 34.

These discrepancies suggest that for each play the setting consisted of stock components brought together for the occasion in a marriage of convenience; the wings of *La Critique* were used again for *Le Sicilien ou L'Amour peintre* (Fig. 9).

Les Précieuses and *La Critique*, though they have interior locations, were not staged in exactly the same way as *Tartuffe* and *Le Misanthrope*. These latter plays were designed to provide an afternoon's entertainment in themselves, at least in their initial runs; and their sets were the only ones that needed to be mounted on the stage on the days when they were performed. But *Les Précieuses* and *La Critique* are one-act

LES PRECIEUSES RIDICULES

Fig. 7. *Les Précieuses ridicules*. Brissart, 1682.

plays, which from the beginning were never performed except as afterpieces; *La Critique*, naturally, always appeared on the bill with *L'Ecole des femmes*, while *Les Précieuses* premiered as an afterpiece to *Cinna* and subsequently shared the bill, and the stage, with other one-set tragedies, most of them by Corneille.

Thus the stage had to change from a tragic palace, or the street outside Arnolphe's house, to a Parisian salon. * * * When the action moved to the interior location, the backdrop, which we must now call a *ferme* (the direct ancestor of the English shutter), was drawn aside to reveal the room. The room was then presumed to encompass the whole stage, and the downstage wings, still in place and visible, were simply ignored. Just such an arrangement is called for in *Jodelet ou Le Maître valet*, an old comedy by Scarron that was an active part of Molière's repertory in the early sixties. In all probability, after the location was

Fig. 8. *La Critique de l'Ecole des femmes.*
Brissart, 1682.

established, the actors gravitated fairly far downstage to perform in the prime acting area, between the rows of seated spectators. The entire procedure traces back directly to the medieval scenic conventions, which were still displaying remarkable vigor as recently as the time of Mahelot.

Both *Les Précieuses* and *La Critique*, then, must have been performed in what amounts to a small box set, situated upstage of the wings belonging to the play that had formed the first part of the afternoon's bill. This arrangement would explain why Brissart's engravings for both plays show the wings set snugly against the backdrop: there was no need to leave a gap there for entrances and exits, which would have been made between these wings and the downstage pair. The set for *Les Précieuses* also provided an entry point through the wing, since the sight gag of Mascarille's entrance requires a visible practical door; but this is an unusual requirement, and the wings for *La Critique*, like those for most plays with interior locations, had no practical opening.

Thus the scenic equipment for a routine day's performance at the Palais-Royal might consist of two settings, the secondary one mounted upstage of the primary one and concealed until the appropriate moment by a *ferme*, which could be drawn aside during a break in the action—either in the interval between acts of the main play or in the interval between main play and afterpiece. It is clear for a variety of reasons that the wings must have been less important in defining the location of the action than the *ferme*, or backdrop. First of all, the backdrop, because of its central position,

was a more prominent part of the stage picture and was less likely to be obscured by the spectators seated onstage. Furthermore, the wings were reused for other plays much more frequently than were the backdrops; this indicates that the actors thought of the wings as being more formal and universal and less particularly identified with individual plays. And finally, the downstage wings remained in place when the *ferme* was moved to indicate a change in location; thus audiences and actors were in the habit of disregarding the wings when they became momentarily irrelevant to the action.
* * *

Fig. 9. *Le Sicilien ou L'Amour peintre*, Brissart, 1682.

P. MUÑOZ SIMONDS

Molière's Satiric Use of the *Deus Ex Machina* in *Tartuffe*†

Molière's use of the unexpected *deus ex machina* in his much criticized tragicomedy *Tartuffe* to resolve the complications of the plot has always provoked mixed reactions from both audiences and scholars. Ordinary logic demands that Orgon pay the full price for his gullibility and for his willful nurturing of hypocrisy within his own household at the expense of his family's honor and welfare. Accord-

† From *Educational Theatre Journal* 29.1 (1977): 85–93. © Educational Theatre Journal. Reprinted with permission of The Johns Hopkins University Press.

ing to Alvin Eustis, however, this contrast between our expectations based on knowledge of the actual world and the final romantic dénouement, which we desire but cannot in fact believe to be true, provides a subtle structural irony in many of Molière's plays and must be seen as intrinsic to his artistic technique.[1] I will argue here that this ironic use of the *deus ex machina* is intended to disturb us and that the result of such structural irony in the theatre is a particularly effective form of socio-political satire. In the case of *Tartuffe*, the satirical force of the *ex machina* ending seems to be very precisely directed against the absurd pretensions of Louis XIV to the divine attributes of omnipotence, omniscience, and omnibenevolence.

The miraculous salvation by the King's Officer of Orgon and his family from the machinations of a vicious hypocrite does not happen in *Tartuffe* until, as Walter Kerr puts it, "the knot about the throats of the principals is tied so tightly that only a divination of the king, delivered by special messenger, can cut it."[2] The comedy first hovers uncomfortably on the brink of tragedy. But, to leave an evil Tartuffe in power would be as offensive to our sense of poetic justice as the miracle of Orgon's salvation is offensive to our Aristotelian expectation of "the credible" in the drama. Molière decided in favor of justice, which could be introduced into Orgon's corrupt world only through the miracle of Divine Grace personified by Louis XIV. However, the tension at this point between our knowledge of the behavior of real kings and the ideal justice we expect from God can find release only in disbelieving laughter.

Critical responses to this emotionally desired but rationally unacceptable *deus ex machina* have ranged from outright condemnation to extravagant praise of the device as the very epitome of the play's major theme of seeing through appearances. John L. Palmer summed up the traditional evaluation when he called the dénouement of *Tartuffe* nothing more than "a politic proclamation of the King's favour and support" which becomes "an excrescence upon the comedy."[3] The second and more modern position is that Molière's ending is in fact not irrational or unexpected for generic reasons. Such critics as Walter Kerr and Alvin Eustis explain that *Tartuffe* is a comedy and therefore *must* have a happy ending; indeed the logic of the genre demands it.[4] On the other hand, William G. McCollom—in a brilliant analysis of *Tartuffe* as a dramatic embodiment of the victory of the new forces of enlightenment over the darkness of superstition

1. *Molière as Ironic Contemplator* (The Hague, 1973), p. 97.
2. *Tragedy and Comedy* (London, 1967), p. 67.
3. *Molière* (1930; reprint ed., New York, 1970), p. 356. Hereafter cited in text as Palmer. See also Robert J. Nelson's contrary argument that the king's "intervention is not a 'convenient' way out of the dilemma but the only way out of it," in "The Unreconstructed Heroes of Molière," *Molière* ed. Jacques Guicharnaud (Englewood Cliffs, N. J., 1964), p. 114.
4. Kerr, pp. 66–70, and Eustis, p. 96.

and medievalism—takes a third position of complete approbation. He describes Molière's *deus ex machina* as the fitting climax to what has been "a hymn to the King's discernment, moderation and vision."[5] There seems to be some truth in all of these observations, but none is completely satisfying.

It is true that, on the surface, the Officer does flatter the King when he arrests Tartuffe instead of Orgon and praises the monarch's ability to see all, know all, and finally to do all: "With one keen glance, the King perceived the whole/Perverseness and corruption of his soul" (V, 6, 59–60).[6] However, the irony behind this elaborate flattery would not have been lost on the sophisticated court audience at private performances or later on the equally worldly Parisian audience at the Palais Royal. The King had indeed been a spectator at the play's first performances and may even have read later versions of the script during Molière's times of residence at Versailles—a period during which the playwright continued to request a license to perform *Tartuffe* on the public stage. Of course the King had seen and understood Tartuffe's perverseness and corruption.

Furthermore, the monarch had been directly involved in the stormy events between the first performance of a three-act version of the play at Versailles in 1664, its resulting prohibition, its expansion into a five-act play with *a deus ex machina* ending, and its final licensing for public performance in 1669. As a matter of history, the King had allowed the real Tartuffes in his government to triumph over Molière (who played Orgon onstage) for five long and discouraging years, even though he knew perfectly well that Molière was attacking false piety and not true religion. By the time that Molière added the *deus ex machina* ending to *Tartuffe*, the play had become historically far more than an entertainment or even a well-wrought work of art. It had become a *cause célèbre* against censorship in the theatre. Thus, since the King was in reality a significant part of the play's life, it should not surprise us unduly to see him utilized as an offstage actor in the plot. After all, Molière as a satirist was famous for reflecting the events of real life (particularly his own) in the comic mirror of his art.

The action of the *deus ex machina* thus becomes a double-edged sword in *Tartuffe*. Public flattery of this sort is also public hyperbole which can be reasonably interpreted as a public challenge. If the King presumes to enjoy divine powers, he will be expected to use these powers in a godlike manner. But if he uses his power arbitrarily, he will himself face divine judgment.

5. *The Divine Average* (Cleveland, 1971), p. 174. See also Martin Turnell, *The Classical Moment* (1948; reprint ed., Westport, Conn., 1971), p. 77.
6. All references to *Tartuffe* are taken from the Richard Wilbur translation in *World Masterpieces*, ed. Maynard Mack et al. 3rd ed. (New York, 1973), II, 34–85.

Such an interpretation does not deny the validity of the genre theory that *Tartuffe*, if it is a comedy, must have a happy ending. But perhaps, as Eric Bentley has suggested, "Happy endings are always ironical like everything else that is happy in comedies."[7] If so, we are then faced with the question of why Molière chose to treat Louis XIV ironically. Was he as interested in unmasking the royal pretensions to divinity as he was in unmasking religious hypocrisy? The answer may lie partly in an argumentative preface to *Tartuffe*, published with the final version of the play in 1669, where Molière stated that "If the function of comedy is to correct men's vices, I do not see *why any should be exempt*. Such a condition in our society would be much more dangerous than the thing itself; and we have seen that the theater is admirably suited to provide correction. The most forceful lines of a serious moral statement are usually less powerful than those of satire; and nothing will reform most men better than the depiction of their faults. *It is a vigorous blow to vices to expose them to public laughter*."[8]

It seems to me significant that we *do* laugh at the sudden reversal of events and at the Officer's extravagant praise of the King's godlike ability to see into the hearts of men. Thus, it may be that in *Tartuffe* Molière was assuming the traditional rights of the court buffoon to mock the pretensions of monarchs and, through the inflated hyperbole of the Officer's speech, to remind his sovereign of the real limitations of mortality, despite the accepted religious nature and responsibility of the kingly role.[9] Molière had previously criticized Louis XIV in *The Impromptu of Versailles* and would do so again in *Amphitryon*.

The Impromptu of Versailles, for example, addresses the problem of unreasonable royal demands for instant entertainment, demands which are inconsiderate of the performers and which encourage artistic failure. When the actors in Molière's company complain in a staged "rehearsal" before the court about the King's order for the performance of a new play they have not yet had time either to create or to memorize, Molière—acting himself—replies contemptuously,

> Good heavens, mademoiselle, what kings like is prompt obedience: they aren't pleased at meeting obstacles. They want things at the time they want them; if they see their amusements postponed, they no longer find them amusing. They like pleasures

7. *The Life of the Drama* (1964; reprint ed., New York, 1970), p. 301.
8. Molière, Preface to *Tartuffe*, trans. and ed. Haskell M. Block, in *World Masterpeices*, II, 26–27. Italics mine.
9. Even Louis XIV, despite all his theatrical extravagances, never claimed superhuman knowledge; on the contrary, he openly admitted his human tendencies to confusion, indecision and even error in his memoirs, although his administration liked to claim the opposite. See Orest and Patricia Ranum, eds., *The Century of Louis XIV* (Chicago, 1972), p. 72.

they don't have to wait for; and the ones they like best are the ones which aren't too elaborately prepared.[1]

This kind of open criticism of kings might be dangerous for a court poet, but it is here softened by a *deus ex machina* somewhat like that in *Tartuffe*. Molière digresses from his rehearsal of an unwritten play by stepping forward to do impromptu imitations of the famous Parisian tragic actors who play either over-weight kings or parts ending in death. Then Louis's impatient courtiers enter, one after another, to demand that he begin the play itself at once. Finally, a message from the King arrives which states that he understands at last Molière's difficulty and will be happy to watch any play currently in the repertory. "Ah, monsieur," cries Molière, "you bring me back to life."[2] Meanwhile, of course, the King has been given a comic lesson on the "proper way" of dealing with artists.

Lionel Gossman reminds us that *Amphitryon* is another case in point: "The King is represented in this work as Jupiter, King of the Gods, the common seventeenth-century metaphor for Louis XIV. But this embodiment of the unity of power and law reveals himself to be the supreme individualist, pleasure-seeker and breaker of laws. It is he, supposedly the incarnation of law, who seduces Alcmena by appearing in the guise of her husband and who argues with her for the supremacy of individual inclination over all law, including, of course, that of marriage."[3] Clearly, the King would not have permitted such defiance of the law by any of his nobles, including princes of the blood royal, as history shows.

But the main problem with the generic theory as an explanation of the *deus ex machina* ending, as I see it, arises from a consideration of the play's history. Most scholars now agree that *Tartuffe* was first written as a light-hearted farce in three acts which ended with Orgon piously inviting Tartuffe to visit Elmire at will—for the good of the young wife's soul, of course.[4] The joke was on the middle-aged gull as performed by Molière, a gull who, like the man Poquelin, had defied the laws of nature by marrying a woman much younger than himself. Such a wife could hardly be expected to remain faithful to a tyrannical fool of a husband. It would be unnatural and therefore unreasonable in what the French court considered an Age of Reason. Hence, *Tartuffe* probably began, in 1664, as a clever seducer of

1. Molière, *The Impromptu of Versailles*, in *Eight Plays by Molière*, trans. Morris Bishop (New York, 1957), p. 129.
2. Ibid., p. 150.
3. "Molière and *Tartuffe*: Law and Order in the Seventeenth Century," *French Review*, 43 (1970), 903.
4. Nelson, p. 114. For reviews of the scholarly debate on the first version of *Tartuffe*, see Henry C. Lancaster, *A History of French Dramatic Literature in the Seventeenth Century: Part Three—The Period of Molière* (Baltimore, 1936), II, 620–23; and Nelson, pp. 114–17.

young wives rather than as a dangerous perverter of religious senti-
ments. He probably used the guise of religion in much the same fash-
ion as Wycherley's Master Horner used the guise of impotence. The
final illicit union of Tartuffe and Elmire, with Orgon's blessing,
would then have represented the witty triumph of fertility over fool-
ish senility, and we would indeed have a true comic ending.

However, after the persecution of Molière by the *Compagnie du
Saint Sacrement,* whose powerful membership included even the
Queen Mother, the author decided that religious hypocrisy was no
laughing matter after all. Tartuffe could no longer be played as a
harmless adventurer in the boudoirs of bored middle-class ladies.
Molière now saw how the practitioners of religious hypocrisy in the
court could easily ruin his personal reputation by accusing him of
atheism and destroy his livelihood as a dramatist by keeping his plays
off the public stage. Such villainy had to be publicly unmasked.

To do this, however, Molière had to transform the character of
Tartuffe from a sympathetic fertility figure into an unconscionable
criminal, a menace to society as a whole. He had to show Tartuffe
literally taking over *all* of Orgon's world—his wife, his daughter, his
son's inheritance, and finally his house (a comment on the order of
bourgeois values). At this point, the character of Orgon abruptly
shifts in the final version of the play from absurd dupe to pathetic vic-
tim, a shift which reflects the change in Molière's own life caused by
the enmity of the *Compagnie du Saint Sacrement.* For, although
Molière may have been personally comic as the deceived husband of
a young wife, he was not comic as the persecuted artist who had
depended upon the King's patronage only to find his play prohibited
from the public stage.

Speaking for the *Compagnie du Saint Sacrement,* the Archbishop
of Paris managed to convince Louis after the first performance that
Tartuffe should be denied a license on the grounds that it was an
insult to religion. Although the King refused to admit the justice of
this accusation, he did decide that it would be politic to submit to the
Archbishop's demands. Molière's later petitions show that he was
unwilling to accept the fact that a king claiming to be an absolute
ruler by divine right should be unable to overcome the objections of
religious zealots, even though the Archbishop could and eventually
did threaten to excommunicate anyone attending a production of
Tartuffe. After all, the Papal Nuncio had found nothing offensive in
the comedy which he saw in a private performance.

In August, 1664, a simple-minded clergyman, Pierre Roullé, vicar
of St. Barthélemy, published an attack on Molière as a "demon in the
flesh" and paid fervent tribute to the piety of Louis XIV whom he con-
sidered "the Most Glorious King in all the World" (Palmer, p. 334).
Roullé praised the King for prohibiting *Tartuffe* and for his godlike

graciousness toward a writer who really "should be burned at the stake": "His Majesty, having severely reproached him, though moved by a strong indignation, has, in the exercise of his ordinary clemency, in which he imitates the essential gentleness of God . . . pardoned the devilish hardihood of this creature in order to give him time to devote the rest of his life to a public and solemn penitence . . ." (Palmer, p. 335).

Is it possible that this incredible passage planted the seed for the *deus ex machina* in Molière's mind? He uses the idea in his First Petition to the King in August, 1664, asking that the play be publicly produced in order to clear his name: "I will not ask, Sire, for what I need for the sake of my reputation and the innocence of my work: enlightened kings such as you do not need to be told what is wished of them; like God, they see what we need and know better than we what they should give us. It is enough for me to place my interests in Your Majesty's hands, and I respectfully await whatever you may care to command."[5] Of course, in the first part of the petition Molière had already informed the King exactly what it was that he wanted. Yet, as John Palmer comments, he "waited for over four years" for satisfaction: "The King was prepared to do anything but authorize a public production" (p. 338).

The new five-act version of *Tartuffe* was given a private performance before the Prince de Condé, a former enemy of the King, in 1665 and was probably shown to Louis between 1 December, 1666 and 25 February, 1667. However, *Tartuffe* was not licensed for public performance until February, 1669, at which time a jubilant Molière wrote his Third Petition to the King, now to ask a favor for his doctor. The jocular tone of the Petition and the continuation of the previously used analogy between the grace of Louis and of God (carried now into the realm of death and resurrection) make it worth quoting in its entirety here. We can hardly fail to detect Molière's blithe irony.

> Sire,
>
>   A very honest doctor whose patient I have the honor to be, promises and will legally contract to make me live another thirty years if I can obtain a favor for him from Your Majesty. I told him of his promise that I do not deserve so much, and that I should be glad to help him if he will merely agree not to kill me. This favor, Sire, is a post of canon at your royal chapel of Vincennes, made vacant by death.
>
>   May I dare to ask for this favor from Your Majesty on the very day of the glorious resurrection of *Tartuffe*, brought back to life

5. Block, p. 31.

by your goodness? By this first favor I have been reconciled with the devout, and the second will reconcile me with the doctors. Undoubtedly this would be too much grace for me at one time, but perhaps it would not be too much for Your Majesty, and I await your answer to my petition with respectful hope.[6]

Molière published the final version of the play that same year complete with a preface and all three of his petitions to the King, thus clearly indicating that *Tartuffe's* history forms an integral part of its artistic texture. Furthermore, in the preface he firmly announced his right to criticize anyone he pleased without censorship, since 1) "comedy for the ancients had its origins in religion and constituted a part of its ceremonies" and 2) the primary "function of comedy is to correct men's vices."[7]

The dénouement of the final version of *Tartuffe* thus reflects the historical events by saving Orgon and his family from Tartuffe just as Louis ultimately saved Molière's play. It is a part of the story of *Tartuffe* and not merely a generic necessity. But, although the flattery of the King is clearly ironic, referring back as it does to years of unjust censorship which in turn caused a severe financial crisis and near demise for Molière's company, McCollom accepts the *deus ex machina* as symbolic of a victory of light over darkness and argues that Molière was attacking the superstitions of the church while upholding the reasonableness of the monarchy.[8]

We are told by other scholars, however, that the style of the poetry actually changes in the Officer's speech to a stately, lyrical expression, perhaps more appropriate to the tragic than to the comic mode and in striking contrast to what Robert Nelson calls the previous "satirical realism" of the comedy.[9] Nelson finds this shift of tone disturbing and artistically "inappropriate": "One cannot sing the praises of anyone with mordant satire; satire is by definition negative and to sing of glories some other form is required. . . . In the final version of *Le Tartuffe* [Molière] has tried with the scene of the *exempt* to 'take back' the negativism of the satire—and failed."[1] Obviously, the effect of satire cannot be undone at the last moment. Yet we should also remember that a major characteristic of irony and satire is the use of striking, sudden, and, above all, "inappropriate" changes of tone. I believe, therefore, that we should assume that Molière's satirical posture is still very much in effect during the apparently solemn apotheosis of Louis XIV in the last scene of *Tartuffe*.

6. Ibid., p. 33.
7. Ibid., p. 26.
8. McCollom, p. 174.
9. Nelson, p. 116. See also Turnell, p. 77.
1. Nelson, p. 117.

A careful analysis of the play reveals that Molière's satire has a number of interrelated targets: religious hypocrisy, tyranny, and political hypocrisy. He shows Mme Pernelle to be a religious hypocrite most pointedly in her cruel treatment of her servant Flipote whom she brutally slaps across the face in the first scene. Molière shows Orgon to be foolish to the point of insanity by contrasting his claims to piety and his elaborate adoration of Tartuffe's false piety with his attitude of absolute tyranny toward his own relatives. Orgon breaks his word to Valère's family and orders his daughter to marry Tartuffe against her will. He insists that his wife accept Tartuffe as a "star boarder" in the house, and he disinherits his own son for daring to accuse the hypocrite of lusting after Elmire. *Hypocrisy* and *tyranny* thus work together in the play to destroy the household of Orgon. But once Tartuffe's hypocrisy is exposed to Orgon by means of Elmire's clever play-within-the-play, the tyrant turns victim and attempts to expel the wolf in sheep's clothing from his home. It is too late.

At this point, Molière shifts his satirical attack from religious to political hypocrisy. In Act V, Monsieur Loyal arrives, offers oily good wishes to Orgon, and proceeds to serve Orgon with a writ of eviction. Tartuffe, having denounced Orgon to the King for befriending a rebel during the Fronde, later arrives with the King's Officer to arrest his former patron.[2]

> TARTUFFE: All deeds are glorious, Madam, which obey
>   The sovereign prince who sent me here today.
> ORGON: I rescued you when you were destitute:
>   Have you forgotten that, you thankless brute?
> TARTUFFE: No, no, I well remember everything:
>   But my first duty is to serve my King.
>   That obligation is so paramount
>   That other claims, beside it, do not count;
>   And for it I would sacrifice my wife,
>   My family, my friend, or my own life.   [V, 7, 15–23]

This remarkably unchristian speech mimics an earlier pronouncement by Orgon in praise of Tartuffe's good influence:

> ORGON: Under his tutelage my soul's been freed
>   From earthly loves, and every human tie:
>   My mother, children, brother, and wife could die,
>   And I'd not feel a single moment's pain.
> CLEANTE: That's a fine sentiment, Brother; most humane.
>   [I, 5, 18–21]

2. W. G. Moore comments on this readjustment of the hypocritical mask in "Tartuffe and the Comic Principle in Molière," *Modern Language Review*, 43, 1 (1948), 51.

The similarity between the two speeches points up, first, a likeness between the two kinds of hypocrisy, religious and political; secondly, it reveals the similarity between the relationship of Orgon to Tartuffe and Tartuffe to the King. Since both Tartuffe and the King ultimately turn against their flatterers in the play, it is quite unlikely that Molière himself would risk the same losses by seriously flattering the real Louis in his tragicomedy.

The symmetrical analogy between Orgon's idolatrous worship of Tartuffe and everybody else's idolatrous worship of the King has been noted by Lionel Gossman, who appears to suspect the kind of subtle political satire I am suggesting in this paper: "The grotesque caricature of the *faux dévot* makes the Sun-King seem even more brilliant by comparison, but at the same time it casts a disquieting shadow over him. Likewise the worship of kings, flags, and other symbols of distinction is at once enhanced and rendered suspect by being set alongside Orgon's infatuation with Tartuffe. Relatively the worship of kings may be better, but it is a phenomenon of a disturbingly similar sort."[3] Walter Kerr also admits having wondered as a student if Molière were not "pulling somebody's leg, if only Louis's" when he makes use of the King himself as the god from the machine in *Tartuffe*.[4]

Like many plays with *deus ex machina* endings, *Tartuffe* is structured around two basic metaphors which promise the eventual appearance of a god figure by their very nature. The first of these is the insane asylum metaphor. Life in Orgon's household is like "a madhouse" (*"la cour du roi Pétaud,"* or house of misrule) as Mme Pernelle describes it, "with the keeper gone" (I, 1,12), implying that there is a sane world outside and a keeper who will one day reappear. The King does eventually bring the light of reason into this bourgeois Parisian madhouse; but France herself is analogous to Orgon's family and still awaits the appearance of Louis's "keeper" to cure, in turn, the royal excesses.

The second basic metaphor compares life to a stage play with unseen divine spectators looking on. This theatre metaphor has implications similar to those of the madhouse metaphor. If the King represents Reason in judgment of madness, he also symbolizes in *Tartuffe* the Divine Spectator of the human comedy. But simultane-

---

3. *Men and Masks* (Baltimore, 1970), p. 144.
4. Kerr, p. 68. Such suspicions are difficult to prove, however, to those who believe that the seventeenth century took literally the royal claims to divinity. Actually, none of the monarchs did make quite such a blasphemous claim. They argued more reasonably that their *office* was divinely appointed, that they had succeeded to that office through the proper rule of primogeniture (England) or Salic law (France), and that they could therefore legitimately exercise divine authority as the Vicar of Christ on earth. John Figgis, referring to the French system, observes: "The essential notion is that the King owes his position directly to Divine Appointment and is therefore accountable to God alone, and not to the Pope. From this naturally arises the sense of the absolute duty of nonresistance upon religious grounds. The King is regarded as above the restraints of positive law, save in the matter of succession" (in *The Divine Right of Kings*, 2nd ed. [Cambridge, England, 1934], p. 128).

ously, he too is being observed, as he enacts his kingly role, by the true Divine Spectator whom he represents in the theatre of the world. Molière sees to it that the audience is always conscious of watching a play during a performance of *Tartuffe*. First, the dialogue constantly reminds us of role playing and masks, as many commentators have pointed out; secondly, we see that consummate actor Tartuffe shifting easily from one role to another; and, finally, we watch Elmire stage two plays-within-the-play before a hidden spectator in order to unmask the hypocrite. Like all such metaplays, *Tartuffe* is clearly designed to suggest a metaphysical significance and presence behind its otherwise absurd events.

Having been thus prefigured in such a theatrical situation, god-figures or messengers from the world of reality who interfere with the unreal action onstage are never totally surprising to the spectators. They remind the audience that their own performances are under scrutiny as well. Plays of this sort often combine the convention of God as spectator with the *deus ex machina* and clearly state that we must all of us, even kings, play our parts well on the great stage of the world or face the critical consequences in a final scene of unmasking. To bring Louis XIV onstage, even by way of a messenger, is therefore to point up his role as an actor like Molière in the theatre and like Poquelin out of it. The Divine Spectator observes both in the Great Theatre of the World.

Thus, Molière's *deus ex machina* is far from being an excrescence on the structure of *Tartuffe*. It is not a fault in the dramatic structure at all but a vital element of the play's structure which contributes directly to the meaning of *Tartuffe*. It is a symbolic action which ironically corrects the assumptions of the characters, and of the audience as well, by overriding normal expectations for the outcome of the plot. Above all, it calls attention to the humbling notion that we live in a *theatrum mundi* overseen by gods, and it reminds Louis XIV (and the audience generally) of his humanity by overpraising his pretensions to divinity.

The seventeenth century cultural point of view in France upheld Reason as a standard against which all human behavior must be judged. Since Orgon's understanding of religion and his idolatry were unreasonable, they became for Molière the objects of laughter. Since the King's claim to superhuman powers of Reason was also patently unreasonable, the action of the *deus* in *Tartuffe* may resolve the plot but (because it is also *ex machina*) it is at the same time unconvincing, even absurd. Molière has in this way subtly employed the *deus ex machina* convention to satirize the unreasonable extravagances in the politics and religion of his time.

PAMELA S. SAUR

Molière's *Tartuffe*[†]

William Jaynes's 1981 article "Critical Opinions of Cléante in *Tartuffe*" offers an excellent and well-researched summary of a somewhat bewildering history of diverse critical opinions on Molière's character Cléante. One much-debated issue concerns the extent to which the character is "the mouthpiece of the author," as he delivers many of the passages on the issue of hypocrisy, which Molière identified as the central moral issue in the play. A related question is the evaluation of Cléante as one of Molière's *raisonneurs*, or representatives of rationality and reason. Some critics have analyzed the content, wit, and rhetorical skill of Cléante's speeches and found them quite impressive. Nevertheless, others do not consider him likable, calling him dull, mediocre, even "a self-important busybody" (91). Much depends, of course, on the decisions and styles of the directors and actors who ultimately bring the character to life. In fact, one could sidestep the controversies and simply conclude from them that this character, as presented by the play's written text, allows a good bit of flexibility for stage interpretation.

Jaynes argues for a positive view of Cléante's wisdom and constructive, admirable role in the play by contrasting him with other, clearly more negative and unbalanced characters. He says of Cléante, "His ability to see things clearly is reflected in his ironic comments to Tartuffe, who distorts reality, and to Orgon, who cannot see it at all" (96). Jaynes also comments. "The play is a struggle between Tartuffe and Cléante to guide Orgon" (96). These statements are true enough: however, I believe that additional characters should be brought into the pattern. If the play were merely "a struggle between Tartuffe and Cléante," the ending would be different. The victory would go to Tartuffe, for Cléante by himself is quite ineffective in making Orgon see the truth about his false friend. For most of the play, Cléante's rhetoric and reasoning are ignored and even ridiculed by Orgon and his mother, Madame Pernelle; only the drastic wiles of Elmire, who gets Tartuffe to try to seduce her while her husband, Orgon, hides under the table, are effective in persuading Orgon of the truth. Even then, Madame Pernelle stubbornly supports Tartuffe until faced with the fact that he is trying to evict the family from their home. For all its wisdom, Cléante's eloquent advice is of little consequence in moving the plot forward or toppling Tartuffe from his seat of power in the household.

[†] From *The Explicator* 60.1 (Fall 2001): 9–11. Reprinted with permission of the Helen Dwight Reid Educational Foundation. Published by Heldref Publications, 1319 Eighteenth Street, NW, Washington DC 20036. Copyright © 2001.

Instead of juxtaposing Cléante to Tartuffe and Orgon, I suggest another foil for him: Orgon's son Damis. If Tartuffe, Orgon, and Madame Pernelle are the "villains" of the play, blockers of Mariane and Valère's rightful marriage and distorters of truth and natural family order, the "good" allies on the other side include the women Dorine and Elmire and the men Cléante and Damis. Dorine seems initially to have some chance at bringing the truth out, but she ultimately succeeds only in bringing some resolve to Mariane and Valère: she fails utterly to shake Orgon's stubborn allegiance to Tartuffe. If we view Cléante and Damis together as the two women's allies, we must admit that neither is of much use. Cléante may represent wisdom and Damis folly, yet both have the same goals and both are ineffectual. Since we expect caricature, distortion, and excess in a comedy, it is worth considering whether Cléante represents an excess of rationality and mental orientation and Damis an excess of irrationality and emotional/physical (violent) orientation, just as Tartuffe represents an extreme amount of hypocrisy and Orgon extreme stubbornness, gullibility, and loyalty to friends (Tartuffe and Argas) at all costs.

In one scene (5.2), Cléante and Damis confront each other. Damis has learned that Tartuffe has turned against Orgon. He responds in a typically impetuous, hotheaded manner, threatening to cut off Tartuffe's ears and beat his head in. Cléante replies, "The voice of youth. Now, will you please calm down! We're living in an age and in a kingdom where violence is never a solution" (lines 10–13).[1] The manner in which these lines are delivered could certainly affect whether the audience thinks that Damis is being confronted by wisdom or just a different kind of foolishness. And even if Cléante is wise, at this point in the play there is no evidence that his wisdom will prevail against Tartuffe's pernicious cleverness.

Cléante's long speech at the end of act 5, scene 1 is also pertinent. Orgon has been persuaded of Tartuffe's villainy and has vowed not to trust any more religious men. Cléante refutes this ridiculous notion well enough, but draws a questionable conclusion: "if you can't help going to extremes, better to make the same mistake again" (55–56). Surely not! Can it be wise to suggest that Orgon once again reject his family, disinherit his son, break his word to his daughter, and risk his property, good name, and wife's honor? Donald M. Frame's translation, which is closer to the original French, is milder: "And if you must fall into one excess / Err on the side of trusting more, not less" (300).[2]

---

1. In the 1984 Royal Shakespeare Company version of the play, based on the translation by Hampton, the actor's voice "cracks" or ascends to an unnaturally high pitch: as a result his words sound foolish.
2. The original French line reads, "Et s'il vous faut tomber dans une extrémité, / Péchez plutôt encor de cet autre côté" (100).

Those words carry the same ridiculous implication if one thinks them through, but the audience is not as likely to notice it.

In act 5, scene 5, after the family has been served eviction papers, Cléante says, "Come on now, let's go and discuss the options" (12). Frame's translation reads, "Let us consider what you'd better do" (308). Cléante's thought here can be defended as reasonable and appropriate, but it can also be regarded as foolish. Discussion, logic, and rational consideration of alternatives have not worked up until now. With so much at stake, is Cléante being ridiculous? Is he "Mr. Too Rational," reverse image of Damis, easily described as "Mr. Too Irrational"?

In the end, it is probably safest to regard Cléante as complex rather than one-dimensional and as a character particularly subject to differing interpretations on the stage. Saying that Cléante is a caricature of overrationality is as oversimplified as saying that he is the voice of the author and nothing else. As I mentioned, there is some textual evidence that he may go too far in his rational approach to life. However, that can also be regarded as evidence that he is, after all, not a walking essay or clear-cut allegory, but a character in a play. As such, he is a unique combination of human and representational characteristics. Moreover, his being is realized not on the written page but on the stage and in interaction with the other characters in his environment. In a more rational environment, his rationality would be admirable and effective; if it is absurd and ineffective, it is because of the extreme traits and behaviors of the other comic characters in the play.

Works Cited

Frame, Donald M., trans. Tartuffe *and Other Plays by Molière*. New York: New American Library, 1967.

Hampton, Christopher, trans. *Molière's Tartuffe*. London: Samuel French, 1984.

Jaynes, William. "Critical Opinions of Cléante in *Tartuffe*." *Oeuvres and Critiques* 6.1 (1981): 91–97.

Molière, Jean Baptiste Poquelin. *Le Tartuffe and Le Médecin malgré lui*. Introd. and notes by Jacques Guicharnaud. Laurel Language Library. New York: Dell, 1962.

Tartuffe, Perf. Antony Sher, Nigel Hawthorne, and Alison Steadman. A Royal Shakespeare Company Production by BBC TV in association with RKO Pictures. RKO Home Videos, 1984.

WILLIAM J. BECK

More on Molière's *Tartuffe*[†]

While many readers of Molière's *Le Tartuffe* would be bewildered if asked to comment upon the origin of the name which the seventeenth-century French dramatist gave to his protagonist, critics themselves have propounded a number of explanations. Some of the latter are ingenious and plausible, others, ingenuous and implausible. Does the name derive from the Italian *truffa*, is it a deformation of Monsieur Tuffes-Tartaux, who came from the region of Pézenas, are its origins to be found in the German word *Teufel*, which ultimately became *tertuffle* around the region of Lyons? In purely literary texts, its possible sources have been detected in Antoine Fusy's *Mastigophore*, in the 1624 collection of the letters of Guez de Balzac, in Scarron's *Hypocrites*, a simple twisting of the name Montufar.[1] And there are still other possible explanations for the origin of this intriguing name. Obviously, Molière's actual source of acquisition is conjectural at best, and the difficulty of solving the question of origin is shown by the numerous theories that have been advanced thus far. Perhaps the most the researcher can do, in an attempt to better understand the name, is to indicate some of the close parallels between the possible meanings of the word and the existence of similar qualities in the bearer.

The sixteenth-century French word for weasel was "tar," and the Burgundian word *truf* or *truffe*, used as an adjective, meant either "sly" or "deceitful."[2] Hence, "Tartuffe" very plausibly signifies "sly weasel," an appellation that is most appropriate in the case of Molière's imposter. The presence of the letter "r" in *truffe* and its disappearance in "Tartuffe" presents no significant difficulty. In his discussion of *truffe*, Emile Littré declares that there very early developed two forms of the word, one with an "r" the other without it. Evidently, in popular usage, the two forms were interchangeable, and Littré suggests other analogous examples.[3] In fact, the omission of the "r" is very timely, since the two syllables, "tar" and "tuffe," evoke, by the heaviness and fullness of the first, and the smooth, slick richness of the second, both the true nature of Tartuffe the man, and that of the weasel, characterized by La Fontaine as "grasse, maflue et rebondie" [stout, chubby, and plump]. Furthermore, there is no doubt that phonetically,

[†] From *Papers on Language and Literature* 6.2 (Spring 1980). Copyright © 1980 by The Board of Trustees, Southern Illinois University, Edwardsville. Reproduced by permission.
1. J. Guicharnaud, *Molière: Une aventure théâtrale* (Paris, 1963), p. 19.
2. Randle Cotgrave, *A Dictionarie of the French and English Tongues* (Columbia, South Carolina, 1968).
3. *Dictionnaire de la langue française* (Paris, 1970), 7, 1392–1393.

the hypocrite's name has the power to evoke qualities of guile, deceit and fraud, all found in the weasel. From the point of view of literary history, the name places its possessor in the tradition of similarly named hypocrites of fiction: Montufar, Onuphre, Panulphe, Truffaldino and Truffa. One might even suggest that symbolically, the hypocrite's name calls to the reader's mind a covert, slippery, slinky animal, one whose very appearance is deceptive: the ferret or weasel.

Internal evidence within the play gives further support to the description of Tartuffe as a "sly weasel." The weasel is striking because of its long, plump body, and above all, because of its dominant, pointed nose. The Larousse French dictionary defines the animal in the following manner "du genre putois, qui a le corps allongé et le museau pointu" [of the skunk family, having a long body and a pointed snout]. Clearly, one of the generalized feelings the careful reader comes away with upon first meeting Tartuffe is a sense of the hypocrite's almost animal-like cunning and slyness, and the evocation of the weasel, a member of the skunk family, is quite appropriate when picturing Tartuffe. An attentive reading of act 1, scene 2, reveals some significant descriptive language, notably on the part of Dorine, who paints an accurate and complete portrait of Tartuffe's physical appearance. In the scene, one is struck by Dorine's response to Orgon, when the latter suggests that while Tartuffe is not exactly a ladies' man, his appearance is most unusual. Unfavorably impressed by Tartuffe's most prominent possession, Dorine replies ironically that his is a "handsome snout."

ORGON   Sans être damoiseau,
               Tartuffe est fait de sorte . . .
DORINE   Oui, c'est un beau museau.
ORGON   Que quand tu n'aurois même aucune sympathie
           Pour tous les autres dons . . . [4]

[ORGON   Although he is not a ladies' man,
          Tartuffe's appearance is such . . .
DORINE   Yes, his is a handsome snout.
ORGON   That even if you have no
          sympathy for his other gifts . . .]

Dorine's use of the word *beau* is clearly ironic, she is really suggesting that Tartuffe possesses a rather large, ugly nose. All of her remarks, while they may on occasion lack elegance, are highly colorful and complete. They supply us with physical details which tell us that Tartuffe is a repulsive, cunning, animal-like individual, most unfit with his prominent, weasel-like snout, for inspiring love and admiration in Marianne or women in general.

The Spanish theatre was a most fertile source for the comedies of

4. *Le Théâtre Complet de Molière*, ed Robert Jouanny (Paris, 1960), 1, 656.

Molière. In Spanish literature, not only did the dramatist find some of his most extensive borrowings but also much of the best material that he eventually adapted to the French stage.[5] Furthermore, thanks to this new wellspring, Molière was able to free himself from a long-standing imitation of Italian sources, directing his attention and creative talents to the Spanish tradition. The novella, *La garduña de Sevilla y anzuelo de las bolsas* [*The weasel of Seville and purse-hooker*], written by the Spaniard don Alonso Castillo Solorzano, was translated into French in 1661 by Monsieur Antoine le Mêtel d'Ouville and published in Paris. Ernest Martinenche affirms,[6] and I agree, that the French translation, *La fouine de Séville ou l'hameçon des bourses*, contains a number of scenes that were directly useful to Molière. This picaresque novella recounts the life and exploits of the prostitute Rufina, particularly her encounter with an old hermit. While the story is not of immediate interest in the present context, the title is, because it is a positive indication that Molière had knowledge of the concept of the weasel-hypocrite. Like several of the weasels in the *Fables* of Molière's contemporary, La Fontaine,[7] Tartuffe has inserted himself into Orgon's house through cunning and deceit, and he has grown fat by his deception. Yet, he will not succeed in extricating himself from the artificial paradise his hypocrisy has created. Certainly, "Tar," "Tuffe," or "sly weasel" is as appropriate as any other characterization suggested heretofore of Molière's impostor, Tartuffe.

MECHELE LEON

The Poet and the Prince: Revising Molière and *Tartuffe* in the French Revolution[†]

Le paradoxe de Molière, à l'apogée de sa vie, fut d'être à la fois homme de pouvoir et de contestation. Personnage officiel en même temps que marginal, il se trouva sans cesse au centre de luttes, dont les négociations pour obtenir son enterrement chrétien ne constituèrent pas le dernier épisode.

[The paradox of Molière, at the high point of his career, was to have been simultaneously a man of power and contestation, an official figure and at the same time marginalized. He was forever at the center of battles. The negotiation that permitted him a Christian burial was not the last of them.]

Michel Delon

5. Ernest Martinenche, *Molière et le théâtre espagnol* (Paris, 1960), p. 271.
6. Martinenche, p. 161.
7. See particularly *La Fontaine, Oeuvres Completes*, ed. E. Pilon and R. Groos (Paris, 1954), vol. 1 livre 2, fable 5, livre 3, fable 17, livre 7, fable 16.
† From *French Historical Studies* 28.3 (Summer 2005): 447–65. Copyright 2005, the Society of French Historical Studies. All rights reserved. Used by permission of the publisher, Duke University Press.

An array of contradictory elements surrounded Molière, but the paradox of his having been both powerful and persecuted acquired special resonance during the French Revolution. Molière's legendary association with Louis XIV and the royal patronage long deemed integral to his artistic success came to the fore in the context of revolutionary anxiety about the culture inherited from the Old Regime—culture at once useful and stained by its association with a rejected past. Molière's ties to the monarch emerged in published debates that raged early in the Revolution about the proper relationship between government and theater. This literature suggests the construction of a new narrative of the poet's life story in which he owes little or nothing to his sovereign. Documents also reveal that performance texts of *Tartuffe* were altered during the revolutionary period to excise the role of the monarch. Together, the reconfiguration of Molière's relationship to Louis XIV and the modifications to *Tartuffe* may be interpreted as complementary processes of revision—one historical, the other literary. They are parallel efforts by revolutionaries to void their cultural inheritance of all traces of Old Regime legitimacy. They are also mutually illustrative of the tenacious nature of the Old Regime political culture embedded in the artifacts revolutionaries so passionately sought to reform.

In this article, I examine both sides of this revisionist coin. My interpretation of the significance of revolutionary revisions to Molière's life and works is informed by Robert Darnton's work on related phenomena. In research presented to the American Society for Eighteenth-Century Studies in 1989, Darnton offered the intriguing thesis that "one of the most important tasks of the French Revolution was to rewrite Molière."[1] What led Darnton to this bold conclusion was his analysis of the revolutionary play by Fabre d'Eglantine, *Le Philinte de Molière, ou Suite du "Misanthrope."* It was so important to rewrite Molière, goes Darnton's argument, because society itself was being rewritten. Revising the literature of the Old Regime was integral to fashioning a new society: "The French Revolution was a literary revolution." Revolutionaries tried to reconstruct their reality "from the rubble of an old regime" and so began with the "sacred center of the old literary system—the space shaped by Molière."[2]

Darnton's interest in Molière's fate during the Revolution was certainly justified. Thanks to extensive quantitative research into the repertory performed in the Parisian theater between 1789 and 1799, we now know that his plays became enormously popular once theater

---

1. Robert Darnton, *What Was Revolutionary about the French Revolution?* (Waco, TX, 1989), 21.
2. Ibid., 38–41.

enterprise was liberated and the Comédie-Française lost its century-long privilege as exclusive presenter of his comedies.[3] Nearly two thousand performances of them were given; *L'école des maris*, *Dépit amoureux*, and *Le médecin malgré lui* figure among the ten most performed plays during the Revolution, and Molière's comedies were produced in more theaters than those of any other author. Unfortunately, little is known about his plays in performance—acting styles, for example, or "corrections" to his texts—or about their reception.[4]

As Darnton's work suggests, the revolutionary treatment of Molière's *Misanthrope* is significant as an example of what contemporary revolutionary historiography understands as the era's defining political strategy, namely, inventing a complete break with the past. Within this historiography, theater (broadly defined to include art, event, gathering, performance technique, and dramatic literature) has come to be regarded as crucial to an understanding of the genesis and contradictory workings of revolutionary political culture.[5]

---

3. Emmet Kennedy et al., *Theatre, Opera, and Audiences in Revolutionary Paris: Analysis and Repertory* (Westport, CT, 1996). These data are now incorporated into the *Calendrier électronique des spectacles sous l'Ancien Régime et sous la Révolution*, www.cesar.org.uk. See also André Tissier, *Les spectacles à Paris pendant la Révolution: Répertoire analytique, chronologique et bibliographique, de la réunion des Etats Généraux à la chute de la royauté, 1789–1792* (Geneva, 1992); and Tissier, "Les représentations de Molière pendant la Révolution," in *Eighteenth-Century French Theater: Aspects and Contrasts*, ed. Magdy Gabriel ([Edmonton], Alberta, 1986), 119–36.

4. The theater press during the Revolution was focused mainly on productions of new drama; relatively rarely would commentators remark on performances of Molière's plays. Studies about Molière in the revolutionary era consequently lean toward quantitative methodologies. In addition to the studies mentioned above, see Roger Barny, "Molière et son théâtre dans la Révolution," *Bulletin d'histoire de la Révolution française* (1994–95): 43–63, 65–79. One exception to this is Otis Fellows, "Molière à la fin du siècle des Lumières," in *Age of Enlightenment: Studies Presented to Theodore Besterman*, ed. W. H. Barber et al. (Edinburgh, 1967), 330–49. Fellows surveys a variety of topics and concludes that Molière's reception during the Revolution was "equivocal."

5. Darnton's assessment of literature as central to revolutionary politics reflects a methodological sea change that shifted the focus for many historians of the French Revolution from socioeconomic determinants to the discursive practices that embody and reveal the ideological underpinnings of revolutionary politics. One result of this shift in focus has been to put attention as never before on the theater. Studies most directly reflecting this shift include Marie-Hélène Huet, *Rehearsing the Revolution* (Berkeley, CA, 1982); Susan Maslan, "Resisting Representation: Theater and Democracy in Revolutionary France," *Representations* 52 (1995): 27–51; and Paul Friedman, *Political Actors: Representative Bodies and Theatricality in the Age of the French Revolution* (Ithaca, NY, 2002). Exhaustive quantitative research undertaken on the repertory of plays and operas performed in Paris from 1789 to 1799 and presented in *Theatre, Opera, and Audiences*, however, has proved that performances of plays written prior to the Revolution—particularly the corpus of Old Regime comedies, in which Molière's works figure so prominently—far outnumbered those of plays written during the Revolution. Given that the plays most often performed on the revolutionary stages of Paris had nothing to do with the politics of the day, Kennedy and coauthor Marie-Laurence Netter argue, it follows that audiences wanted simple entertainment: light, amusing, and frivolous. Rather than a theater that spoke to the events and concerns of the time, it was, *grosso modo*, "oblivious to the Revolution" (34). I criticize this position in my review of Kennedy and Netter's book in *Theatre Insight* 9, no. 2 (1998): 71–73, in which I cite Pierre Frantz's salient point that a play "can take, in the context of its revolutionary mise-en-scène, meanings that its mere inscription on the repertory does not reveal" ("Pas d'entracte pour la Révolution," in *La carmagnole des muses*, ed. Jean-Claude Bonnet [Paris, 1988], 390).

If Darnton helps us situate revisions of Molière's plays squarely within the context of revolutionary political culture, it is important to add that the notion of rewriting Molière can be found in other domains of his revolutionary afterlife: in plays and theatrical performance, of course, but also in biography, dramatic criticism, political discourse, iconography, and memorializing events. In contrast to the respectful *drames* of the prerevolutionary period, for example, revolutionary biographical dramatic literature depicted Molière not as an acolyte of the court but as a man of the people, drawing inspiration from the common folk and rejecting aristocratic values.[6] The revolutionaries did not stop at revising his corpus: they exhumed his corpse with the explicit intention of avenging the ignoble burial given him under the Old Regime.[7] In this sense, we can broaden the notion of what constitutes "rewriting Molière" to include both text and author. Doing so provides an important methodological opportunity, one that Dominick LaCapra describes as exploring the "mutually challenging interaction" between the study of history and literature.[8] What is beneficial about this dialogical interaction is not that it validates or harmonizes discoveries between these domains but that it can uncover the disarticulations, the fault lines, in seemingly coherent phenomena in both domains. The rewriting of Molière's plays, this article aims to show, should be considered in tandem with the rewriting of his life history, because literary revision helps expose the lingering presence of ideas and structures that revisions of history may occlude.

Reflecting this two-pronged approach, the first part of this article considers debates concerning the theater early in the Revolution to analyze how revolutionaries articulated the relationship between Molière and Louis XIV. They sought to liberate theater enterprise and end the monopolies on different dramatic genres held by the privileged theaters. The issue at stake was how to write legislation to replace the long tradition of royal authority over the theater. Molière's relationship with Louis XIV, as I discuss below in a brief summary of

6. A chapter in my book manuscript in progress is devoted to biographical plays about Molière. Several of these plays appeared in the form of vaudevilles and demonstrate a marked shift in theme and emphasis from the plays of Louis-Sébastien Mercier, *La maison de Molière* (1787), and Michel Cubières-Palmezeau, *La mort de Molière* (1788).
7. What were believed to be Molière's remains were exhumed in July 1792. The Parisian section calling itself "Molière and La Fontaine"—one of forty-eight centers of community governance during the Revolution—that initiated the exhumation intended to honor him with a sepulchral monument in the chapel adjoining the cemetery. Instead, his bones were moved from one place to another for seven years before Alexandre Lenoir laid them to rest in the garden of the Musée des Monuments Français. The exhumation of Molière is one of the more intriguing events in his afterlife, and one I analyze in my book in terms of the tension between history and memory. A thorough account of the exhumation is provided by Louis Moland, "Histoire des restes mortels de Molière," *Revue de la Révolution* 2 (1883): 405–25.
8. Dominick LaCapra, "Reconfiguring French Studies," in *History and Reading: Tocqueville, Foucault, French Studies* (Toronto, 2000), 169.

his professional biography, was a strange combination of both extraordinary benefit and frustrating inconsistency. This complex relationship between the poet and the prince was promptly seized on by revolutionaries eager to use it to shore up arguments for theater regulation in the name of a new regime.

The second part of this article considers the implications of revisions to *Tartuffe* in the revolutionary theater.[9] Although censorship of dramatic literature as it was practiced under the Old Regime officially ended in 1791, it became common for theater practitioners to "correct" Old Regime plays still deemed acceptable for the stage. According to the little evidence we have, these corrections ranged from the relatively innocuous substitution of *citoyenne* for *madame* to more substantive alterations of language, character, and plot. Despite their popularity, Molière's plays were not spared the vilification heaped on the Old Regime dramatic repertory during the Terror.[1] In May 1794 the Committee of Public Instruction reestablished preemptive censorship by ordering theaters to submit their repertory lists to government committees for approval. Almost all of Molière's plays were declared unacceptable. *Tartuffe* was an exception; it was admitted "with revisions."[2] While the precise nature of these revisions is unknown, they appear to have affected most specifically the denouement of the play—an exemplary deus ex machina in which the king intervenes, by proxy of a royal officer, to exonerate Orgon and rescue him from the hypocrite Tartuffe. This article shows different strategies that the revolutionaries employed to excise the sovereign from the play. My analysis of the inconsistencies introduced by these "corrections" suggests that rewriting Molière was less an instance of revolutionizing Old Regime literature than an illustration of this literature's ability to sustain Old Regime political culture.

9. The matter of *Tartuffe* during the Revolution has attracted the attention of literary historians, most notably William D. Howarth, "Les 'Tartuffes' de l'époque révolutionnaire," in *Il teatro e la Rivoluzione francese: Atti del convegno di studi sul teatro e la Rivoluzione francese, Vicenza, 14–16 settember, 1989*, ed. Mario Richter (Vicenza, 1991), 65–77. Howarth focuses on revolutionary-era plays that imitate *Tartuffe* in their portrayal of social or political hypocrisies. My approach focuses on revisions to the play itself.

1. Two important studies by André Lieby discuss the fate of the Old Regime dramatic repertory during the Revolution: "La presse révolutionnaire et la censure théâtrale sous la Terreur," *Révolution française* 45 (1903): 306–53, 447–70, 502–29; 46 (1904): 13–28, 97–128; and "L'ancien répertoire sur les théâtres de Paris à travers la réaction thermidorienne," *Révolution française* 49 (1905): 146–75, 193–219. See also Beatrice Hyslop, "The Theater during a Crisis: The Parisian Theater during the Reign of Terror," *Journal of Modern History* 17 (1945): 332–55; and Suzanne J. Bérard, "Aspects du théâtre à Paris sous la Terreur," *Revue d'histoire littéraire de la France* 4–5 (1990): 610–21.

2. Records of the Committee's work on these repertory lists were destroyed by fire during the Commune. According to the researcher who consulted the documents in 1844, in the space of three months 151 plays were examined, 33 were rejected, and 25 were accepted with revisions. Auguste Vivien, "Etudes administratives III: Les théâtres et leur situation actuelle en Angleterre et en France," *Revue des deux mondes*, n.s., 6 (1844): 399.

Revising History

The history of the paradoxically powerful/persecuted Molière begins with the return of his company to the capital after thirteen years of touring the provinces following his failed attempts to establish a theater in his native Paris between 1643 and 1645.[3] After performing before the court in October 1658, Molière was granted a theater at the Petit-Bourbon palace, which his company, under the patronage of the king's brother, was to share with the Italian players then in residence. The actors and playwrights of the premier theater of Paris, the Hôtel de Bourgogne, were less than pleased about the competition from the Troupe de Monsieur. While they and their sumpathizers took little notice of Molière's company when it began performing in November 1658, the success of *Les précieuses ridicules* a year later brought Molière to their attention and began the attacks that would plague him throughout his career.

Criticism of Molière's plays during his lifetime was as varied as his repertory. Clearing away the nuances, however, it came down to a few basic accusations: that Molière's work was artless, unoriginal, obscene, and irreligious. Although severe, much of this criticism was in keeping with aesthetic, moral, and religious concerns of the time. So why the enduring image of Molière as persecuted? To many in the eighteenth century, the negative assessments of Molière by his contemporaries appeared both harsh and specious. They were understood to be the product of cabals led by powerful rivals whose agendas had little to do with his plays. While commentators of the Enlightenment questioned the salutariness of his plays, they did so on social, not religious, grounds. The church's condemnation of the theater—a centuries-old obsession—made the clergy's attacks on Molière appear a matter of sweeping parochial policy.[4] More egregiously, Molière's enemies launched personal attacks on him. He was ridiculed in the plays *Le portrait du peintre* (1664) and *Elomire hypochondre* (1670). As an actor, his detractors charged, he was incapable of playing anything but a clown; his formidable comic skills were nothing more than aping of the great Italian farceur Scaramouche, leading actor of the Comédie-Italienne in Paris.[5] Molière was also mocked as a beleaguered husband, a cuckold worthy of the

3. The summary that follows draws on a number of biographies, including, most recently, Virginia Scott, *Molière: A Theatrical Life* (Cambridge, 2000).
4. For an excellent comprehensive analysis of eighteenth-century opinion of Molière, see Monique Wagner, *Molière and the Age of Enlightenment* (Banbury, U.K., 1973).
5. The frontispiece to *Elomire* (an anagram of "Molière"), for example, sported the engraving "Scaramouche enseignant, Elomire étudiant" and depicted Molière with a mirror in his hand trying to reproduce Scaramouche's grimaces. Molière, *Oeuvres complètes*, ed. George Couton (Paris, 1971), 2:1551n. References to the plays are to act, scene, and line in this edition.

most memorable *cocus* in his own plays. He was accused, in barely disguised terms, of marrying his own daughter.

Louis XIV was Molière's powerful ally against the onslaught of professional criticism and personal calumnies that plagued him throughout his career in Paris. Molière's company was favored at the court: twenty-eight of his thirty-two plays were performed there, and most of them premiered before the king. Molière's talents were placed at the center of elaborate festivals staged at the palaces of Versailles, Saint-Germain-en-Laye, Vincennes, Fontainebleau, and Chambord. Louis XIV supported Molière in real and symbolic ways at strategic moments in his career. At the height of the controversy over *L'école des femmes* in June 1663, the monarch awarded the playwright and his company generous pensions, to be renewed annually. Molière immediately brought this victory to the attention of his rivals by publishing his *Remerciement au Roi*. Molière also publicized the king's active interest in his plays. In the dedication to *Les fâcheux* (1661) Molière thanked Louis XIV for his contribution to the play. The monarch had suggested that he add a character to the parade of pretentious pests and bores that populate this piece—a character "qui a été trouvé partout le plus beau morceau de l'ouvrage [found by all to be the finest part of the play]," Molière remarked (1:481). Not long after a rival actor had accused Molière of incest, the sovereign became the godfather of the playwright's son Louis, born in February 1664. During the battles that raged over *Tartuffe*, the king gave Molière's company seven thousand livres and awarded them the title of Troupe du Roi. But Louis XIV's support for Molière was not consistent. When in 1672 he gave Jean-Baptiste Lully, the Italian-born composer with whom Molière collaborated on many of his *comédie-ballets*, exclusive privilege to musical performance, Molière was forced into the humiliating position of seeking permission from the king to maintain a small orchestra and dancers for his theater. A year later Molière's wife, Armande, had to petition Louis XIV to intervene against the church's decision to deny her husband a Christian burial. The monarch remained silent on the matter.

The defining event in the history of Molière's association with Louis XIV was undoubtedly his five-year battle to bring *Tartuffe* to the public stage. The facts are well known: Molière presented a performance of his three-act play *Tartuffe, ou L'hypocrite* to Louis XIV at Versailles in May 1664. Although reportedly the king was impressed by the play, he deemed it politically unwise to allow public performances of it. Over the next several years and with the monarch's tacit approval, Molière continued to revise the play and gave several private performances at the command of Condé. Meanwhile, the powerful *dévots* used their influence to keep the play from the public. In August 1667 Molière, having the verbal consent of the king, pre-

sented the five-act *Panulphe, ou L'imposteur* at his theater in Paris.
Louis XIV was with his army in Flanders at the time. In his absence
the city was under the authority of Guillaume de Lamoignon, presi-
dent of the Parlement of Paris and a prominent member of the Com-
pagnie du Saint-Sacrement, a secret and militant Catholic society.
Lamoignon promptly forbade a second performance of the play and
obtained an interdiction from the archbishop of Paris stating that
anyone presenting, reading, or attending this play, publicly or pri-
vately, risked excommunication. Two actors from Molière's troupe
were immediately dispatched to the king's camp in Lille with a peti-
tion from Molière. They obtained the sovereign's promise that he
would consider the matter as soon as he returned to Paris. Shortly
afterward, a lengthy description and defense of the play appeared in
print in the anonymous *Lettre sur la comédie de "L'imposteur."* With
the issue now before the public, the monarch gave his consent and
Tartuffe, ou L'imposteur opened in February 1669 for a record num-
ber of performances before packed houses.

The denouement of *Tartuffe* was the coup de grâce for those ene-
mies of Molière who believed that their machinations, like Tartuffe's,
could deceive "un Prince dont les yeux se font jour dans les coeurs [a
Prince who sees into our inmost hearts]" (5.7.1907). "Voici une
comédie dont on a fait beaucoup de bruit, qui a été longtemps per-
sécutée [Here is a comedy about which much fuss has been made
and which has been long persecuted]," wrote Molière in the opening
sentence of the preface to the play, published the same year—thus
leaving for posterity both an elegant argument in his own defense and
an indictment of those who opposed him (1:883). The battle for
Tartuffe and Louis XIV's role in the affair were inscribed for poster-
ity in Molière's *pétitions* to the king, reproduced in the first edition of
his complete works (1682). For La Harpe, the denouement of
Tartuffe was the best evidence of Molière's "gratitude toward Louis
XIV."[6] Meanwhile, the persecution he suffered at the hands of his
contemporaries was a "humiliation" for the nation, according to
Voltaire in *Vie de Molière*.[7] Similarly, La Harpe writes: "What! At the
moment when you surpassed even your own genius, instead of being
rewarded, you were greeted with persecution!"[8]

Given this legendary history of Molière's relationship to the mon-
arch, and particularly to the royal patronage that was widely under-
stood to have played a central role in his career, it is not surprising
that we find it recalled in the ardent debates that occurred early in

---

6. Jean-François de La Harpe, *Lycée, ou Cours de littérature ancienne et moderne* (Paris,
1799–1805), 8:287.
7. Voltaire, *Oeuvres complètes* (Paris, 1879), 23:119.
8. La Harpe, *Lycée*, 8:209.

the Revolution over government regulation of the theater. After July 1789 the bond between the king and the privileged theater founded in Molière's name was severed when authority over the Comédie-Française—the *maison de Molière*—passed from the Crown's bureau charged with its management to the municipal government of Paris. Later that year spectators decried the interdiction of performances of Marie-Joseph Chénier's historical drama about the Saint Bartholomew's Day massacres, *Charles IX*. Throughout 1790 playwrights, politicians, commentators, and actors voiced their opinions concerning issues pertaining to the theater: free enterprise, dramatic censorship, and the proprietary rights of authors.[9] In addition to Chénier's prolific production of letters and pamphlets defending his cause, Millin de Grandmaison's *La liberté du théâtre* and La Harpe's *Discours sur la liberté du théâtre* (both 1790) were greatly influential in shaping the legislation passed in January 1791 that destroyed all but a few governmental restrictions on theater while eliminating the proprietary claims of theaters on different dramatic genres.

Molière is regularly invoked in the arguments of the theater reformers. Sometimes he is mentioned in passing, as in La Harpe's *Discours* supporting the rights of authors and denouncing the monopolies held by the royal theaters. "It seems to me absurd, incredible, ridiculous," writes La Harpe, "that we should believe twenty men of genius worked for over a century and a half just to nourish the laziness and vanity of a single privileged acting troupe, sole inheritor of their efforts." In the name of liberty, he continues, "all actors must be permitted to perform Racine, Crébillon, Molière, et cetera, just as any publisher is permitted to print them."[1] Chénier, in the course of condemning the subaltern status of actors, reminds his readers of the ignoble treatment accorded Molière, "a great man," who "only narrowly received a burial in France." The celebrated English actor David Garrick, Chénier writes, "was offered a seat in the House of Commons alongside the representatives of the English nation. Molière, in France, would not have been given the post of a churchwarden."[2]

The history of Molière's career is given more prominence in a 1790 pamphlet arguing that, instead of liberating theaters, royal authority over theater should be replaced with strict government regulation. This pamphlet, *Influence de la Révolution sur le Théâtre-Français*, takes the somewhat ambiguous position that Molière owed the perfection of his

9. G. Charles Walton, "*Charles IX* and the French Revolution: Law, Vengeance, and the Revolutionary Uses of History," *European Review of History* 4 (1997): 127–46.
1. Jean-François de La Harpe, *Discours sur la liberté du théâtre, prononcé par M. de la Harpe, le 17 décembre 1790, à la Société des Amis de la Constitution de Paris* (Paris, 1790), 7.
2. Marie-Joseph Chénier, *Courtes réflexions sur l'état civil des comédiens* (Paris, 1789), 7–8.

art not specifically to Louis XIV but to the inspiration provided by the occasions of state theater. The anonymous author argues that, as royal authority over the Comédie-Française (Théâtre de la Nation) was now dissolved, the government should take responsibility for controlling theaters to maintain their dignity and protect the quality of the national stage from unworthy competition. Louis XIV's support for Molière illustrates the benefits of such patronage. The author asserts that Molière's art flourished by virtue of his association with the court. He describes pre-Molièrean comedy as a kind of dramaturgical dark age that amused "the imbecility of the people" with farces performed by unskilled itinerants on "boards in public squares and fairgrounds." The king's military triumphs and the court festivities that were designed to celebrate them provided both the occasion for Molière's art to flourish and the inspiration for him to perfect it: "One was obliged to sing of the conquests and celebrate the conqueror." In glorifying the king, Molière's genius was animated by "a noble ambition." Louis XIV rewarded Molière with protection and preference, defended him against rivals, and conferred on him the honor of organizing his festivals. All this, the author summarizes, "chained Molière to his king."[3]

The ties between Molière and Louis XIV are portrayed far less favorably in another pamphlet by Chénier, *De la liberté du théâtre en France* (1789). While acknowledging that Molière received support from the monarch, the author of *Charles IX* considers Molière's struggle to bring *Tartuffe* to the stage indisputable proof of the necessity for legislation to protect theater from arbitrary censorship and equally arbitrary patronage. Chénier argues that Louis XIV eventually approved public performances of the play only because "Molière, tormented and slandered by a cabal of priests and insulted in church by Bourdaloue, knew how to flatter Louis XIV's pride and to ensure his support by inserting in his play a panegyric of him."[4] Chénier then emphasizes the inconsistency of the monarch's support for Molière. Louis XIV, "weakened by age and worry" and passing his time no longer at spectacles but "between his Jesuit confessor and his Jansenist mistress," neglected Molière shamelessly in the last years of his life. "Thus everything varied in France under the despotism of those aristocrats whose yokes we now shake off. Thus the law changed from one day to the next. The slightest friend of a prince, a favored servant or courtesan, the mistress of a minister or a head clerk, could rudely challenge the law, or more rudely defend it."[5]

The texts I have discussed thus far allow that Molière's artistic production owed something to Louis XIV's patronage. But in an article

---

3. *Influence de la Révolution sur le Théâtre Français: Pétition à ce sujet, adressée à la Commune* (Paris, 1790), 4–5.
4. Marie-Joseph Chénier, *De la liberté du théâtre en France* (Paris, 1789), 10.
5. Ibid., 10–11.

from *Révolutions de Paris* in December 1790 we find an interpreta-
tion of the relationship between the poet and prince that is strikingly
different. In this text Molière neither flourishes under Louis XIV's
patronage nor benefits from his fair-weather protection. Instead, he
is painted as a cunning and audacious rebel, seething with hatred for
the monarch:

> Although Molière was obliged and forced to remain silent in hor-
> rible servitude, liberty seeped from his pores. Forced to praise
> Louis XIV, he wrote detestable prologues and broke the rules of
> versification. He employed platitudes and the most vulgar
> common-places intentionally so as to reveal for posterity the dis-
> gust and horror he had for a task imposed on him by circum-
> stances, his position, and the desire to diffuse his talents and
> ideas. Read *The Impromptu at Versailles* and judge for yourself.
> His cynicism and disdain, shielded by an exquisite and sublime
> talent, found the means to express themselves, even to the point
> of reproaching Louis XIV for puerile vanity, despotism, and the
> domination of nobles. And this he did right to his [Louis's] face,
> making the prince laugh at his own ridiculousness.[6]

This passage is fascinating for its configuration of Molière as a kind
of republican *avant la lettre*, sending a message in a bottle to be fished
out by some future free society capable of deciphering its code.
Instead of willingly serving his king, Molière is depicted here as
antagonistic to him. Never, declares the journalist, has anyone been
"more ahead of his time." It is worth noting that this opinion is strik-
ingly different from one expressed only two years before. In an argu-
ment invoking similar prescience—this time attributed to Molière's
royal patron—Grimod de La Reynière writes that "Louis XIV, who
loved art and recognized it in men, foresaw that Molière would
immortalize his reign. He was consistently his protector and sup-
porter. He stood behind him with all his authority against les *faux-
dévots*, les *précieuses ridicules*, ignorant doctors, and impertinent
boors. Without the resolve of this prince, *Tartuffe* never would have
been performed."[7]

Presenting a portion of the *Révolutions* article under the section
heading "Le courtisan malgré lui," Paul d'Estrée describes the opin-
ion as a "grotesque" interpretation of Molière's works.[8] But neither
d'Estrée nor Marvin Carlson after him provides the full context in
which these remarks appear.[9] They are found in a long footnote to an

6. *Révolutions de Paris*, no. 74 (1790): 457–58n.
7. A.-B.-L. Grimod de La Reynière, *Peu de chose: Hommage à l'Académie de Lyon* (Paris, 1788), 14.
8. Paul d'Estrée, *Le théâtre sous la Terreur* (Paris, 1913), 415–16.
9. Marvin Carlson, *Theater of the French Revolution* (Ithaca, NY, 1966), 84.

article in which the author urges the National Assembly to cease its delay in rendering legislation on the theater. He argues that the government should be deeply concerned with theater because drama has proven to be enormously beneficial to the nation. *Tartuffe* is the case in point: the Jesuits would never have been expelled from France if Molière's chef d'oeuvre had not opened the public's eyes to "the hypocrisy, greed, charlatanism, and cruelty of that terrible sect."[1]

This "grotesque" characterization of Molière as a protorepublican occurs alongside the argument to abolish monarchial authority over the theater. Admittedly, the opinion expressed by the journalist is extreme, but it is not unlike efforts, such as those of Chénier, to represent a Molière whose professional career owed little or nothing to royal patronage. It is no more grotesque to recast Molière as a seething critic of despotism than it is to depict *Tartuffe* as revolutionary literature. The interpretation of *Tartuffe* as a drama effecting a radical change in a corrupt society harmonized with the notion of Molière as foreign to the world in which he produced his works. As for *Tartuffe* in this new context, the record of censored drama in 1794 indicates that all that was needed for approval of the play during the Terror were some "corrections." Revising history, however, is not revising literature. Taking Molière out of the Old Regime would prove easier than taking the Old Regime out of *Tartuffe*.

Revising Literature

"In the course of all these crises," wrote a leading actor of the Comédie-Française about the Terror, "what became of the theater? We sansculottized [*sans-culottisa*] it as we sansculottized everything. Our masterpieces underwent purifying scrutiny. . . . We mutilated Corneille. . . . We even dared to lay a sacrilegious hand on Molière."[2]

As it concerned *Tartuffe*, defiling Molière meant tampering with the denouement of the play. It is common to regard the ending of *Tartuffe* as effected by a deus ex machina. The miserable Orgon, on the verge of losing his home and freedom to the impostor, is saved when the king's officer (the Exempt), accompanying Tartuffe ostensibly for the purpose of arresting Orgon, arrests Tartuffe instead. The king by proxy of his officer is therefore that "character external to the plot who intervenes in extremis to resolve an apparently insoluble intrigue." In fact, the *Dictionnaire encyclopédique du théâtre*, in which this definition appears, refers the reader to *Tartuffe* as the exemplar.[3]

1. *Révolutions de Paris*, no. 74 (1790): 457.
2. Fleury [Joseph Abraham Bénard], *Mémoires de Fleury de la Comédie-Française*, ed. Henri d'Alméras (Paris, 1903), 239–40.
3. *Dictionnaire encyclopédique du théâtre*, ed. Michel Corvin (Paris, 1995), s.v. "deus ex machina."

A few points of plot about this unusual intervention at the end of the play: Orgon technically does not have a case against eviction from his home and arrest. In anticipation of marrying Tartuffe to his daughter, and after banishing his son from his home, Orgon deeds Tartuffe his house and fortune with a contract "en bonne forme [in proper form]" that "on n'y peut rien dire [one cannot question]" (5.4.1757). Furthermore, Orgon, in possession of a strongbox containing secret papers belonging to an exiled friend, entrusts the incriminating coffer to Tartuffe "par un motif de cas de conscience [by a scruple of conscience]" (4.1.1585). Thus Orgon has been cornered by Tartuffe, as he will discover when he tries to order him from his house. To extricate Orgon from this situation will require an extralegal solution. The monarch annuls Tartuffe's contractual claim on Orgon's home and exonerates Orgon for aiding an exile. He does so at the last moment and to the surprise of all. The king's intervention, as La Harpe correctly points out, introduces "a foreign jurisdiction" to the play. The intervention is necessary, however, because Tartuffe "cannot be punished by the law."[4] Modifications to the denouement of the play that were made during the revolutionary period, however, sought to do just that. The inconsistencies that surface in the text as a result of the attempt to replace the sovereign's will with republican justice demonstrate the difficulties inherent in the revolutionary political dream of erasing the past.

As a practical matter, eliminating the king from the denouement of the play is all the more difficult because of the officer's speech in the final moments of the play. Forty lines extol the virtues of the prince. While no definitive evidence exists about alterations made to the text for performance,[5] a few telling indications about changes appear in contemporary sources. Historians of the revolutionary theater have noted Cailhava's remarks that the opening verses of the officer's speech,

> Nous vivons sous un Prince ennemi de la fraude,
> Un Prince dont les yeux se font jour dans les coeurs,
> Et que ne peut tromper tout l'art des imposteurs
>
> [We live under a prince who despises fraud,
> a prince who can read into the hearts of men,
> who is not fooled by the impostor's art] (5.7.1905–7)

---

4. La Harpe, *Lycée*, 8:286.
5. No researcher has yet uncovered manuscript evidence of changes to *Tartuffe* for performance in the revolutionary theater. This is not true for *Phaedra* and *The Misanthrope*. See Antonio Sergi, "*Phèdre* corrigée sous la Révolution," *Dix-huitième siècle* 6 (1974): 153–65; and Jules Janin, "'Le Misanthrope' de Molière en 1793 d'après un exemplaire approprié à cette époque," *Journal des débats politiques et littéraire*, Aug. 12, 1833, 1814–55.

were replaced in performance with the lines

> Il sont passés, ces jours d'injustice et de fraude,
> Où doublement perfide, un calomniateur
> Ravissait à la fois et la vie et l'honneur

> [They have passed, those days of injustice and fraud,
> When a slanderer, doubly perfidious,
> Devoured both life and honor].[6]

Cailhava does not indicate precisely when these changes were introduced, but evidence suggests that they date from late 1793 or early 1794. This is confirmed in a report by a police agent who attended a production of *Tartuffe* in January 1794 at the Théâtre de la République. From the agent's description of the play, it appears that the officer's speech was cut in its entirety; indeed, the play was markedly altered following Tartuffe's entrance in the final scene. According to the report, Tartuffe calls on the officer to arrest Orgon for harboring "unpatriotic [*incivique*] intentions in collusion with the enemies of the Fatherland." This anachronistic denunciation received "most enthusiastic applause" from the public. In the ending's surprise reversal, "a municipal officer" arrests Tartuffe with words, according to the agent, "that should be engraved in the hearts of all true republicans: 'Your villainous schemes are discovered, and no longer does a vile slanderer rule over the lives of true patriots. Follow me!'"[7]

Purely in terms of plot, accusing Orgon of treason is in keeping with Molière's *Tartuffe*; Orgon is culpable of aiding a traitor. What is curious here is the report that, on hearing the perfidious Tartuffe— *the villain of the play*—make his accusations against Orgon, the audience broke out in "enthusiastic applause." Audiences attending a performance of Molière's play without such "corrections" to the text might be impressed with Tartuffe's audacity and cunning, but an act of incriminating Orgon would hardly elicit approval. How can we understand the incongruity in the revolutionary audience's energetic endorsement of the acts of a hypocrite in one moment and of his ruin in the next? In part, this incongruity may reflect the exceptional logic of the revolutionary government after the Convention suspended the constitution in October 1793. The law lost its authority in favor of "the circumstantial necessity of arbitrary violence against the enemies of liberty."[8] The audience endorses Tartuffe's accusations

---

6. Jean-François Cailhava d'Estendoux, *Etudes sur Molière* (Paris, an X [1802]), quoted in d'Estrée. *Théâtre sous la Terreur*, 8, and Carlson, *Theater of the French Revolution*, 158.
7. Report of 13 nivôse II (Jan. 2, 1794), in *Paris pendant la Terreur: Rapports des agents secrets du Ministre de l'Intérieur*, ed. Pierre Caron (Paris, 1910–64), 2:143–44.
8. François Furet, "Gouvernement révolutionnaire," in *Dictionnaire critique de la Révolution française: Institutions et créations*, ed. François Furet and Mona Ozouf (Paris, 1992), 241.

against Orgon in the name of revolutionary justice aimed above all to punish the enemies of the state. Tartuffe's arrest by "a municipal officer" was applauded for the same crime of treason. The audience's reception of *Tartuffe* in this instance seems similarly to have been ruled by "circumstantial necessity"—in other words, not by fascination or disgust with the vile behavior of Tartuffe, or by amusement and pity for Orgon's plight, but by the enjoyment of an abstract application of acts of denunciation and arrest.

I have noted that La Harpe points out that Tartuffe, having committed no crime, can only be punished by the exceptional measures at the disposal of a king. During the Terror the revolutionary government similarly displayed extralegal powers to punish "vile slanderers" for crimes against "true patriots." We might pause here to consider this homology. "Under the Old Regime," writes François Furet, "the idea of public safety came from the absolute authority of the king; under the Revolution, it supported a dictatorship employed in the name of the people. The two regimes were fueled by comparable situations or identical pretexts. They have in common putting public usefulness above the law and accepting the arbitrary actions of the state as the price for its efficacy."[9] In this sense, even these sizable revisions to the denouement of *Tartuffe* do not effect a real transformation of the terms by which Tartuffe will be punished in the absence of a prince. The next clues to appear about revisions to the text surface in 1798. Here law is emphasized as the principle by which Tartuffe is judged, but again the Old Regime retains its power over the text.

According to a 1798 article in Grimod de La Reynière's *Censeur dramatique*, "for the last five years, these verses [the denouement of *Tartuffe*] have been altered in ten or twelve different ways. In 1794 it was the intervention of the Revolutionary Tribunal, two words that were strangely discordant with Molière's verses." This confirms that it had been the practice to cut the officer's speech in its entirety. Grimod continues: "These days it is customary to remove only the first twenty-eight verses of the officer's speech, for which are substituted eight or ten verses that signify nothing, but in which it is the law that does everything, and just in time."[1]

Even if "only" the first twenty-eight verses are eliminated (suggesting for Grimod an improvement over previous cuts), replacing the authority of the monarch with the law remains troubling for the editor of the *Censeur dramatique*. Grimod argues that the law cannot intervene against Tartuffe because "what Molière gives a king to say cannot be transferred to the law, as it is a metaphysical entity that can neither 'pardon an offense' [5.7.1936] nor 'remember one's

9. Ibid., 242.
1. *Censeur dramatique*, 30 ventôse an VI (Mar. 20, 1798), 148.

virtues' [5.7.1943].”[2] He also takes issue with replacing *roi* with *loi*
because, if the latter noun is used, "one must not, in the twelve verses
that follow [5.7.1932–43], use the pronoun *il*, which is repeated four
times, as it does not agree in gender with the feminine *loi*.”[3]

Now, the *il/loi* disagreement is glaring in French, so naturally it
elicits a response from an attentive reader. The correspondent
writes—referring to the first time the pronoun appears in the speech
(5.7.1932)—that *il* was indeed used, but only once and only to refer
to Tartuffe, not to the law. This was made clear onstage by the actor,
who as he spoke used a gesture to indicate Tartuffe. The editor of the
Censeur dramatique responded to the reader that, no, the author of
the article had been sitting in the front row and had distinctly heard
the masculine pronoun used repeatedly, as he reported in his article,
to refer to the law.[4]

What is happening here? Did the actors substitute *elle* for *il* as
necessary in the officer's speech? Did the auditor's familiarity with
the play make *il* an anticipation instead of a reality? Is the power of
an expurgated prince such that an *elle* is spoken and an *il* is heard?
Moreover, why is Grimod concerned, on the one hand, by the
thoughtful question of the nature of the law and, on the other, by a
grammatical annoyance? Perhaps these two issues are not unre-
lated. A closer look at the officer's speech shows that indeed, if one
eliminates the first twenty-eight lines, the speech begins by refer-
ring to the character Tartuffe: "Oui, de tous vos papiers, dont il
[Tartuffe] se dit le maître" (5.7.1932). The remaining four pro-
nouns refer to the monarch (5.7.1933, 1934, 1938, 1943). More-
over, there are two objects (*lui*), one referring to Tartuffe (5.7.1935)
and the other to the prince (5.7.1942). In short, the last eighteen
verses of this speech are innately susceptible to deictic confusion—
a referential disorder that the attempt to erase the king from the
speech only exacerbated and that the actor's physical gesture failed
to overcome. The deeper sense of this linguistic confusion is sug-
gested by the intriguing juxtaposition of Grimod's two seemingly
discrete complaints. The law, that stubbornly abstract "metaphysi-
cal entity," is incapable of remembering and forgiving, as Grimod
correctly points out. To endow the law with volition—as happens
when the prince is replaced with the law—is disturbing because to
do so personifies the law and thus invokes the potentially arbitrary
will of an individual. The ungrammatical *il* is the trace of that indi-
vidual expunged from the speech. The monarch is amputated from
the play, but he haunts the denouement—like a phantom limb—in
the form of the pronoun *il*.

2. Ibid., 148–49.
3. Ibid., 147–48. *Il* is actually repeated five times, in 5.7.1932, 1933, 1934, 1938, and 1943.
4. *Censeur dramatique*, 20 germinal an VI (Apr. 9, 1798), 261–63.

The alterations to the denouement of *Tartuffe* thus failed to perform the shift from monarchial intervention to republican jurisprudence. Some implications of this failure are suggested by an interesting exchange of letters in the *Journal des théâtres* toward the end of 1798. The debate begins with a letter from a reader who argues that the theater, while it can inspire spectators to hate vice and love virtue, has no business with criminal behavior and should not attempt to address something that only the law can properly punish. Comedy should unmask vice in all its seductive colors, but "where the authority of the law begins, there ends the influence of the playwright."[5] Another reader countered that exposing crimes, not just socially undesirable behavior, is precisely what Molière does in *Tartuffe*. Tartuffe's scheming is not just a passing vice, he insists, but a crime. This is proven by the fact (and here the circular reasoning is apparent) that the *law* intervenes at the end of the play: "Taking one of his best comedies, perhaps his greatest, *Tartuffe*, I see not merely a harmless vice or an amusing rascal but an infamous hypocrite, ungrateful toward his benefactor, a wife seducer and a thief. Molière did not stop where 'the authority of the law begins,' because the denouement is achieved by the intervention of this same authority. One cannot deny that Tartuffe is a man for hanging."[6]

In a final counterresponse, the first author notes that Tartuffe is not, in fact, a criminal, even if his schemes merit "universal animadversion." The correspondent points out that Tartuffe has the law on his side. The intervention of the prince at the end of the play is therefore a *perversion* of the law. The monarch abused the law in the name of moral correction:

> The government, aware of [Tartuffe's] nefarious machinations, appalled by the horrible abuses of confidence perpetrated by this scoundrel, this traitor to those who gave him board, transgressed the law in order to punish this monster on moral grounds, and with a *lettre de cachet* removed him from society. This is the truth of it, and I will add that Molière has always been reproached for this denouement and with good reason: the law has no business resolving a comedy.[7]

On the one hand, therefore, we have an argument that recognizes the indelibility of the Old Regime in the text: the title character is not a criminal; he is guilty of a social vice, and only with the special powers at the disposal of a king—the *lettre de cachet*—can he be punished for the public good. On the other hand, the authority of a new sovereignty reconceptualizes Tartuffe's behavior as criminal and thus

5. *Journal des théâtres*, 11 frimaire an VII (Dec. 1, 1798), 6.
6. *Journal des théâtres*, 21 frimaire an VII (Dec. 11, 1798), 46.
7. *Journal des théâtres*, 23 frimaire an VII (Dec. 13, 1798), 55.

punishable by law. I suggest that if Molière was "rewritten," if revolutionaries succeeded in erasing Old Regime authority from his legacy, they did so in instances like this criminalization of Tartuffe. Not surprisingly, the same correspondent adds that *Tartuffe* is not the only example of criminality in Molière's plays. One need only look at the scheming valets and eloping lovers to see crime everywhere: scams, thefts, even kidnappings—all of them punishable by law. The representation of crime, the correspondent is saying, is all over Molière's work. In other words, Molière is no longer a painter of the social trespasses of the Old Regime that were once disciplined at the discretion of a monarch; he is now the denouncer of Old Regime crimes, punishable by the rule of law.

Conclusion

To conclude, I wish to reentangle the revisions of both history and literature, emphasizing them again as complementary processes. Rewriting the history of Molière's career appears more coherent than rewriting his literature. The paradox, forged by the events of his career, that Molière was powerful yet persecuted was exploited by revolutionaries to appropriate for the new nation this premier figure of Old Regime culture. His close alliance to the monarchy might have troubled his successful relocation to the shifting mosaic of revolutionary approbation. But in the incoherencies of Louis XIV's sponsorship, in the interstices where Molière was persecuted by his contemporaries, the revolutionaries found what they needed to rewrite an important aspect of the history of his career by aligning him with republican ideals. In opinions expressed in debates about government legislation of the theater, this ran the gamut from moderate viewpoints that acknowledged some association between the genius of Molière's art and the patronage of Louis XIV, to a more extreme view in which Molière not only owed nothing to his time but wrote his plays in seething anger over his forced servitude to the monarch. However coherent these revisions of history may appear, the revisions to *Tartuffe* tell another story. While the history of Molière's career becomes the means by which to illustrate the abuses of the Old Regime and to celebrate the authority of the law, his masterpiece *Tartuffe* refuses to cooperate in this construct. Here, literary revision exposes the fragility in the reinterpretations of the past that historical revisionism aims to achieve.

WILMA NEWBERRY

The New Spanish *Tartuffe*†

Ever since his creation in 1664 Tartuffe, Molière's monstrous caricature of saintliness, has had a turbulent existence because there have always been people who are antagonized by the satirical comedy, of which he is the title character, directed against hypocritically pious men who use religion for profit. *Le Tartuffe* was first performed in a three-act version before Louis XIV in Versailles, but it provoked a scandal among ultrareligious Parisians who soon forced the King to forbid future performances. Molière persistently continued to plead for the right to perform his play in public, and in order to soothe the opposition inserted many lines which served to stress that the play was not an attack against sincerely religious people. In spite of the fact that Molière was able to convince many influential men that his play was not pernicious, it was again prohibited when the five-act version called *L'Imposteur* was performed in 1667. It was not until 1669 that the ban was finally removed.

The barriers against the incorporation of translations and adaptations of Molière's play into the Spanish repertory were even more formidable than in France because the Inquisition guarded against any public performance which even indirectly criticized the Catholic religion. Cándido María Trigueros' adaptation of *Le Tartuffe* entitled *El gazmoño o Juan de Buen Alma* produced a scandal when it was performed in Sevilla about 1769.[1] In 1777 when Pablo de Olavide, a Sevillian intellectual who was imprudent in religious matters, was tried in an inquisitorial court,[2] one of the misdeeds of which he was accused was his involvement in the production of Trigueros' adaptation of Molière's comedy. When the play was performed in Madrid in this same year by Eusebio Ribera's company in El Teatro de la Cruz it enraged many spectators and was immediately denounced to the

---

† From *Hispania* 55.4 (December 1972): 922–25. Reprinted by permission of *Hispania*, American Association of Teachers of Spanish and Portuguese.

1. I was surprised that a whole century passed between the time the play was written and the first Spanish production. Emilio Cotarelo y Mori explains this by saying that in general Spaniards preferred their own Golden Age plays and even preferred other French playwrights to Molière at that time. He believes that Molière's humor lost much in translation, and adds that since French was often the cultured Spaniard's second language most Spaniards who were likely to be attracted to Molière could enjoy his plays in the original. "Traductores castellanos de Molière," *Extracto del Homenaje a Menéndez y Pelayo* (Madrid, 1899).

   Two articles by Marcelin Defourneaux may be consulted for more complete information about the early Spanish translations of Molière's plays: "Une Adaptation Inédite du 'Tartuffe': *El gazmoño ou Juan de Buen Alma* de Cándido María Trigueros," and "Molière et L'Inquisition Espagnole" both in *Bulletin hispanique* 64 (January-June 1962).

2. A very interesting biography of this man has been written: Marcelin Defourneaux, *Pablo de Olavide* (Paris, 1959).

Inquisition which forced the play to close, even though it had been cleared by the religious and secular authorities prior to its performance.

In 1779 Trigueros' adaptation, under the title *La hipocresía castigada o Juan de Buenalma*, was placed on the Index of books prohibited even for those who were authorized to read proscribed books. In face of this opposition, the play was neglected for many years.

Although the French domination of the years 1808–1814 is generally regarded as an inglorious period in Spanish history, one of its fortunate by-products was the abolishment of the Inquisition. Of course the intellectual climate during this period favored the performance of Molière's plays. In 1810 José Marchena's translation entitled *El hipócrita* was well-received by the public and was published the following year. During this time a copy of the play found its way to Peru where it was denounced in 1818 when it was performed in Lima. The director of the theater excused himself by saying that it had been printed and performed in Madrid, not taking into account that this had occurred during the French occupation. Of course *El hipócrita* was then added to the list of forbidden plays in Lima. Finally, Riego's revolution in 1820 ended this type of censorship in Peru and saved *Tartuffe*.

In the Madrid theater season of 1969–70 a version of Molière's play again became the object of excitement, discussion and polemics, but this time there was nothing innocent about the intentions behind the production as Molière and his early Spanish adapters tried to maintain. The new version, entitled *El Tartufo*, translated by Enrique Llovet and staged by Adolfo Marsillach, is a direct attack against Opus Dei, and additions were made so that there is no possibility of mistaking the symbolism already contained in the original which makes it the perfect vehicle for criticism of Opus Dei.

Probably by coincidence, the première of *El Tartufo* took place just before Franco's October 1969 cabinet changes which gave technocrats who are associated with Opus Dei, a Roman Catholic organization of laymen and priests, pre-eminence in Spanish politics. *Time* magazine comments in discussing the new Cabinet:

> Opus Dei (the Work of God) might also be called Octopus Dei. Most of its lay members are professional men who pledge to strengthen their Christian lives by improving the world around them. They accomplish this in part by appointing fellow members to key government and commercial posts. Opus Dei adherents are known to control almost all of Spain's banking and a large share of its communications media. "They have the frying pan by the handle and the handle as well," runs a Spanish expression, meaning that members have both power and the will to use it. (November 7, 1969, p. 34)

Criticism of Opus Dei's extensive involvement in government and business through its members is evidently condoned, perhaps because the Falangists are among its most violent opponents. However, many Spaniards, unaccustomed to hearing public criticism of the government, seem to be somewhat amazed that *El Tartufo* has been permitted. Surely, no Spanish play within anyone's memory has been the object of such interest, as evidenced by the long run to capacity audiences and the huge crowd which packed into an auditorium on December 10, 1969 to attend a *Coloquio* entitled *Tartufo, personaje contemporáneo*, which consisted in a very open discussion of the play.[3]

During the colloquium, Jesús Aguirre, a Jesuit priest, suggested that the people should be concerned about the possible reason that the play has been allowed to continue. His tentative answer was that "they" have so much power that now it no longer matters, and he evinced his own concern about this possibility.

Although this was not mentioned during the colloquium, in Llovet's version of the play there is a perfect answer to the question of why it has been permitted. After the scene in which Orgón's family unsuccessfully attempts to drive Tartufo from the house, he says the following:

> Ya sé que este no es el momento de las lecciones. Pero, por otra parte, hermano . . . "¡Qué bien que se nos discuta y combata! Porque eso: a), engendra esfuerzo y sacrificio; b), hace disminuir el favor público, que es siempre un mal y pone a la opinión en cautela contra nuestra obra; c), obliga a hacer mejor las cosas . . . Único mal: a), el que ellos se hacen; b), la mala pasión que despierta en nosotros y en nuestros amigos. . . ."[4]

The damaging effects of censorship upon a country's intellectual life were brought into sharp focus during the colloquium. Marsillach said that he envied the liberty with which Aguirre was able to speak, and even suggested the possibility that the frank discussion taking place would cause the play to be discontinued: "Si *Tartufo* tiene una vida larga como espero incluso después de este coloquio. . . ." There had been rumors that the play would be stopped. Living theater existed in Madrid two years ago, according to one member of the audience, but it is not permitted now.

Marsillach assured the spectators that he had made no concession to censorship, but then one spectator accused him of playing a game

---

3. The members of the panel were Adolfo Marsillach, Jesús Aguirre, José Monleón (drama critic), and Jean Poutet (Philosophy Professor at the Liceo Francés).
4. Quotation marks are placed around this passage in the script, so this may be assumed to be a statement made by an Opus Dei member. Enrique Llovet, *El Tartufo* (Madrid, 1970), p. 62.

to make it appear that it is possible to criticize in Spain. However, another man remarked that perhaps there has been a change. Aguirre insisted upon stressing the fact that the play represents only "una crítica parcial."

Regardless of the venturous feeling accompanying the production of the play, and the generally discreet way in which the publicity was handled, especially early in the season as if the climate were being tested, Llovet has been much more fortunate than Molière's earlier Spanish imitators. The play continued all season, even though there were some hostile spectators, and it has been published.

Compared to some of the earlier Spanish versions in which names are changed and important scenes and even characters are omitted or transformed, Enrique Llovet's rendition is very close to the original. Llovet describes his attitude as follows: "Esta versión—y este cáustico y entusiasta montaje de Adolfo Marsillach—no es fiel, ni siquiera respetuosa, con 'la letra' de Molière. Nuestra devoción al autor está en tratar su 'Tartufo' como si hubiese sido escrito anoche. Claro está que es muy delicada la tarea de actualizar a los clásicos. Pero el 'Tartufo' parece tan claro que no temo haber traicionado los enfoques del gran creador de la comedia moderna."[5]

The most important single addition which Llovet has made to Molière's play is the song "Los ejecutivos" which the actors sing as they approach the stage at the beginning of the play and as they leave it at the end. This song provides the key for the understanding of the production, as it alerts the spectators to the fact that although they are to see a classical comedy they must also understand it in terms of the present.

> El mundo nunca ha sido para todo el mundo,
> mas hoy al parecer es de un señor,
> que en una escalerita de aeropuerto,
> cultiva un maletín, pero ninguna flor.
>
> Sonriente y afeitado para siempre,
> trajina para darnos la ilusión,
> de un cielo en tecnicolor donde
> muy poquitos aprendan a jugar al golf.
>
> ¡Ay, qué vivos,
> son los ejecutivos,
> qué vivos que son!
> Del sillón al avión,
> del avión al salón,
> del harén al Edén,

5. This statement is part of the "Autocrítica" which appears in the above-mentioned publication of Llovet's play, p. 5–6.

> siempre tienen razón,
> y, además, tienen la sartén . . .
> La sartén por el mango . . .
> ¡y el mango también!

The other stanzas repeat the same general ideas in different words, followed by a repetition of the refrain.

The translation of Molière's text (Llovet uses the term *trasladado* rather than *traducido* to describe what he has done) is, for the most part, a natural present-day prose rendition of Molière's verse. Comparatively few lines are added and nothing important is omitted. The most consistent change effected is Llovet's use of words which clearly allude to technocrats. For example, this is part of Orgón's enthusiastic description of Tartufo:

> ¡Te encantaría conocerle, estoy seguro! . . . ¡Te fascinaría! . . . Verás . . . Es un hombre que . . . Bueno . . . Una clase de ser . . . ¡Fenomenal! . . . Analítico . . . Crítico . . . Ejecutivo . . . Tranquilo . . . Eficiente . . . Quien sigue su ejemplo, adquiere la paz de los seres superiores y aprende a mirar a los demás como si fueran basura . . . A mí me ha convertido en otra persona . . . Ya no siento ninguna debilidad . . . No tengo amigos . . . A nada me siento encadenado . . . Ya se pueden morir mi hermano, mis hijos, mi madre y mi mujer, si hace falta, que lo soportaré con toda tranquilidad. (p. 21–22)[6]

And throughout the play there are reminders of the intention behind the new translation. For example, Dorina states that Orgón behaved like a man during the Civil War, but afterward . . . and leaves the sentence unfinished. Mariana asks what can be done about a father who was born to be a dictator, which, after all, is a fairly exact translation of the French "Contre un père absolu que veux-tu que je fasse?" (p. 657) and is an excellent example of the uncanny appropriateness of Molière's comedy for the situation in Spain.[7] Orgón states that Tartufo devised a perfect plan for the development of his home, which refers to the Spanish Plan de Desarrollo which is associated with Opus Dei and especially with Laureano López Rodó, an Opus Dei member who is the Minister for Economic Planning in Franco's new Cabinet. Dorina sarcastically tells Mariana that Tartufo

---

6. The French reads: "Mon frère, vous seriez charmé de le connoître, / Et vos ravissements ne prendroient point de fin. / C'est un homme . . . qui, . . . ha! un homme . . . un homme enfin. / Qui suit bien ses leçons goûte une paix profonde, / Et comme du fumier regarde tout le monde. / Oui, je deviens tout autre avec son entretien; / Il m'enseigne à n'avoir affection pour rien, / De toutes amitiés il détache mon âme; / Et je verrois mourir frère, enfants, mère et femme, / Que je m'en soucierois autant que cela."

7. A strange coincidence is that in Molière's play Monsieur Loyal, who carries Tartuffe's message of eviction to the family, states that he has served in his official capacity for forty years, and Opus Dei was created in 1928, forty years before Llovet translated the play.

would be a good match for her—after all, with a little luck he will soon be "presidente de esto . . . , director general de lo otro, consejero de lo más allá . . ." (p. 37). She also tells her that they must "organizar la resistencia" (p. 45), and the compromising papers, more specifically than in Molière's original, are "listas de personas de la oposición, octavillas (the form in which political verse is written in Spain), y manifiestos" (p. 81).

Especially Tartufo's own conversation, regardless of the subject of his discourse, is sprinkled with technocratic jargon. He will be in the prison "coordinando la distribución de las limosnas" (p. 49), he has only one guideline "la idoneidad recíproca equilibrada" (p. 65), and he will know how to administrate Orgón's money "con la competencia de un ejecutivo de nuestro tiempo" (p. 66).

Adolfo Marsillach's staging and direction often seem to invade the field which playwrights reserve for themselves, because he adds a few scenes and even inserts some lines. In the colloquium Marsillach explained how he understands the characters. Orgón, for Marsillach, is not Tartufo's victim because Orgón needs Tartufo and even invents him. Orgón is a despot, and justifies his tyrannical power over his family through Tartufo who seems to be a slave at the beginning of the play. Each member of the family represents a different possible attitude and course of action. Dorina, the voice of the people, speaks the truth. Elmira attempts to negotiate, Cleante reasons and tries to mediate, Mariana wishes to escape, Valerio comes from the outside world and never completely understands what is happening. Of course most of these character interpretations are already clear in Molière's original, but it was also stressed in the colloquium by other participants that Tartuffe's motivation has always been open to interpretation.

CHERYL KENNEDY McFARREN

Mnouchkine's *Tartuffe:*
Unleashing the Text's Potential[†]

A Director's Prerogative

The work of a director presupposes making choices. From choosing a script on which to work, to casting actors in roles, to blocking the characters' movement patterns, to approving scenic and costume designs, to coaching actors in their development of characters, the director selects from a vast array of possibilities. The options them-

† From *On-Stage Studies* 21 (1998): 87–112. Reprinted with the permission of the Department of Theatre and Dance, The University of Colorado at Boulder.

selves are evoked by the text and derive from a variety of sources: the director's education and training, creativity, historical research, political sensibility, as well as from contact with other productions and other theatre practitioners. For every choice made, potential choices are refused. Therefore, a production's choices always illuminate the director's bias vis-à-vis the script as much as—and in some cases more than—they express the play's meanings. Indeed, in contemporary practice, the director not only unearths meaning *in* the play; the director brings meaning *to* the play.

We may view the staging of a play, then, not only as a site in which meaning is constructed, but also, consequently, as a site in which meaning is contended. Indeed, the text as "monument" has been demystified in the postmodern world, and the stage provides a meaningful location wherein even canonized classics are *re*read. In the contemporary theatre, as James Carmody asserts, "The script . . . need not be seen as a writing that exists before the performance but, instead, as a writing that is completed in performance."[1] To the traditional question, "What constitutes a 'faithful' representation of a classic script?" the contemporary stage responds, "By 'faithful,' what do you mean? On our stages, any production which completes the text—that is, any production that communicates the playwright's message to its audience—is a 'faithful' one."[2]

In what follows, I will discuss the choices made by France's Théâtre du Soleil, under the direction of Ariane Mnouchkine, for their 1995–6 staging of *Tartuffe*, arguing that the production emerges as an extraordinarily faithful one. Ultimately, this production's explicit political rereading not only delivers Molière's text, but also, by finding a context oddly analogous to that of the seventeenth century original, enables the audience to experience the play's disturbing subtext.

Locating the World of the Play

Molière specifies that "the scene is in Paris, in the home of Orgon."[3] Mnouchkine takes this direction selectively, as a point of departure. The production places the scene in the courtyard of Orgon's house, yes. But the city of residence? *Le Monde* states, "Ariane Mnouchkine's mise en scène has transported the play to the banks of the Mediterranean."[4] The *London Times Literary Supple-*

---

1. James Carmody, *Rereading Molière: Mise en Scène from Antoine to Vitez* (Ann Arbor: U of Michigan P, 1993) 11.
2. Clearly, this statement rests on the assumption that each playwright *has* a message.
3. Molière, "Le Tartuffe ou L'Imposteur," *Oeuvres Complètes* (Paris: Éditions de Seuil, 1962) 255. Unless noted otherwise, all translations are mine.
4. Olivier Schmitt, "Le Tartuffe: théâtre de guerre contre tous les fondamentalismes," rev. of *Tartuffe*, dir. Ariane Mnouchkine, *Le Monde* 7 Nov. 1995, online, Lexis-Nexis.

ment also notes the evocative ambiguity of the setting: "Ariane Mnouchkine's modern-dress production of *Tartuffe* is set somewhere between North Africa and Pakistan, in a space lined with carpets and cushions, and bordered by railings. This is the home of Orgon."[5] *Western European Stages* comments, "There is no hint of the French *Grand Siècle*, except for the wrought iron gate enclosing Orgon's domain, a replica of that of Paris' Palais de Justice."[6] *Theatre Journal* adds:

> Mnouchkine situates the drama in the inner courtyard of an earth-toned Mediterranean villa, walls laden with bougainvillea, crickets relentlessly pulsing, and an upstage entrance marked by a magnificent wrought-iron gate. Representatives of the outside world—in skull caps, flowing robes, and veils—penetrate through this opening in hysterical flourishes.[7]

As designed by Guy-Claude François, the stage represents an enclosed courtyard with a "Middle Eastern" feel.[8] The presence of a "rusting" gate upstage symbolically includes European (Parisian) cultural influences; in fact, while the decor most overtly represents an Orientalized world,

> we are in a land of shared cultures. The decor has Christian, Islamic and Judaic features. This could be southern Spain in the 16th century, when Moorish, Christian and Jewish civilizations mingled with and fertilized one another; or Egypt or somewhere in the Levant, where the architecture shows Venetian, possibly French, influence. We are in the forecourt of a prosperous but somewhat neglected house: the once elegant tall iron railings are in poor repair and the gate is rusting badly.[9]

The side walls of the courtyard and its cupboards and doors, according to *The Observer*, "offer a bleached scribble of texts and images from the great faiths that have, up to now, lived together on this spot."[1] Suggesting several plausible locales for the play's action, the stage setting *evokes* more than it definitively *signifies*.

Although we may accept this choice to relocate the action of the play as one that completes the writing of the text, we must nevertheless consider how spectators might read the written/spoken text

5. Dominique Goy-Blanquet, "Molière: TARTUFFE," *Times Literary Supplement* 18 Aug. 1995: 16.
6. Rosette C. Lamont, "Tartuffe and the Imams," *Western European Stages* 7.3 (1996): 13–16.
7. Judith G. Miller, "Tartuffe," rev. of *Tartuffe*, *Theatre Journal* 48 (1996): 370–1.
8. Lamont 13.
9. John Peter, "Power Points," rev. of *Tartuffe*, *Sunday Times*, 12 Nov. 1995, online, Lexis-Nexis.
1. Michael Ratcliffe, "Paris Theatre: Molière's Mullahs," rev. of *Tartuffe*, *Observer* 10 March 1996: 10.

through the visual elements provided by the production. In other words, how might scenically transposing *Tartuffe* affect an audience? First, Mnouchkine effectively destabilizes the familiar world represented by *Tartuffe*. François's set alienates, in the Brechtian sense; an audience attending *Tartuffe* likely anticipates seeing the seventeenth-century home of a member of the Parisian *haute bourgeoisie*.[2] By defamiliarizing the location, the set calls attention to its denial of the audience's expectations. The world (the play) represented is not one they *know implicitly*. The set thus engenders a critical awareness in the audience, permitting them to weigh the issues presented and make judgments about the play and about their society.

Second, the appearance of the stage affords a multiplicity of interpretations. Where indeed does Orgon live? In a relatively distant place like Pakistan or the West Bank? Or nearer to the audience's frame of reference, in the former French colony of Algeria? Or nearer still, within a Muslim community in France? In fact, the design suggests the ubiquitousness of the *intégristes*, Muslim fundamentalists, perhaps playing upon the French audience's naturalized discomfort with and/or fear of a stereotypical Oriental Other.

Setting the play among the *intégristes* allows an audience to connect the doctrine of Tartuffe and his followers, including his host Orgon, with contemporary militant Islamist fanaticism. Reactionary intolerance, like Madame Pernelle's, begets violence. She slaps her maid,[3] displaying a volatility which has in it the seeds of the Ayatollah issuing a death warrant for Salman Rushdie, or of *intégristes* murdering Algerian pop (raï) singer Cheb Hasni in 1994. In fact, Hasni's music, emanating from a merchant's boom-box outside the gate, serves as the production's first clear statement that the action of the play takes place in our era.[4] The visual elements of Mnouchkine's production present an exotic, sensual and potentially menacing world, one that is recognizable to its audience as a stereotype, but one that remains unknown in its specificity. The imprecision of the locale thus allows Théâtre du Soleil to play with and against the audience's familiarity with Molière's text.

Tartuffe: Everything Old Is New Again

The theme [attracted me to Molière's comedy]! It's a play which, every ten years, becomes actual . . . That's the point of a real classic masterpiece . . . If you believe what Molière says in the

---

2. James F. Gaines, *Social Structures in Molière's Theatre* (Columbus: U of Ohio P, 1984) 200.
3. In the Mnouchkine production, Madame Pernelle is accompanied not by a single maid (Flipote), but by two women, Flippe and Pote. Here, to underscore the power and menace of Madame Pernelle, Mnouchkine cast the same three women who played the Furies in her production of *The Forsworn City*, running in repertory with *Tartuffe* (Lamont 15).
4. Lamont 14.

play you see that it's a war play; Molière describes a state of war, a sort of hostage situation. He shows that the house, the family, is taken as hostage not only by a man but by a movement. In Molière's time the movement was La Compagnie du Saint-Sacrement but now it happens in other countries, not completely in our country. It's the same though, exactly the same.[5]

There are at least three issues in *Tartuffe* that Mnouchkine's production problematizes. First, like the play performed in the seventeenth-century by Molière's company, the Troupe de Monsieur, Mnouchkine's production foregrounds the issue of religious hypocrisy. However, in the Théâtre du Soleil production, Tartuffe and his followers espouse fundamentalist doctrine of the Islamic—not Christian—persuasion.[6] Second, the production enables a pointed examination of patriarchal power structures as well as the location and role of women within those structures. Finally, in its fifth act, the production questions the beneficence of the King's Officer and, in so doing, contemporary governmental justice. Each one of these problematic issues will be examined separately in the context of Mnouchkine's production choices. Collectively, these issues exist in the text, lying beneath the comic surface of Molière's play. It is Mnouchkine's production, however, that shows us these issues anew.

Fundamentalism and the Performance of Faith

Without question, Molière satirizes religious hypocrisy in *Tartuffe*; even Tartuffe's name means "hypocrite." Scholars generally acknowledge the Compagnie du Saint-Sacrement, a group of casuist spiritual directors with great access to Louis XIV, as the targets of this satire. As scholar J. L. Kasparek states, "Molière had excellent reasons for looking at the Compagnie with the satirist's eye. The organization developed rapidly away from whatever ideals first motivated it, becoming spies and moral censors with their own police system."[7] It

---

5. Ariane Mnouchkine, "Ariane Mnouchkine," *In Contact with the Gods? Directors Talk Theatre*, ed. Maria M. Delgado and Paul Heritage (New York: St. Martin's Press, 1996) 175–190.

6. Interestingly, the play quite naturally affords this shift of faith due to Molière's use of "le Ciel" (Heaven) for any reference to divinity. The use of the name "dieu" (God), which would have definitively branded Molière a heretic in his day, would have necessitated substituting the name "Allah" in the Théâtre du Soleil production. Mnouchkine makes clear that, even in relocating the action of the play, Théâtre du Soleil did not alter the script: "It's strange but only yesterday people came out of the play and asked me, 'Did you publish your adaptation of *Tartuffe*?' And I say, 'What adaptation?' And they reply, 'Well, the one we just saw.' And I have to tell them, 'There is no adaptation. This is it. It's Molière's text'" (qtd. in Delgado 182). We know that "Molière's text" went through two incarnations (1664 and 1667) before Louis XIV accepted a third version in 1669. Since neither of the two earlier versions is extant, we can say with certainty that the text to which Mnouchkine refers is that of 1669.

7. Jerry Lewis Kasparek, *Molière's Tartuffe and the Traditions of Roman Satire* (Chapel Hill: U of North Carolina P, 1977) 6.

is important to note that Molière's play does not condemn *faith*, but rather the *performance* of faith, as reprehensible. For instance, Tartuffe's performs his entrance (3.2) once he notices Dorine watching. Even Orgon is capable of characterizing Tartuffe's shows of piety, though he fails to recognize their hollowness:[8]

> He used to come into our church each day
> And humbly kneel nearby[9] and start to pray.
> He'd draw the eyes of everybody there
> By the deep fervor of his heartfelt prayer;
> He'd sigh and weep, and sometimes with a sound
> Of rapture he would bend and kiss the ground.[1]

Tartuffe's dramatic ardor, his sighs, his "humble" kissing of the ground all demonstrate his zeal *to Orgon*; these shows are directed at him.

Since faith is not mocked, the religious issue the text calls into question is neither Christianity nor Islam, but rather fundamentalism. Appearing "holier than thou" becomes imperative to the point that Orgon would sacrifice his family for his fundamentalist beliefs. He says, "My soul's been freed / From earthly loves, and every human tie: / My mother, children, brother, and wife could die / And I'd not feel a single moment's pain."[2] Moreover, for the satire to succeed, an audience must be able to distinguish faith from fundamentalism. Detachment from worldly concerns may be a positive practice in moderation, but blind adherence to any set of precepts poses significant problems for an individual or a society. Apparently Mnouchkine's audience, unlike Molière's, understood the distinction, due (perhaps in part) to the insistence of the Press on this point: "This show passionately denounces the yoke of fundamentalism of all faiths;"[3] "Fundamentalism as mass manipulation is Mnouchkine's target here;"[4] "When Tartuffe arrives . . . preceded by the offstage roar of a fundamentalist mob, you are in the past, the present and a possible future all at once."[5]

Although the production pokes fun at fundamentalism rather than at a particular faith, Mnouchkine's choice of the Islamic faith as the

---

8. The fact that Orgon fails to pick up on Tartuffe's chicanery is puzzling. It seems that he has been, metaphorically, seduced. The excessive religiosity directed at him feeds his narcissism. In *Men and Masks*, Lionel Gossman alludes to the collusion of Tartuffe and Orgon: "Those who are duped by impostors are themselves impostors in their own way . . . Dupe and deceiver—and which is which?—are seen to be partners in the same enterprise" (Baltimore: John Hopkins UP, 1963) 101.

9. Line 284 of the original French reads "Tout vis-à-vis de moi se mettre à deux genoux" or "Directly across from me he got down on both knees." Molière emphasizes Tartuffe's physical placement, showing that the charlatan contrives to become Orgon's reflection. This image is sadly lost in Wilbur's fine verse translation.

1. Molière, "Tartuffe," trans. Richard Wilbur, *The Misanthrope and Tartuffe* (1954; New York: Harcourt, 1965): 187.

2. 187.

3. Olivier Schmitt, "L'Objection de conscience culturelle: Ariane Mnouchkine."

4. Della Couling, "Avignon Festival," *Independent* [London] 2 Aug. 1995: 10.

5. John Peter, "Power Points."

fundamentalist vehicle is clearly not accidental. Islam serves as a plausible contemporary frame for the action of the play:

> Where do men still exist like Orgon, men who wield life or death powers over their wives and children? Where exists a clergy with despotic powers? The answer to both questions, Ms. Mnouchkine concluded, is in certain [Islamic] fundamentalist societies.[6]

Many Westerners paint Islam only in the broadest strokes. Mnouchkine plays upon this lack of nuanced understanding: Islam in Mnouchkine's *Tartuffe* is a theatrical device, a "type" like the characters of the *commedia dell'arte*. However, Mnouchkine portrays and manipulates three real beliefs that are central to Islamic thought: the virtue of following the *Sharia* (divine law of Islam); the primacy of the *ummah* (religious community); and the resurgence of the ideology of *jihad* (striving in the path of God) among fundamentalists.

Following the *Sharia* defines a Muslim. The *Sharia*—based on the Koran, the teachings of the prophet Mohammed, tradition, consensus of the Muslim community, and argument from analogy—offers guidance for Muslim conduct in every situation and "is the final authority in all areas of social interaction."[7] Transposing *Tartuffe* into Islam requires no verbal adaptation; the hypocrite recites conservative platitudes of an indeterminate faith. But while his words may be construed as "universally" virtuous, his actions reveal him to be a universal impostor.

Any community living according to the *Sharia* constitutes an *ummah* (religious community). All followers of Islam can be considered part of the *ummah*; conversely, the *ummah* excludes and legitimately antagonizes anyone or anything un-Islamic.[8] Mnouchkine represents the *ummah* on stage by adding a community of religious brothers:

> Mnouchkine's most important addition is in her creation of a silent chorus of imams. Orgon does not move without them. He arrives with a group of black-clad, black-bearded men. Under their influence, Orgon grows insanely tyrannical. He insists that his only daughter marry Tartuffe, much as the Imaginary Invalid requires his daughter to marry a doctor. The imams are the physicians of his soul; they will insure his safe passage to paradise.[9]

Under Mnouchkine's direction, the *ummah* is an exclusively male group. Further, she links the fundamentalist group not to the justice

6. *International Herald Tribune* [Neuilly-sur-Seine] 8 Feb. 1996, online, Lexis-Nexis.
7. Seyyed Vali Reza Nasr, "Islamic Society," *Multimedia Encyclopedia*, 9th ed., CD-ROM (Novato: Grolier, 1997).
8. Nasr, "Islamic Society."
9. Lamont 15.

of the *Sharia*, but rather to the injustices of a corrupt world. In the fifth act, the imams are at the gate as the "friends" of Monsieur Loyal.[1]

Jihad is a basic duty of certain Muslims. The term is defined variously as "striving in the path of God"[2] or "legitimate struggle."[3] Significantly, however, Westerners may have come to learn the term *jihad* only for its meaning "holy war," as it was repeatedly heard in connection with the Gulf War. Bearing in mind that the *ummah* excludes all that is un-Islamic and that the un-Islamic is thus considered part of the abode of war, or *dar al-harb*:

> Relations between the [Islam and the *dar al-harb*] can be antagonistic, especially if the religion of the *dar al-harb* is not one that is recognized by Islam. The doctrine of *jihad* (holy war) in the military sense has meaning only against the *dar al-harb*. It is permissible to wage war against the *dar al-harb* and take booty from it.[4]

Fundamentalists (*intégristes*) arguing for the integrity of Islamic culture may advocate the violent defense of Islam against the *dar al-harb*. Mnouchkine exploits this trait: certainly, Madame Pernelle's slap, the omnipresence of five identically-clad observers (spies?), and the music of a recently murdered young man all bring this more sinister meaning of *jihad* to life on the stage.

The Politics of Patriarchy

In Islam, the *Sharia* determines the status of women whose "rights and responsibilities differ from those of men. A modern reading of that difference would suggest that women's position is subordinate to that of men."[5] The choice to make Tartuffe an imam and to locate the play in a world governed by the *Sharia* foregrounds patriarchal authority in Mnouchkine's *Tartuffe*.

Dorine proposes opposition in response to Orgon's power over his female child, thus challenging the *Sharia*'s containment strategy. Dorine's outspokenness strikes at ideological foundations; the challenge to absolute authority, already provocative in Molière's day, once again finds its troubling voice. The voice and speech metaphor, apt in any situation where one without power is expected to be "seen and not heard," is quite pronounced (pun intended) in the following dialogue from act 2, scene 3 (emphasis added):

1. 16.
2. Seyyed Vali Reza Nasr, "Islam," *Multimedia Encyclopedia*, 9th ed., CD-ROM (Novato: Grolier, 1997).
3. Nihad Awad, Interview with Liane Hansen, *Weekend Edition Sunday*, Natl. Public Radio, KCFR, Denver, 23 Aug. 1998.
4. Nasr, "Islamic Society."
5. Nasr, "Islamic Society."

Dorine:	Well, *have you lost your tongue* girl? Must I play
	Your part, and *say the lines you ought to say?*
	Faced with a fate so hideous and absurd,
	Can you not utter one dissenting word?
Mariane:	What good would it do? A father's power is great.
Dorine:	*Resist* him now, or it will be too late.
Mariane:	But . . .
Dorine:	*Tell him* one cannot love at a father's whim;
	That you shall marry for yourself, not him.[6]

Dorine suggests at least verbally resisting Orgon's plans for Mariane. Richard Wilbur's translation retains only a vestigial reference to Orgon's power; in the original French, Orgon is Mariane's "père absolu" or "absolute" father, a phrase that evokes the unquestionable authority of an absolute monarch. The authoritarian structures of both seventeenth century France and twentieth century Islam, socially—even morally—justify Orgon's "disposal" of his daughter in the way he chooses. Dorine recognizes that remaining passive (mute) in such a system is dangerous. She pushes Mariane to identify more options than mere obedience or death.

Mnouchkine further questions the role of women in this fundamentalist patriarchy by casting a woman in the role of Damis.[7] The choice gives Orgon increased motivation to disbelieve his son (a feminine presence) when Damis confronts him about Tartuffe's attempted seduction of his wife. Damis—disinherited, made powerless by circumstance (namely, Tartuffe)—is literally feminized by this cross-gender casting decision. The choice additionally motivates Damis' pervasive anger: in this production, Damis becomes the manifestation of Dorine's call for feminist opposition of the patriarchy, not solely to benefit of women, but all oppressed people.

---

6. The speech conceit is more detailed in the exchange between the two women in the original French (emphasis added):

Dorine:	*Avez-vous donc perdu, dites-moi, la parole?*
	Et faut-il qu'en ceci je fasse votre rôle?
	Souffrir qu'on vous propose un projet insensé,
	Sans que du moindre mot vous l'ayez repoussé!
Mariane:	Contre un père absolu que veux-tu que je fasse?
Dorine:	Ce qu'il faut pour parer une telle menace.
Mariane:	Quoi?
Dorine:	Lui *dire* qu'un coeur n'aime point par autrui;
	Que vous mariez pour vous, non pas pour lui;
	Qu'étant celle pour qui se fait toute l'affaire,
	C'est à vous, non à lui, que le mari doit plaire,
	Et que si son Tartuffe est pour lui si charmant,
	Il le peut épouser sans nul empêchement.
Mariane:	Un père, je l'avoue, a sur nous tant d'empire,
	Que *je n'ai jamais eu la force de rien dire.*
Dorine:	Mais *raisonnons.* (2.3.585–99)

7. Miller 371.

Tartuffe's attempted seduction of Elmire, the famous table scene, is also reread in light of the fundamentalist patriarchal system's subjugation of women. "Mnouchkine has staged the funniest seduction scene, the one in which Tartuffe is finally unmasked. Yet we are shown how dangerous the bigots are particularly since their presumed religiosity is a cover for usurpation of power."[8] The context of Islam, where women's social roles are "different" (viz. less important) than men's, divests the scene of safety for Elmire. In the trap set to catch the impostor, Elmire is nothing more than the bait. The scene provides a chilling illustration of the seventeenth century adage, "La verité est une femme nue" or "Truth is a naked woman":

> Tartuffe's attempted seduction of Orgon's wife is sometimes played as almost farcical: you can gloat over the pseudo-saint getting randy while wondering if it could really happen. Ghalam [as Tartuffe] leaves you in no such doubt. He is a hungry man, a member of a new master race. His sensuality is methodical but unbridled. I have never before felt, during this scene, that Tartuffe was such a predator. Ghalam has made immediate the brutish side of all fundamentalism.[9]

Comedy and calamity are here interwoven: Elmire is at the mercy of a rapist in a society which, by subordinating women to the will of men (and/or Allah), comes dangerously close to condoning rape.

Deus Ex Machina

Molière creates a climactic impasse when Orgon gives Tartuffe his wealth, including his family's home. The gift demonstrates the extent of Orgon's unwitting surrender to his beliefs,[1] particularly his blind faith in the spiritual director prior to the attempted rape of Elmire. In act five, scene four, Monsieur Loyal, a solicitor, arrives to seize the property for Tartuffe, and shows the Pernelle family the ramifications of Orgon's leave of his senses. Loyal takes the house keys and offers the family a slight reprieve: they may stay the night before "bright and early, Sir, you must be quick / And move out all your furniture, every stick." Dorine comments ironically on the state of affairs: "This man Loyal's a most disloyal sort!" Mnouchkine's staging of the fifth act

> make[s] palpable the horrors of fanatic religious rule. No longer enmeshed in their own internal battles, the family members, necks bruised by guns and hands pinioned behind heads, look on helplessly as Tartuffe and what appear to be his military assistants appropriate everything that had been the family's.[2]

8. Lamont 16.
9. John Peter, "Power Points."
1. Incidentally, Islam means "surrender" to the will of God.
2. Miller 371.

In this chillingly contemporary idiom, Mnouchkine realizes on the stage what fundamentalist ideology looks like when paired with force.

With the crisis at its greatest intensity, the plot requires resolution. Molière found in this necessity an opportunity to pay tribute to his sovereign: "We serve a Prince to whom all sham is hateful, / A Prince who sees into our inmost hearts, / And can't be fooled by any trickster's arts."[3] The Officer's commendation, given during the reign of Louis XIV, reveals nothing unusual in its overdone language; praising *Sa Majesté* was the norm.[4] Yet, it is difficult to view this moment of the play without sensing a contradiction implicit in Molière's facile use of the *deus ex machina* device: In oversimplifying the questions raised by the play's action, the resolution disturbs. Given that Louis XIV withheld approval for Molière's play from 1664–1669, one wonders what underlies the lengthy hymn of praise. Molière paints a portrait of the King idealizing him, perhaps emptily extolling his virtues because Louis insisted upon such praise. Perhaps, however, Molière pleads for His Majesty's cooperation, depicting Louis the way Molière sincerely wished he were.[5]

Mnouchkine's staging of the Officer's speech delivers this cynical undercurrent in a particularly eloquent metaphor for her predominantly French audience:

> In this production . . . the King's Officer arrests Tartuffe and restores order only after filling his own pockets with whatever loot he can find. A direct reference to the daily outrages perpetrated by both fundamentalists and government in France's former colony Algeria, these last scenes bring the production to an uneasy close.[6]

The staging reveals that the government (in Molière's terms, "le prince") is corrupt, polluted, and thus the order restored is far from ideal. The production's allusion to Algeria's ongoing civil war incriminates the *intégristes* and recriminates the French colonialists. Mnouchkine's staging implies that the play's resolution is ideological stalemate.

Completion

Mnouchkine presents the play with renewed urgency, and one is amazed to hear how well . . . Molière's lines express our contemporary plight. In this *Tartuffe*, we see fundamentalism destroying the natural bonds at the very heart of a community.[7]

---

3. Molière, *Tartuffe*, trans. Richard Wilbur (5.7).
4. See Boileau's "Epître VIII Au Roi."
5. The portrait here painted recalls the verbal portraits Madame Pernelle paints in the opening scene of the play.
6. Miller 371.
7. Goy-Blanquet 16.

In satirizing the *faux dévots* or, "falsely pious," Molière overesti-
mated the ability of his audience to laugh at itself and, through com-
edy "to correct the vices of men."[8] Mnouchkine knowingly takes up
the gauntlet of Molière's politico-moral campaign. Her targets, the
intégristes, like Molière's *faux dévots*, have no sense of humor about
their beliefs. They legitimize their actions based on their ideology: a
narrow interpretation of the *Sharia*, conditional admission to reli-
gious communities (based, in part, on gender), and the duty to
defend Islam from the pollution of everything un-Islamic.

Does Mnouchkine's transposition succeed? Reviews are mixed;
most balance enthusiasm for the production's concept and criticism
for elements of its delivery. The play, after all, lasts four hours! But,
according to *The Sunday Times* of London, four hours "never feels
like it, such is her control of rhythm and pace."[9] Judith Miller calls
the production's focus "divided" between the "caricatured quarrels"
of the "first half" and the "different emotional and political universe"
of the second. Yet even Miller acknowledges Mnouchkine's "joyous
optimism and ebullient creativity."

Mnouchkine, in selecting the idiom of Islamist fundamentalism,
has not made the only choice possible for Molière's play in our time.
She has, however, chosen an effective context in which to deliver
Molière's message, faithfully, to her audience. In her words, "The
nature of the Théâtre du Soleil, I think, is not to be provocative or
anything. It just aims to follow the path of traditional theatre, of pop-
ular theatre."[1] Her comment recalls Molière's formation as a theatre
artist—touring, training with the great *commedia* actor Tiberio Fior-
illo, at times struggling to have his work produced. Mnouchkine
claims she thinks of Molière frequently: "I have a love for the man,
Molière, I love him! . . . I'm *faithful* to him, because I think, in a way,
he is the boss of all theatre companies. You can't live in France and
do theatre and have a theatre company, without thinking at least once
a week of Molière" (emphasis added).[2] Mnouchkine as director likens
herself to a midwife: "[The midwife] doesn't create the baby. She
doesn't create the woman, and she's not the husband. But still, if
she's not there, the baby is in great danger and might not come out."[3]

The midwife metaphor complements Carmody's description of the
relationship of performance to text. We may think of the text as
potential, a child awaiting birth. The contemporary director/midwife
brings the energy and excitement of the text/baby into the world. The

8. Molière, "Preface [à *Tartuffe*] (1664)," *Oeuvres Complètes* (Paris: Editions de Seuil, 1962)
256.
9. John Peter, "Power Points."
1. Mnouchkine in Delgado 185.
2. 181.
3. 187.

delivery of the child is an act of dedication and humility, of risk and of love. The faithful resemblance of the child, *Tartuffe*, to his father, Molière, is perhaps best summarized by Olivier Schmitt in his review in *Le Monde* (emphasis added):

> One cannot help but think that Molière himself worked on this *Tartuffe*'s mise en scène. In it, we rediscover his passion to tell the truth armed by comedy, to comment on his time using the eternal ammunition of the stage where mime, song and dance combine creating a singular play between delight and utter seriousness. A handful of *Tartuffes* marked the half century, whether they were attempted by Louis Jouvet, Roger Planchon or Antoine Vitez. This production inscribes itself in that memory, with an *exemplary fidelity and obvious presence*.[4]

In asking spectators to consider that contemporary Islamist fundamentalism is analogous to seventeenth century Christian fundamentalism, Théâtre du Soleil unleashes *Tartuffe*'s potential to unsettle its audience. Mnouchkine's faithful direction and the daring artistry of Théâtre du Soleil thus permit us to experience the dangerous comic genius of Molière.

4. Olivier Schmitt, "Le Tartuffe: théâtre de guerre contre tous les fondamentalismes."

Molière: A Chronology

1622   January 15. Jean-Baptiste Poquelin was baptized at the church of Saint-Eustache in Paris. Presumably, he was born on that day or the day before, the second son of Jean Poquelin, a merchant who sold bedding, and his wife, Marie Cressé.

1632   Marie Cressé died, leaving Jean-Baptiste and three other children.

1633–39?   For some years during this period, Jean-Baptiste Poquelin attended the collège de Clermont, a Jesuit school that was also attended by sons of the nobility.

1642   Young Poquelin is said to have studied law at Orléans and to have received a license to practice. At about this time he met Madeleine Béjart, a beautiful red-haired actress, and gave up the law for the theatre.

1643–45   June 16. Jean-Baptiste Poquelin signed—along with his mistress, Madeleine, her brother and sister, and several other young Parisians—an act founding l'Illustre Théâtre (The Illustrious Theatre), which opened in a remodeled tennis court on the Left Bank on January 1, 1644. Although never successful and forced to move to another venue, the Illustre Théâtre survived until the end of July 1645; in August Jean-Baptiste went to debtor's prison.

1644   June 28. Jean-Baptiste Poquelin, for the first time, signed a document as "de Molière."

1646–58   By April 1646, Molière and Madeleine had joined the provincial troupe of Charles Dufresne, supported by the duc d'Épernon, governor of the province of Guyenne in the southwest of France. This troupe, which eventually became the troupe of Mlle Béjart and Molière, played primarily in the cities and town of Languedoc, but also in Lyon, Grenoble, and Rouen. For a time, the prince de Conti, a cousin of the king, sponsored the troupe, although in later years he became one of the most ruthless enemies of the theatre. At some point during these years, Molière began to write and perform in a series of short farces, but only *La Jalousie de Barbouillé* (*The Jealousy of*

the Barbouillé, also titled The Jealousy of Gros René) and
Le Médecin volant (The Flying Doctor) have survived.
Although he wanted to play tragedy, Molière was not
applauded in serious roles. He first became noted as an
actor when he created for himself two wily servants, Mas-
carille and Sganarelle, based on the masks of the Italian
commedia dell'arte.

1655   Molière's first full-length play, L'Etourdi (The Scatter-
brain) was performed in Lyon, according to Molière's
friend and biographer, Charles Varlet de La Grange.
Molière played Mascarille.

1656   Le Dépit amoureux (Unrequited Love), Molière's second
full-length play, was performed in Béziers, in Languedoc,
in December. Molière again played Mascarille. Both of
these early plays were written in verse.

1658   October 24. Molière led a troupe of ten actors and
actresses back to Paris and performed for King Louis XIV,
who gave them the right to play in a royal theatre at the
Palace of the Petit-Bourbon. The legend is that the trag-
edy by Corneille, with which they opened the evening,
was not successful, but that Molière saved the day with
the farce of The Amorous Doctor.
November 2. The troupe, now sponsored by the king's
brother, Monsieur, opened at the Petit-Bourbon. Once
again, the actors were found inadequate in tragedy, but
both l'Étourdi and Le Dépit amoureux were successful.

1659   November 18. Molière opened his first great hit in Paris:
Les Précieuses ridicules (The Pretentious Young Ladies).
This short afterpiece ridiculed the cult of preciosity
affected by many Parisian society women. Molière played
Mascarille as a bogus Marquis smothered in lace and rib-
bons.

1660   May 28. Molière starred as Sganarelle, another type char-
acter, in Le Cocu imaginaire (The Imaginary Cuckold).
Sganarelle remained one of Molière's characters through-
out the remainder of his career, although the character
did not stay the same from play to play. Sometimes an
old man, sometimes a servant, sometimes masked, some-
times not, Sganarelle did retain his costume of white dou-
blet and pantaloons, decorated with braid.

1661   Having been dispossessed from the theatre at the Petit-
Bourbon, the troupe of Monsieur was granted use of
another royal theatre at the Palais-Royal, originally built
for Cardinal Richelieu. They opened there on January 20
with Le Dépit amoureux and Le Cocu imaginaire.

February 14. Molière tried his hand at a tragicomedy, *Dom Garcie de Navarre, ou Le Prince jaloux* (*Don Garcie of Navarre, or The Jealous Prince*), in which he played the romantic prince. Jean Donneau de Visé wrote of it that it failed and that "it's enough to tell you that it was a serious play, that he played the leading role, and that no one found it very entertaining."

June 24. The first of Molière's important comedies of manners, *L'École des maris* (*The School for Husbands*) opened successfully. Molière again played Sganarelle, this time as an irascible old gentleman.

August 17. The king's superintendent of finances, Nicolas Fouquet, gave an elaborate party to inaugurate his splendid new country house at Vaux-le-Vicomte. Molière was invited to provide a play to entertain the guests, which included the king and his court. He responded with *Les Fâcheux* (*The Boors*), in which he played at least five roles. The play was a resounding success with His Majesty, who offered the playwright an idea for an additional boorish character; Molière took the king up on his suggestion. The evening was a disaster for Fouquet, who soon found himself permanently in prison for misuse of state funds; but for Molière, for the architect Le Vau, the painter Le Brun, the garden designer Le Nôtre, and the musician Lulli, the evening was a triumph. All were soon invited to undertake commissions for the king.

1662 February 20. Molière, now forty, married the twenty-year-old Armande Béjart, either the daughter or the sister of his first love, Madeleine Béjart. The marriage created a scandal, with Molière even accused of having married his own daughter.

December 26. The scandal was magnified when Molière opened *L'École des femmes* (*The School for Wives*). He played Arnolphe, a bourgeois obsessed with marital fidelity, who wanted to marry the young ward he had raised to be sexually innocent. The play was hugely successful and had an amazingly long run for the period, amplified when Molière added two afterpieces: *La Critique* (*The Critique*) on June 1, 1663 and *L'Impromptu de Versailles* (*The Impromptu of Versailles*) on October 14 at Versailles and on November 4 in Paris. This latter afterpiece was the first play Molière wrote specifically for Louis XIV and his court.

1663 At some point in this year, Molière received from the king a "gratification," a pension of 1,000 livres paid every year "in consideration of the works of theatre he gives to the public."

1664   February 17. The king had danced on January 29 in *Le Mariage forcé* (*The Forced Marriage*), a royal ballet for which Molière wrote the libretto. As a prose comedy (his first) and without the ballet, it opened at the Palais-Royal to moderate success.

February 28. The king put an end to rumors that Molière had committed incest by serving as godfather to the actor's first son, Louis. The boy died on November 11.

May 5–13. Louis XIV's great festival, *Les Plaisirs de l'Île enchantée* (*The Pleasures of the Enchanted Isle*) was held at Versailles. Molière served as a producer of the festival, providing four plays and appearing with his troupe in various spectacular parades. Written specially for *Les Plaisirs* was *La Princesse d'Élide* (*The Princess of Elis*) a romantic comedy that introduced the young Mlle Molière to the court. It was toward the end of the festival, on May 12, that Molière presented the three-act version of *Tartuffe*. The king, influenced by the devout party at court, forbade any further performances.

1665   February 15. Furious after the interdiction of *Tartuffe*, Molière lashed out at religious hypocrisy among the nobility with *Don Juan*. Although censored after its opening, the play survived for fourteen more highly successful performances, closed for the Easter recess, and was not performed again in the lifetime of Molière. When it was finally published in 1682, it was again censored.

August 4. Esprit-Madeleine, Molière's second child and the only one to survive her father, was born and baptized.

c. August 14. The Troupe of Monsieur became the King's Troupe and began to receive an annual pension of 6,000 livres.

September 14. *L'Amour médecin* (*Love Is the Doctor*) was first performed at Versailles. A bitter satire on medicine, in it Molière had the idea of using portrait masks representing four fashionable doctors. The doctors apparently did not have the same power as the religious fanatics; *L'Amour médecin* opened in Paris on September 22 and settled in for a long run.

1666   Probably ill during the winter of 1666 with the tuberculosis that would eventually kill him, Molière leased an apartment in the suburb of Auteuil and wrote his great verse comedy, *Le Misanthrope*, which opened on June 4 to limited success.

August 6. After poor box-office receipts during the summer, the troupe presented the farcical *Médecin malgré lui* (*Doctor in Spite of Himself*), and Molière once again took the stage as Sganarelle, in this instance a hapless woodcutter turned doctor. Played as an afterpiece to *Les Fâcheux* and *Le Misanthrope*, it produced a substantial increase in income for the actors.

1666–67   December 1–January 20. All the Paris theatre troupes were at the palace of St.-Germain-en-Laye for the king's *Ballet des Muses*. Molière furnished three short plays: *Mélicerte*, *Le Sicilien* (*The Sicilian*), and *La Pastorale comique* (*The Comic Pastoral*).

1667   August 5. The first public performance of *Tartuffe*, retitled *L'Imposteur* (*The Imposter*), was given at the Palais-Royal. Molière played Orgon, another obsessed bourgeois. The next day, further performances were forbidden by the president of the Paris Parlement, in charge while the king was out of town besieging Lille.

August 11. The archbishop of Paris forbade all the Catholics in his diocese to perform in, read, or hear read *L'Imposteur*, publicly or privately, under pain of excommunication.

August 21–22. Molière was living much of the time in Auteuil and was unofficially separated from his wife, although they continued to work together.

1668   January 13. The Troupe de Roi opened Molière's *Amphitryon*, played for the king and the court three days later at the Tuileries.

July 18. *George Dandin*, a sour comedy about a peasant who marries above his station, was the centerpiece of a ballet performed at Versailles as part of a Grand Divertissement Royal that celebrated the Peace of Aix-la-Chapelle.

September 9. At the Palais-Royal, the troupe opened *L'Avare* (*The Miser*) to something very close to failure—odd, since the play has been one of Molière's most frequently produced. After several poorly attended performances, it was alternated with *George Dandin*, which did no better. Molière's tuberculosis was at this point obvious enough that he had to write in coughing fits for his character of Harpagon.

1669   February 5. At long last, apparently with the king's approval, *Tartuffe* opened at the Palais-Royal, with Molière as Orgon. It was the most successful and most profitable of all of Molière's plays, a triumph of playwriting and the ultimate *succès de scandale*.

October 6. A comedy-ballet, *Monsieur de Pourceau-gnac*, with music by Lulli, was produced at the Château of Chambord "for the entertainment of the King." This was the first of a series of entertainments with music by Lulli that, with the exception of *Le Bourgeois Gentil-homme* (*The Middle-Class Gentleman*) are rarely performed today. They include *Les Amants magnifiques* (*The Magnificent Lovers*, never produced at the Palais-Royal), *Psyché*, and *La Comtesse d'Escarbagnas* (never produced at the Palais-Royal), all written as commissions for the court. *Monsieur de Pourceaugnac*, which includes another pointed attack on doctors, opened in Paris on November 17 and played constantly until mid-January 1670.

October 14. *Le Bourgeois gentilhomme* was first performed at the Château of Chambord with Molière as the middle-class merchant who is trying to learn how to be a gentleman. The "Turkish ceremony" in Act IV is said to have been devised at the request of the king, himself. The play opened in Paris on November 23 and ran successfully through the Christmas season.

1671   January 17. The play and musical extravaganza titled *Psyché* was written in prose by Molière and versified by himself and Pierre Corneille, with lyrics by Philippe Quinault and music by Lulli. It was the most elaborate and most expensive theatrical entertainment ever produced at the French court; it was also a great success in a more restrained production at the Palais-Royal, where it ran continuously from July 24 to October 25. Molière played the relatively minor role of Zéphir, but his wife starred as Psyché.

May 24. Molière returned to farce and the *commedia dell'arte* with *Les Fourberies de Scapin* (*The Tricks of Scapin*) at the Palais-Royal. His friend Boileau complained: "I no longer recognize the author of *The Misanthrope* wrapped up in Scapin's ridiculous sack."

December 2. The last play that Molière devised for the king, *La Comtesse d'Escarbagnas*, was performed at Saint-Germain-en-Laye, as was a pastoral, now lost. In the last year of his life, with Jean-Baptiste Lulli's star in the ascendant, Molière appears to have retreated from the court.

1672   February 17. Madeleine Béjart, Molière's former mistress and long-time colleague, died in Paris at the age of fifty-four.

March 11. Apparently reaching into his trunk, Molière pulled out a play, *Les Femmes savantes* (*The Learned Women*) that was several years old and may have been originally written for Madeleine Béjart, who had been too ill to play for some time. Although her role, Philaminte, was eventually played by a male actor, Hubert, and the satire of literary Paris was dated, the play was reasonably successful. Perhaps this reflects the fact that this play was the first that Molière had fully versified since *Amphitryon*. His role, Chrysale, is relatively undemanding, suggesting that Molière's health may have begun to inconvenience him on stage.

September 15. Molière's second son, Pierre Jean-Baptiste Armand, was born in Paris, the product of a reconciliation between his parents. He died on October 11.

1673   February 10–17. *Le Malade imaginaire* (*The Imaginary Invalid*), Molière's last play—and last comedy-ballet, with music not by Lulli but by Charpentier—opened in Paris, not at court. It was seen by the king only after Molière's death, which happened unexpectedly after the fourth performance on February 17. During the *divertissement* that ends the play Molière began coughing blood, and a few hours later he died of a tuberculer hemorrhage. Denied a grave in the church's cemetery by the pastor of his parish because he was an actor, he was finally buried—after the king intervened—at night and without ceremony. The theater reopened after a week with *Le Misanthrope*; the run of *Le Malade imaginaire* continued successfully after March 3 with another actor in the leading role.

1682   The *Oeuvres complètes* (*Collected Works*) of Molière, including eight plays that had not been published before, appeared in an edition supervised by Charles Varlet de La Grange, who also added a brief biography of the playwright.

Selected Bibliography

• indicates works included or excerpted in this Norton Critical Edition.

Works of Molière

The Misanthrope. Verse version by Constance Congdon based on a translation by Virginia Scott. New York: Broadway Play Publishing, 2003.
The Misanthrope and Tartuffe. Trans. with intro. Richard Wilbur. New York: Harcourt, Brace, 1993.
The Misanthrope, Tartuffe and Other Plays. Trans. and ed. Maya Slater. Oxford Classics. Oxford: Oxford University Press, 2001.
Oeuvres complètes. Ed. Georges Couton. 2 vols. Bibliothèque de la Pléiade. Paris: Gallimard, 1971.
Oeuvres complètes. Ed. Eugène Despois and Paul Mesnard. 12 vols. Éditions des Grands Écrivains de la France. Paris: Hachette, 1875–1927.
Tartuffe and Other Plays. Trans. Donald M. Frame, intro. Virginia Scott. Signet Classic. New York: Penguin Group, 2007.

Documents

• Boileau, Nicolas. *Correspondance entre Boileau Despréaux et Brossette avec Mémoires de Brossette sur Boileau*. Ed. August Laverdet. Paris: J. Techner, 1858.
Jurgens, Madeleine, and Elizabeth Maxfield-Miller. *Cent ans de recherches sur Molière, sur sa famille et sur les comédiens to sa troupe*. Paris: S.E.V.P.E.N., 1963.
• Loret, Jean. *La Muze historique*. Ed. J. Ravanal and V. de La Pelouze. 4 vols. Paris: Jamet, 1859–78.
• La Grange, Charles Varlet de. *Registre*. Ed. Bert E. and Grace P. Young. 2 vols. Facsimile ed. Paris: Droz, 1947.
Mongrédien, Georges. *Recueil des textes et des documents du XVIIe siècle relatifs à Molière*. 2 vols. Paris: Centre National de la Recherche Scientifique, 1965.
• Rothschild, James M., ed. *Les Continuateurs de Loret*. 3 vols. Paris: Margand et Fatou, 1881–82.

Biographies

Bulgakov, Mikail. *The Life of Monsieur de Molière*. Trans. Mirra Ginsburg. New York: New Directions, 1986.
Palmer, John. *Molière*. New York: Benjamin Bloom Reprint, 1970.
Scott, Virginia. *Molière: A Theatrical Life*. Cambridge, Cambridge University Press, 2000.

Directors Work with Molière

- Jouvet, Louis. *Molière et la comédie classique, extraits des cours de Jouvet au Conservatoire (1939–1940)*, Paris: Gallimard, 1965.
- "Stanislavsky Works with *Tartuffe*." Trans. James B. Woodward. *Drama Survey* 5 (Spring 1966): 73–75.

Critical Studies and Reviews

Ackerman, Marianne. *L'Affaire Tartuffe, or, The Garrison Officers Rehearse Molière*. Montreal: NuAge Editions, 1993.

- Beck, William J. "More on Molière's *Tartuffe*." *Papers on Language and Literature* 16 (Spring 1980): 203–6.

Bermel, Albert. *Molière's Theatrical Bounty: A New View of the Plays*. Carbondale: Southern Illinois University Press, 1990.

Bold, Stephen. "Molière and Authority: From the Querelle de *L'École des Femmes* to the Affaire *Tartuffe*." *Romance Quarterly* 44 (1997): 80–92.

Bradby, David, and Andrew Calder, eds. *The Cambridge Companion to Molière*. Cambridge: Cambridge University Press, 2006.

Cairncross, John. *New Light on Molière: Tartuffe; Elomire hypocondre*. Geneva: Droz, 1956.

Calder, Andrew. *Molière: The Theory and Practice of Comedy*. London: Athlone Press, 1993.

Carmody, Jim. *ReReading Molière: Mise-en-scène from Antoine to Vitez*. Ann Arbor: University of Michigan Press, 1993.

- Chill, Emanuel S. "*Tartuffe*, Religion, and Courtly Culture." *French Historical Studies* 3 (Fall 1963): 151–67.
- Clurman, Harold, "Theatre" [Review of *Tartuffe* at Circle in the Square]. *The Nation*, October 8, 1977, pp. 348–49.

Dock, Stephen V. *Costume and Fashion in the Plays of Jean-Baptiste Poquelin Molière: A Seventeenth-Century Perspective*. Geneva: Slatkine, 1992.

Gaines, James F. *A Molière Encyclopedia*. Westport, Conn.: Greenwood Press, 2002.

Gaines, James F. *Social Structures in Molière's Theatre*. Columbus: Ohio State University Press, 1984.

Gaines, James F., and Michael S. Koppisch, eds. *Approaches to Teaching Molière's "Tartuffe" and Other Plays*. New York: MLA, 1995.

Gossman, Lionel. "Molière and Tartuffe: Law and Order in the Seventeenth Century." *The French Review* 43 (1970): 901–12.

Gutworth, Marcel. "*Tartuffe* and the Mysteries." *PMLA* 92 (1977): 33–40.

Harrison, David. "The Problem of Friendship in *Tartuffe*." *Dalhousie French Studies* (Fall 2006): 3–12.

- Herzel, Roger W. "The Decor of Molière's Stage: The Testimony of Brissart and Chauveau." *PMLA* 93 (1978): 925–54.

Hilgar, Marie-France. "Modern and Post-Modern Interpretations of *Tartuffe*." *Theatre Journal* 34 (1982): 384–88.

Hope, Quentin M. "Place and Setting in *Tartuffe*." *PMLA* 89 (1974): 42–49,

Howarth, W. D., ed., with Jan Clarke, Edward Forman, John Golder, Michael O'Regan, and Christopher Smith. *French Theatre in the Neo-Classical Era, 1550–1789*. Cambridge: Cambridge University Press, 1997.

Howarth, W. D. *Molière: A Playwright and His Audience*. Cambridge: Cambridge University Press, 1982.

Hubert, Judd D. *Molière and the Comedy of Intellect*. Berkeley: University of California Press, 1973.

Koppisch, Michael S. *Rivalry and the Disruption of Order in Molière's Theatre*. Madison, NJ: Fairleigh Dickinson University Press, 2004.

Knutson, Harold C. *The Triumph of Wit: Molière and Restoration Comedy*. Columbus: Ohio State University Press, 1988.

Lalande, Roxanne Decker. *Intruders in the Play World: The Dynamics of Gender in Molière's Comedies*. Madison, N.J.: Fairleigh Dickinson University Press, 1996.

• Leon, Mechele. "The Poet and the Prince: Revising Molière and *Tartuffe* in the French Revolution." *French Historical Studies* 28 (Summer 2005): 447–65.

LePage, Raymond. "Brian Bedford's *Tartuffe*: The Erotic Violence of Hypocrisy." *Theatre Journal* 34 (1982): 389–96.

McBride, Robert. *The Skeptical Vision of Molière*. London: Macmillan, 1977.

McCarthy, Gerry. *The Theatres of Molière*. London and New York: Routledge, 2002.

• McFarren, Cheryl Kennedy. "Mnouchkine's *Tartuffe*: Unleashing the Text's Potential." *On-Stage Studies* 21 (1998): 87–112.

Mercier, Vivian. " 'No Second Miracle' Review Richard Wilbur's trans. of *Tartuffe*." *The Hudson Review* 16 (1963): 634–36.

Moore, W. G. *Molière: A New Criticism*. Oxford: Clarendon Press, 1949.

Nadin, Mihai. "Sign Functioning in Performance: Ingmar Bergman's Production of *Tartuffe*." *TDR* 23 (1979): 105–20.

• Newberry, Wilma. "The New Spanish *Tartuffe*." *Hispania* 55 (December 1972): 922–28.

Norman, Larry F. *The Public Mirror: Molière and the Social Commerce of Depiction*. Chicago: University of Chicago Press, 1999.

Peacock, Noël. "*Tartuffe* on Screen and/or the Metaphysics of Performance." In *Theatrum Mundi*, ed. Kathleen Wine. Charlottesville: Rookwood Press, 2003.

Peter, John. Review of *Tartuffe*, *The Sunday Times* [London], November 12, 1995.

Phillips, Henry. "Molière and *Tartuffe*: Recrimination and Reconciliation." *The French Review* 62 (1989): 749–63.

Riggs, Larry W. *Molière and Modernity: Absent Mothers and Masculine Birth*. Charlottesville: Rookwood Press, 2005.

• Saur, Pamela. "Molière's *Tartuffe*." *The Explicator* 60 (Fall 2001): 9–12.

• Senior, Nancy. "Translators' Choices in *Tartuffe*." *TTR: traduction, terminologie, rédaction* 14 (2001): 39–63.

• Simonds, P. Munoz. "Molière's Use of the *Deus ex Machina* in *Tartuffe*." *Educational Theatre Journal* 29 (March 1977): 85–93.

Tobin, Ronald W. *Tarte à la crème: Comedy and Gastronomy in Molière's Theatre*. Columbus: Ohio State University Press, 1990.

Wine, Kathleen. "*Le Tartuffe* and *Les Plaisirs de l'Île enchantée*: Satire or Flattery." In *Theatrum Mundi*, ed. Kathleen Wine. Charlottesville: Rookwood Press, 2003. 139–46.

Whitton, David. *Molière/Don Juan*. Cambridge: Cambridge University Press, 1995.